# THE BOOK THAT GOES BEYOND GRIEF OFFERS NEW HOPE, NEW HELP FOR MILLIONS

"It is impossible to leave *Ended Beginnings* without feeling infinitely grateful for its existence, intensely moved by its content, and uplifted by its simplicity and effectiveness."
—**Nancy Wainer Cohen, author of *Silent Knife***

"*Ended Beginnings* is one step toward helping grief-stricken couples confront our death-denying society and themselves."
—*Childbirth Educator*

"Supplies a total healing process for pregnancy-related losses. Intended for those willing to give maximum commitment to personal healing."
—**"Best Birthing Books,"** *Los Angeles Parent*

"Each area is treated sensitively.... The major thrust of this book is the healing aspect of grieving: helping people to handle a loss

...motionally, and spiritually.... a

...*e Caring Unlimited*

*MORE...*

"Painful, profound, and ultimately healing."
—*New Age Journal*

"This truly remarkable book will help us all to face and grow from the losses we must face. It should be required reading."
—*Positive Pregnancy Fitness*

\*            \*            \*            \*

**CLAUDIA PANUTHOS** is director of Offspring, a childbirth counseling network in Massachusetts. She is the author of *Transformation Through Birth: A Woman's Guide*, and is a national lecturer and consultant and a frequent guest on TV and radio discussion shows.

**CATHERINE ROMEO**, co-director of Offspring, is a certified childbirth-educator; a founder of Birthchoice, an organization for childbirth education; an instructor of parent education in the Massachusetts prison system; and a national lecturer/consultant.

# Ended Beginnings

## Healing Childbearing Losses

**Claudia Panuthos & Catherine Romeo**

Foreword by Peggy O'Mara McMahon

WARNER BOOKS

A Warner Communications Company

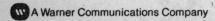

# CONTENTS

# ACKNOWLEDGMENTS

"And to you, my dear devoted friends,
Whose love and compassion never ends...
I honor you."*

We have both, individually and together, been blessed with the love and support of family and friends while *Ended Beginnings* was being written. Without that support—our children cared for, meals prepared, studies researched, pages typed, suggestions offered, and our spirits bolstered— *Ended Beginnings* would not be what it is. And so, dear friends and loved ones all, you share in this book. We thank you from the depths of our hearts and souls.

We honor you... Elaine Bontempo, Lee Longchamps, Nancy Brown, Claudia Greenfield, Kim Cavanaugh, Peter Panuthos, Pat Flagg, Nancy and Paul Cohen, Rita and Dick Bemis, Joan and Peter Collins, Pat and John Stegelmann, Jean Cavanaugh, Bunny Antonellis, Eleanor and Vincent Carreiro, Rick Bemis, Ann Landry, Ellia Manners, Mary Ann Miller, Tom Bemis, Rosalie Meropol, Sally Dempsey, Lori Lovezzola, Diane Parfenuk, Ralph Johnson, Barbara Dill, Dianne Boyce, John Miller... and we especially thank the entire Offspring staff.

And to John Romeo and Peter Janney, our eternal love and infinite gratitude, for without *your* unconditional love and endless support, this book would not be.

And to Jonathan, Sharon, Paul, and Allison, our pride-filled love and our thanks for your wise-beyond-years understanding of the need for this book and for loving us enough to let us go a little while it was being written.

And to Peggy O'Mara McMahon, Nancy Wainer Cohen, and Peter Janney, our love and our heartfelt thanks for your faith in us and in *Ended Beginnings* and your willingness to grace these pages with your words.

And to all the women and men who shared with us their stories of ended beginnings, our deepest gratitude. We honor you all.

———————

*From the song "I Honor You," by Robbie Gass

*To all families bound together*
*in life and in death by love...*
*and most especially to our own dear ones*


*Jonathan Panuthos*
*Peter Janney*


*John Romeo*
*Sharon, Paul and Allison Romeo*


*Your love has been the gift of my life.*

# FOREWORD

As you read this book, you may feel embarrassed. If you have experienced some form of childbearing loss yourself, you will relive and release the feelings associated with that loss; if you have not, you may feel embarrassed at the naked honesty of others' sufferings. Your embarrassment will tell you something about yourself as a child of our culture. Ours is a death denying culture, and an emotion denying culture. It is this denial which immobilizes us in our attempts to reach out to others in open acceptance of real grieving, no matter how inappropriate, antisocial or "crazy" it may seem.

We say to one another, "Oh, it happened for a reason." or "It could have been worse." or "Everything will be all right." Statements like these close the door on communication, minimize the intensity of grief and give us the message that our feelings are *not* all right, cannot be understood or shared and thus we are blocked from releasing them. *Should* we be depressed? Should we *still* be grieving after so many years? *Ended Beginnings* gives us back our feelings and grants us permission to have them—all of them.

We are embarrassed and fearful about death because the experience leaves us helpless. It threatens our spiritual foundation and our will to live. There is nothing we can do in the face of loss to make the experience go away or return our lives to "normal." We are terrified to accept the awful awareness that we cannot escape death, that tomorrow it will still be here. Our resistance causes us to deny loss and the intense emotions that accompany it. In a society which values achievement and a rigid striving for perfection, death forces us to face those aspects of life that are beyond our control.

Once we begin to accept the embarrassment and awkwardness of grieving emotions and say yes to death by accepting our feelings of loss without reservations or judgments, we rise from the ashes to live again. Surely there is no life *without* death. While it may be normal in our culture to fear death and to feel terrified when its emotion touches us and those we love, accepting all of the uncomfortable feelings that death reveals facilitates the transformation and resurrection inherent in the nature of death.

The embarrassment we feel in the face of the raw emotions generated by loss tells us also how we judge and compare our feelings in an effort to validate them. "Well, what is she getting *so carried away* about?" or "What happened to him wasn't *that* bad." Because we do not give ourselves permission to experience our own griefs, we judge others harshly for theirs.

In reading this book, I am put in touch with my own feelings toward loss and death. I relive my numbness and inability to respond eight years ago when my friend, Stephanie's, son died at six weeks; and the painful worry we suffered together more recently when her third son underwent surgeries for a brain tumor. I relive the birth six years ago of my own dear son born with a cleft lip and palate. I relive his early feeding difficulties, weight loss and weaning, his surgeries at three and sixteen months. I relive the eleven day hospital vigil I shared with my five month old daughter when she contracted spinal meningitis. I compare my sufferings to that of others. I chalk up the friends I have lost to death and the childbearing losses I have suffered. I wonder if I too have suffered enough to grieve as I read of these other parents' grieving. And as I read I am transformed. For the tears that come from reading *Ended Beginnings* still my comparing and my judging, still my rationalizing and intellectualizing, release my emotions. I am allowed to cry for them and for me too. I am allowed to have *my* feelings and *my* tears too.

But more than that, this book gives us back a sense of hope. It gives us back our will to live. For as we release the grieving and the sorrow, we accept the fatigue, the angry and suicidal thoughts, and the sounds of our dead babies crying in the night. We accept ourselves as good people not because we have *escaped* suffering, but because we have *survived* it. Then we can face the ultimate transformation of death—for death gives new life to the living. As the dead leave their lives behind they transform, through us, the miracle of each new day, the beauty of each new moment, the significance of each thought, action and emotion.

When we cannot change reality, we can only change ourselves. "Yea, though I walk through the valley of the shadow of death, I will fear no evil." This is the ultimate challenge of death. Death puts us squarely in the present. We live each moment more fully thereafter because it has become our constant companion.

Peggy O'Mara McMahon
Albuquerque, New Mexico

# A WOMAN'S DREAM

My dreams are often very vivid. Last night, for example, I dreamed that the following people came together:

*My friend from the midwest* (who called me last week and told me that her first pregnancy had just resulted in a miscarriage. "Alas, it wasn't even a baby that I lost," she told me. "It was a . . . a . . . 'conceptus.' A misguided sperm and a cockeyed egg. I guess it was for the best.");

*my sister* (a DES daughter with a history of tubal pregnancies and miscarriages, and a baby girl—premature and stillborn at 28 weeks gestation);

*Mrs. J.*, one of the receptionists at my husband's office (whose seven-year-old daughter died in 1972. She was her only biological child and her heart had been defective since birth);

*A woman* (who had just had her third abortion);

*A cousin* (whose first twin was stillborn. The other, a little girl was "like a vegetable" and would live in a state home. Three years later the baby died. In the meantime, my cousin got pregnant right away and had a beautiful healthy baby);

*Mary H.* (whose fourth child was a SIDS baby);

*That friend of my mother's* (whose baby was delivered

by [doctor-elected] cesarean section in 1955. The doctor miscalculated the due date and the baby died of hyaline membrane disease—a disease of prematurity. The neighbor had a fertility problem and apparently was unable to conceive again);

*her doctor;*

*my mother* (whose twin sons—my brothers—died two days after their birth. "Perhaps we'd not have our two beautiful daughters," we often heard. Still, I often wondered, growing up, why my mother couldn't stand to have anything out of place);

*my father* (who cries at movies that aren't even all *that* sad);

*a friend* (who has two children, and tied tubes);

*the woman at the copy center* (sixty-ish, who glanced at the article I had asked her to reproduce on miscarriage and infant death, and who looked at me and said "My third baby would have been sixteen this October. They put me on the *maternity* floor: Do they still do that?" Of course, she went on, it would have been ridiculous, having a teenager now, at her age. But could she make a copy of the article for her friend? "Now she, *she's* never gotten over her child's death. And I'll tell you," she leaned over confidentially, "her ten-year-old is suffering for it, too.");

*that teenager,* Carol (who called and asked if I knew any good homes for the baby she was due to have and planning to give up for adoption);

*Carol's mother;*

*her boyfriend;*

*Diane, the women from my childbirth classes* (who delivered a baby boy with multiple chromosomal abnormalities);

*the man I heard on a TV talk show* (who said he had four

daughters and was going to "keep his wife going" until she "produced him a son.");

*and his wife;*

*all the women* (all 40,000 of them—who have written to me who have had unexpected cesarean sections or disappointing birth experiences);

*and me* (with three beautiful, no magnificent! children and a miscarriage [in between #2 and #3]. In a letter to a friend five years ago I remember writing "I often feel as if something, no someone, is missing." And it's funny, but when someone asks me how many children I have, I want to shout "four!");

*along with Joanne* (who has her "perfect, completed, family: a boy, a girl, a station wagon, a dog and a cat—not to mention my husband!"—but who *loved* being pregnant and who misses it);

In my dream, I found a safe and loving place where these people—and all the people who have ever lost a conceptus, embryo, fetus, pregnancy, baby, labor, birth, tube, uterus, child, or a dream of their own, are together. It is a place where they release the pain, heartache, suffering, sorrow, or numbness they have carried with them, created, or taken on since their loss (since we know, in my dream, that all of these situations, planned or unplanned, welcome or not, constitute a form of loss; and that all of the people associated with the loss—including grandparents, siblings, friends, and hosptial staffs—grieve the losses in some way, whether they admit to it or show it and whether they care to or not). In my dream, all these people are helped to mend their hearts, revitalize their soul, restore their spirit. They are given the opportunity to release the hurt, anger, pain, confusion and replace these with dignity, self love, self respect. They take that opportunity to affirm themselves and to use their time together to change and to grow, to love.

In my dream, each person comes away after just a few hours with more self esteem, more feelings of being whole, more peace than they have felt in all the weeks, months and years since their loss.

\*            \*            \*

In *Ended Beginnings* we learn that over one-third of all women who conceive lose their babies (do they ever find them, I keep wondering?) each year through miscarriage, stillbirth, or infant death. Another 1½ million pregnancies result in abortion. Of the women who carry to term, thousands deliver a "less than perfect" child. A number of babies are put up for adoption, some publicly, some privately. In addition, an estimated 20–35% of all women are delivered of their infants via cesarean section, and others are separated from their babies at birth, even though both their births— and their babies—were normal. Is it any wonder we have a country of grieving women? And if the women are grieving, can we not expect their babies, their children—*society itself*—to be in pain?

With *Ended Beginnings* we find a whole new understanding of pregnancy related loss—not only the emotional signs and symptoms, but the effects, the impact—*and even an explanation. Ended Beginnings* provides an opportunity for those who have experienced a loss to heal (and for anyone who has been close to, or affected by loss as well). *Ended Beginnings* helps us acknowledge our pain as a sign of health: *healthy* bodies ready to he healed, healthy minds ready to stop "going unconscious" on emotional pain, healthy spirits ready to soar. It gives grieving hearts concrete, practical, and loving suggestions for beginning that health process—and for completing it as well.

My respect for this work, and for the women who have written it is boundless. Their dedication, their unique and effective approach to grieving and healing, and their love for women, is unparalleled. One has only to be with them for a few moments to understand this. I have had the privilege of watching these beautiful women work, of learning from them. Many lives have been deeply enriched by their work and their love, and in turn, each of those lives has been able to help others.

*Ended Beginnings* provides you with an opportunity to be with Claudia and Cathy for a few moments. It is a workshop of its own. I applaud those of you who have chosen to read this, for to do so is to be open to one's own set of losses. It is impossible to leave this book without feeling infinitely grateful for its existence, intensely moved by its content, awed by its power and truth and uplifted by its simplicity and effectiveness. It is impossible to leave it without feeling ready to grieve: to be ready to acknowledge without judgment; to forgive without forgetting; to affirm, to grow, to seek peace, to move on.

And as I see people, by the hundreds, writing to Claudia and Cathy, calling them, attending their "grieving and healing" workshops in pain and leaving them in peace, I realize it wasn't really a dream after all.

Nancy Wainer Cohen
Needham, Massachusetts

# PREFACE

And ever has it been that love knows
not its own depth until the hour of separation.

—Kahlil Gibran

Every year in the United States well over one-third of all the
babies conceived will not survive. *One in every three
women who conceive is touched by childbearing loss.* Countless others—women *and* men—grieve over *their* broken
dreams of pregnancy, childbirth, and parenthood.

What is the impact of all these ended beginnings? What
of the parents whose lives are so deeply affected by such
loss? What of all the other lives affected, domino fashion,
by the spreading ripples of grief? Is knowing the depth of
one's love, as Gibran so poignantly termed it, a source of
comfort or of pain? Can parents who feel the anguish of loss
ever recover and reach healing? Will a manner of grieving
affect how well and how soon one heals? Can the unforgivable
be forgiven?

Our personal search for answers to these and other piercing questions led to our work on *Ended Beginnings*. Most
works on the subject of grief have been written by those
personally touched by loss and in need of emotional healing. The written word seems to offer a means for expressing
that which otherwise might remain unexpressed. In this
sense, *Ended Beginnings* is no exception.

However, this book was also written to document a successful program for healing childbearing loss, a program that we developed at Offspring, our counseling center for childbearing parents. We are grateful to all those who inspired its development: the thousands who wrote or called Offspring crying out for help—for support and healing of pregnancy related losses. Each letter or call expressed a uniquely different story; yet almost all sought physical, emotional, mental or spiritual guidance in the healing process with a depth of longing for relief that has been the true inspiration of this work.

We define childbearing loss as not only miscarriage, stillbirth, and infant death (including sudden infant death syndrome), but also infertility, release to adoption, the birth of handicapped children, and abortion. We include as well losses inherent in surgical deliveries, traumatic birth, and the postpartum period. Although the latter three categories may be considered minor losses in comparison to the excruciating burdens of the former, *no* loss should remain unhealed, and no one should endure pain unacknowledged. True healing cannot be reached by comparing one person's pain with another's, for in the final analysis we all deserve—and desperately seek—resolution. The pain of grief already causes enough division. We have seen far too many bereaved parents struggling on alone, assuming that their losses are beyond the scope of others' understanding or support. While each loss *is* unique, each person's grief is truly understandable, if we view one another with compassion and acceptance.

We each weave our threads of sorrow into the human fabric of loss, and the combined threads produce a pattern. We can try to see that pattern, to see the similarities in grief in all of us—whether we are grieving a stillborn infant, a handicapped child, or a birth that didn't meet any of our dreams and expectations. We can try to act in a way that supports each other, to accept each other's genuine feelings and grief, regardless of the events and circumstances. *Ended Beginnings* is a plea that we choose a united path of healing, not only for ourselves, but for all others in sorrow.

*Ended Beginnings* is also a manual dedicated to the healing of the *whole* being: body, mind, heart, and soul. Full healing requires that peace and harmony be restored to one's total being—physically, mentally, emotionally, and, perhaps most important, spiritually.

Our focus is first on physical needs. The physical body is weakened and disrupted by the stresses inherent in pregnancy loss. The body, therefore, requires direct care through nutritional consciousness and physical support. Without such attention, mental anguish and emotional heartbreak are often unnecessarily prolonged because the physical being is too weak and malnourished to provide enough strength for effective grieving and healing. Further, the likelihood of future pregnancy losses *increases* when a physically stressed body attempts once again to sustain another fetal life. For many parents, then, loss follows loss. Answering physical needs is absolutely essential.

Once the physical body is restored, emotional and mental resolutions are possible. There are no shortcuts or quick fixes in these phases of healing, for grief is relentless, and it will not be shortchanged. We cannot completely evade its presence in our lives no matter how desperately we may try. Yet peace *is* possible in the mind and the heart when grief and pain are embraced, released and openly expressed. It is no easy task to feel fully our pain, our doubts, our moments of despair. But the alternative to such wholehearted courage is undue emotional suffering, prolonged mental anguish, and possible physical illness as well. We believe that emotional and mental resolution can surely be reached.

It is not enough to seek a return to normalcy, for no such return is possible. No one who has suffered loss is ever again the same; we are either further enlightened and in harmony with our spiritual beliefs, or we are imprisoned in the darkness of our own bitterness, resentment, and self-pity. However entitled we are to such feelings, they are the spiritual killers of our own souls. Love cannot coexist with bitterness and resentment, nor can we ever grow through self-pity. Spiritual resolution, then, is the final step to healing.

*Ended Beginnings* is intended for those willing to give maximum commitment to personal healing. For too long we, especially women, have sought assistance for our life conflicts and lessons externally—in pills, "rescuers," and other ineffective solutions—rather than reaching into our own inner depth of resources and strengths. In so doing, we have weakened ourselves, suffered unnecessarily, and all too often lost our way.

We believe that we who suffer loss *can* find our way. We believe that parents in grief can live without self-inflicted suffering. Pregnancy losses cause enough distress without the additional physical hurt of malnourishment or illness, the emotional pain of blocked feelings, the mental anguish of denied thoughts, and the spiritual imprisonment of bitterness.

And so, to the thousands of parents who have experienced childbearing losses and cried for help and relief, we offer *Ended Beginnings*. We are grateful for the inspiration to present a work dedicated to total healing—of body, mind, heart, and soul. Our hope is that it may guide you through the haze of grief and lead you to an enveloping peace and a restful acceptance. At the very core of peace will live our eternal love for the children who have entered our lives. Even when their time with us has been brief, their impact has been infinite, and they have offered us undeniable opportunities for our own spiritual growth. *They* are the highest inspiration of all.

Claudia Panuthos & Catherine Romeo

# ONE

# PERSONAL INSPIRATION
## Journey Through Loss

Our personal journeys through childbearing loss ultimately led us to the writing of this book. As we worked through our grief and struggled toward healing, we felt a deep kinship—what one of our grandmothers called a sense of "kindred spirit"—with other bereaved parents. Without our personal experiences of loss and without our sense of unity with others who mourn, *Ended Beginnings* might never have been written, and our counseling center, Offspring, might never have been born. Before we share with you our knowledge and ideas about healing childbearing loss, we would like to share something of ourselves. Although the endings we experienced have surely been painful, they have always opened the next set of doors in life's unfolding journey. We feel the truth of bereaved parent Paul D'Arcy's words in *Song for Sarah:* "When we reach one conclusion we only become part of another beginning." Here then are the stories of the endings that transformed our lives.

## CLAUDIA'S STORY

In early August 1972, I drove home from the campus infirmary slightly shocked but mostly delighted at the news that I was pregnant. Both my partner and I were second-year graduate students in a social work degree program. We hadn't planned this pregnancy, consciously at least. But there was clearly no resistance from either of us to the thought that our baby would be arriving the following spring, hopefully after graduation.

Although we both thought ourselves worldly wise—Lee at the age of twenty-six and I at the age of twenty-three—we were painfully naive about the full responsibility and even burden of parenthood. We were newly in love and life was full of beginnings—the romantic kind reflected in freshly cut flowers, newly fallen snow, and a dawning day. Our pregnancy seemed rightfully a part of these beginnings—a reflection of spring love manifested in the childhood dream of becoming a parent.

Lee, even in those early weeks, would touch my belly, talking to our baby. He encouraged growth and health and communicated aloud his dreams of becoming our child's father. This was Lee's second child. Jody, his daughter, lived in Georgia, several hundreds of miles away from our Connecticut home. He saw her a few times a year but had grieved over her departure when she moved south with her mother several years before.

In some ways, Lee longed for Jody and to be reconnected to the "father" in himself and was easily caught in the dream of a new baby. We were both so excited that we waived the tradition of waiting through the first trimester before announcing the pregnancy, and we openly shared our news. Neither of us was able to consciously consider that this pregnancy would not result in a full-term, live, healthy baby.

In mid-September I visited the infirmary for my monthly checkup. The nurse practitioner said that I was fine. She warned me about my weight, although I hadn't gained any. The warning seemed a routine practice, well-meant but not in tune.

The physician, however, was concerned that I would be pregnant during my second year of graduate school. In a paternal voice, he asked if I had considered an abortion. His words pierced my insides—not because I thought abortion wrong—but for the first time I remembered that not all pregnancies result in babies.

I felt horrified but calmly responded that Lee and I felt assured that we were doing what was right for us. He then went on to let me know that I could miscarry and that if I did I would be in good company because many women "failed" the first time around. In those days, I was too unconscious to know when I and my sister women were insulted so I thanked him for his time and went home.

The next day school reopened. It was great to see all our old friends and to share summer stories, including the news of our pregnancy. At week's end, our friends took us to a local pub for a celebration drink, which, for me, was a glass of orange juice. The juice was better than champagne because it symbolically stood for the "specialness" that pregnancy affords every woman.

Lee beamed with pride. I saw in his face the manly awareness of the power of being able to create a child. Although I disliked the "macho" implications, I must admit I enjoyed the attention in his newfound protective role as father-to-be. Little did we know that this would be our only celebration.

On Saturday morning, I awoke early to start our weekend chores. We lived in a country house with a wood stove that provided our only heat. Lee and I had agreed to remodel the house in exchange for rent. Since we both enjoyed physical labor and were short on finances, the house seemed like a student's delight.

Just after lunch, I felt some slight cramping in my lower

abdomen. I stopped carrying the wood pieces into the shed and went inside to sit down, thinking that I'd probably overrexerted myself. I slept for several hours and awoke to keep a supper date that Lee and I had made with friends. In hindsight, we realized that we did not discuss our pregnancy throughout the meal as if we already knew that something was wrong.

Lee and I were both unusually quiet driving home. I was very tired and longing to sleep. We pulled into our driveway, and Bernard, our dog (a St. Bernard), ran over to greet Lee. I opened my door and fell to the ground. The pain in my abdomen was severe. Lee carried me into the house. We still clung to the idea that I had done too much physical labor but agreed to go to the hospital just to be sure.

By this time the cramping had increased. The attending physician, a young resident, discovered some vaginal bleeding, which I had not been aware of, and told us we were having a miscarriage. He gave me a dose of Demerol and sent me home, telling Lee that this hospital didn't provide obstetrical care so we'd have to go elsewhere if I needed further medical assistance.

We cried silently to ourselves until the Demerol took effect and I slumped into the car seat. I awoke in our room vomiting out of control and unable to move. Lee cleaned our room and me and nestled in next to me with a bucket in hand. For me the night was a timeless, unconscious Demerol stupor. For Lee it was a prolonged, lonely nightmare as he fearfully sat watch.

At dawn, the drunken-like condition caused by the drug lifted. Lee was asleep sitting up. I tried to stand but passed out in pain. Now we knew this was more than a miscarriage, and the emotional energy of grieving over our lost child was redirected. Our new focus was physical survival as the pain increased and I began to lose my breath.

The next sound I heard was the alarming siren of the ambulance Lee had summoned. Lee screamed at them to move quickly and not let me die. Again I faded out. Every bump in the road reverberated in my pelvis.

Quickly physicians rushed from the emergency entrance. The voices said, "She's in shock!" And then all was dark. Before my eyes surrounded by a white moving mist stood my grandaunts Molly and Nel, both of whom had died during my junior year of high school. They smiled. It wasn't frightening. I thought they would reach out to me but instead they just watched and walked away. I awoke in the recovery room, and Lee was whispering in my ear, "Don't die, Dooby [a nickname he'd given me], don't, Dooby."

When I finally regained consciousness, we were both so relieved that I had survived that we were light years from grieving over our lost pregnancy. We soon learned that I had had an ectopic pregnancy—a condition where a fertilized egg lodges itself outside the uterus. In my case, the condition was undiagnosed and resulted in a ruptured tube.

Lee was thrown into terror at the thought of my dying. He later told me that a physician warned him before my surgery that I was in serious condition and could die. His eyes were glazed for months after the incident. I was grateful to be alive and experienced a new, deeper sense of purpose in my life. Although I felt this sense of spiritual growth in a genuine way, I also buried my grief for months—a healthy condition considering the physical recovery alone that needed to occur.

The hospital stay was a nightmare. No one spoke to me about what had happened. The staff avoided my room unless some physical care had to be given. I knew that even my presence had activated unresolved emotions, particularly in the nursing staff. Twice when I rang my buzzer for blankets at night, I was told to go back to sleep and stop bothering people for blankets because there weren't any I could have. The second time I questioned the response by asking if someone could possibly walk to another floor in search of extra blankets, and I was told to get up and put my clothes on if I was that cold. I did and the next morning the day nurses screamed at me for being in bed with my clothes on.

After this, I knew I would be better at home, so I signed myself out of the hospital and went home with Lee, who wrapped me in sleeping bags in front of the wood stove. The only objection to my leaving the hospital came from my physician, who was concerned that I had not yet moved my bowels. I assured him that if I failed to go, he'd be the first to know.

It is clear to me now that Lee and I were both in a state of deep shock. In an attempt to ground ourselves emotionally, we returned to our normal school routine the following week. Neither of us was able to evaluate my physical condition appropriately so we both basically ignored it. The grieving body, however, has a relentless way of being heard. Although I somehow managed to function for three months after the surgery, I developed severe anemia coupled with a case of mononucleosis. The blood disorders resulted in my missing six weeks of school. Fortunately, my professors allowed me to work at home to complete my graduation requirements.

Lee and I had basically closed ourselves off to any discussions of feelings about our pregnancy. When I bordered on mentioning it, his eyes would open wide in fear and his body would tighten. These signals were enough of an excuse for me to back off since, for the most part, I was still more hurt that I could touch. Both of us seemed to need time.

However, the relationship between Lee and me was never the same again. Our dreams of family, future, and parenthood had literally burst. We would have no baby in the spring and little ability to communicate our pain in the present.

I'm not sure whether Lee ever really let himself have his disappointment or acknowledge his inner hurt. Mine came to a head one Thursday afternoon in downtown Hartford.

I was back at my field placement in a local alternative

high school. My field adviser took kindly to me and gave me the opportunity to make up lost days. The school was located in an old railroad station across from a municipal parking lot.

On this particular Thursday, I was anticipating no unusual occurrences. I drove to what I thought was the parking lot. I was just across from the school at an odd angle. However, I somehow had taken what I thought was a wrong turn and lost my way, I circled back around and again looked upward for the lot.

At this point, I was frustrated and mildly anxious. I remember warning myself not to ask a passing policeman where that lot was located. I was feeling a little crazy and was afraid he'd notice it.

Then I began to cry. I sobbed and sobbed for over an hour and a half. I had lost much more than a parking lot. I had lost my baby, a part of my husband, and a thousand tender moments in a family's life.

The images of a little girl of three dressed in pink-checked gingham, of a six-year-old starting her first day of school, of a twelve-year-old who began her menstrual cycle, and an eighteen-year-old ready for her high school prom paraded before my eyes. I felt that I needed to speak to her, and she needed a name. I named my child Elizabeth. I told her how upset I was—how angry I was that she had checked out on Lee and me.

I told her now very much I loved her and that I was very much with her and with my lost dreams of mothering my child.

It made no difference to me whether Elizabeth was actually a girl. My heart told me this is so. What did matter was that I found a way to reach the part of myself that had been lost as well.

The tears subsided and a passing fire engine jolted me back to the reality of downtown Hartford traffic. The parking lot was on my right—a stark reality and a reminder of the present. I started my car and paused one last moment to mourn Elizabeth.

Lee and I were unable to recover both from our own overidealized dreams and from the genuine reality of our loss. Our lives went on but always separated by the unspoken words and unexpressed despair. Certainly it would seem that two clinical social workers supposedly trained in communication and emotional expression should have healed more fully. We could not.

A year later we got pregnant again. I was a clinical social worker in a mental health center at the time. I did not allow myself to become excited because I knew the other side of elation all too well.

It didn't matter much because when I miscarried, I was still heartbroken to once again not become a mother with a child whose face I could see and whose hand I could touch.

A little less than a year later, we got pregnant again. Again, we miscarried. This time the loss was too much to bear. No more babies, we thought. No more pregnancies, dreams, hopes left unfulfilled. No more physical hurt, stress, bleeding.

Our grief was silent and our mourning muffled by our own unconsciousness and our culture's failure, at that time, to be awakened to such loss. It took almost seven years before I opened my eyes and all my senses to the external cultural denial of grief and the internal unresolved pain of pregnancy loss.


## CATHY'S STORY

Soon after our marriage in 1968, John and I began to hope for a child. The hopes just didn't turn into a baby. We groped through more than three years of infertility, praying every month that I wouldn't get my period and losing a measure of faith and trust in our bodies every time I did.

Our youthful confidence and blithe expectations seeped away with each nonpregnant menstrual flow.

After almost a year of trying to conceive, we consulted a gynecologist. He confirmed our suspicions that something must be wrong by telling us that if a couple did not conceive within a year, they were assumed infertile until proven otherwise. He would begin a series of tests, attempting to ascertain what the problem was. I left the office that day feeling branded; no scarlet letter could have made me feel more conspicuous than I already did. I was certain that people *knew* and that my failure to conceive—to do what women are expected to do—was written all over me. John later expressed similar feelings to me—feelings of inadequacy, lost masculinity, humiliation. Funny, though, that we each blamed our own selves. I wanted to crawl into a hole and hide from the world.

The world wouldn't let me do that. Our immediate families were sensitive to our feelings, but those feelings were considered to be so private then; we didn't share them easily, for somehow we were caught in webs labeled "failure" and felt too deeply ensnared to share ourselves. However, extended family and some friends allowed us no such seclusion. "Well," one aunt prodded, "Isn't it about time you two started a family? Your parents aren't getting any younger, you know, and they want to enjoy grandchildren before they die." "What are you trying to do," another demanded, "make a fortune before you have children? Don't you know kids need *young* parents?!" Someone else commented within earshot that "maybe we were too selfish, too wrapped up in ourselves" to have children. If a pregnant woman was near, someone might remark that maybe we could ask how it was done.

Interestingly, it was usually I who came in for the criticism and judgments, the assumption being that I, being female, controlled the situation. People would wait until I was alone and then level their opinions. I always felt shattered by each barrage of insensitivity. The comments we heard would be in poor taste in any circumstance, but given our deep desire to conceive, they were intolerable. John took to staying by my side at social gatherings and responding to pregnancy questions with joking comments like "Listen, I must be shooting blanks!" People laughed and the tension eased, but John would cringe inside; maybe he was shooting "blanks." Maybe I wasn't receiving. We just didn't know. The tests we were taking were initially inconclusive. They were also degrading, humiliating, and devoid of respect or reverence for life. The memories flood my mind: catching sperm in a specimen envelope, keeping it warm, and rushing it to a lab; having intercourse at a prearranged time and then rushing me to a fertility clinic so my body could be examined under glaring lights right after the act; having bits of my uterine lining manually——and painfully—removed so that they could be microscopically examined; having my uterus and fallopian tubes shot full of fluoroscopic dye so a group of medical people could determine whether there were clear pathways for conception.

Lovemaking, the most intensely personal and deeply intimate connection between John and me, became a clinical function laid bare to a battery of white-coated doctors and probing technicians. No wonder we protected what shreds of our privacy were left; no wonder we shrank from discussing the whys and wherefores of our non-pregnant state with the rest of the world. I search in my mind for any memory of human understanding from our medical care givers. There just isn't any there; there was none then. Doctors either glibly advised us not to worry, "it will happen"; or they coolly and impersonally related test results overlaid with impassive medical opinions.

We felt like malfunctioning machines; we were treated that way. Not one of them, *not one*, put a hand on my arm, looked into my eyes, and said, "This is really tough. It must feel just awful. I'll work with you until we run out of questions to ask." The world's callousness was painfully hard to bear. My faith in my body and John's in his, our images of personal health and well-being, our expectations of ourselves and our marriage—all these were being drained from us with every menstrual period I marked off on my calendar.

It was such a sad and bewildering and painful time. We lived month to month, looking for signs of pregnancy. We were told that pregnancy seemed possible; we both were judged somewhat less fertile than average, but we seemed capable of conception. Finally, the bands of anxiety were released when Sharon was conceived. Hearing that we were, in fact, pregnant was one of the most joyous, exciting, liberating moments of our lives, only eclipsed by Sharon's birth. Becoming pregnant worked so much healing for me, but I often think, with aching compassion, of all those who do not conceive. My desire to foster healing in others was born before Sharon was, as I thought about all the women whose times of waiting for a child stretch on and on and on.

A year after Sharon's birth, I miscarried after what seemed to be a four-week pregnancy. I believed that I was pregnant, but we hadn't yet confirmed the pregnancy with a lab test when I began to bleed. An examination indicated that I had probably been pregnant. The experience shook me, frightened me, and resurrected all my fears of body failure. Maybe there really was something very wrong, very inadequate, or very incomplete inside. Was I really a woman who had safely given birth? I didn't *feel* safe or secure or confident any more. What of the baby I had lost? Did my body fail my child? What happened? Where was my child? Was he or she whole and complete somewhere outside my body? I felt wrapped in a murky fog for weeks, and moving through that fog was such an effort. Nothing was clear; my doctor couldn't even prove that I had been pregnant. But I knew that I had been pregnant, and I felt that the child I lost deserved at least recognition of his existence (I even felt that I had lost a boy). No one seemed to understand. Almost everyone forgot within days that I had miscarried.

Finally, I just pushed past the murkiness and buried my instinctive feeling of loss deep inside. I didn't know then that buried sorrow can be drawn to the surface by a later loss and magnify grief and pain.

Two years passed before our attempts to conceive were successful again. That pregnancy was difficult. The specter of miscarriage haunted days that would otherwise have been filled with joy and expectancy. My body gave some signals of stress, some signs that I might deliver too soon, yet I did carry to term. Paul was safely delivered, and we were joyous.

Three years later we conceived our second daughter, and it was Allison's birth that ultimately dictated my involvement in this book. Strange, some may think. A healthy child. A lovely family. Yet Allison's birth was to plummet us into loss—genuine, grief-stricken, honest-to-God, angry-with-God loss. And that loss called up the other unhealed losses I had experienced in the past, until I was overwhelmed with sadness.

My pregnancy with Allison was the most positive, comfortable pregnancy I had had. The spectres of failure and loss had faded into the background, and we began to look forward to our baby's birth. Our first two children had been born in a major Boston hospital. At each birth we had felt so vulnerable; some aspects of the care we received frightened or angered us. We had felt anxious for our babies' well-being and weren't confident that the medical care we received would safeguard them. So, as time passed in that third pregnancy, we grew fearful of returning to that same hospital. Our years of infertility had left us with a lack of confidence and trust in medical care givers. We hadn't felt honored or respected in most of our medical interactions related to pregnancy, nor had we felt that the hospital atmosphere itself was one of deep respect for life.

We had attended the home birth of our dear friends' daughter, Andrea. At her birth we felt the reverence. We even felt a deep spiritual sense that perhaps God was guiding us to such a birth as well in order to safeguard our child. To find more answers, we attended a weekend spiritual retreat for couples, and we felt more sure that God was guiding us to rely on truly natural birthing.

So, after months of fact-finding and soul-searching, we decided to give birth at home. It was a deeply spiritual, prayerful decision for us. We felt safe there; we found superb, well-trained midwives and excellent obstetrical back-up; we were confident we were making a responsible and safe choice for our child's birth; we envisioned a birth with all of us, our two excited older children and several loved ones, welcoming our new baby; and above all else we dreamed of a peaceful, *safe* birth smiled upon by God and with all of us surrounded by protective guardian angels.

The reality was far from peaceful or heavenly. Active labor was only forty minutes long, overwhelmingly intense and precipitate. Allison was almost delivered, when her heart rate began to drop, and then suddenly it disappeared. The midwife listening for a heartbeat shook her head—there was no heartbeat! I *had* to push my baby out of my body *immediately* to save her life. I poured all of my strength into birthing her. She slipped out of my body, and for a few seconds I blanked out, overcome and traumatized by so rapid and frightening a labor. It had been breathtaking, overwhelming, terrifying.

And then, there she lay, my daughter—not breathing, blue-white, and without a heartbeat. Despite all our plans and prayers, Allison hadn't even been kept safe. The thought that she might die stunned me. I watched, helplessly, as our skilled midwives worked on her tiny body, applying CPR. It was the most excruciatingly painful moment of my life, to see one of my children in such need, in mortal danger, and to merely watch. I remember praying aloud and hearing John pray too as he held me. We begged God not to let our daughter die. Where *was* God? Where was our spiritually-felt guarantee of a safe birth? We spoke to Allison, too, imploring her to breathe. Her heart began to beat again, and she drew a ragged breath—and stopped. Four endless minutes passed, with our midwives breathing into her, and then she began to breathe, first intermittently, and then more steadily. She seemed to be coming around, but we called for an ambulance to take us to the nearest hospital immediately.

And then our birth dreams fell into even greater shreds. Our call intended only for an ambulance brought the entire "911" emergency team. Our quiet residential street was overtaken by a fire engine, a police car, an ambulance, and at least one hundred people. We lost our gentle chorus of angels to the blaring of sirens. Yet Allison continued to improve even during our ambulance trip to the hospital. The first doctor who met us there pronounced her fine, and I began to breathe more evenly myself. I also began, in that moment, to deny my grief. After all, he had just told me I had a healthy baby so what cause did I have for sorrow?

It took such effort to hide that grief. And the guilt—had I endangered my baby by the choices I had made? Why hadn't my body worked "right" this time? Was it my fault, something I did or didn't do? My pasted-on smile hurt my jaws. My shoulders and neck ached from the effort of holding my head high. I felt exhausted, more exhausted than I've ever felt in my life, and yet my new baby was sleeping longer stretches than either of her siblings had. Why was I so tired? I didn't understand at all. Nor did I understand why my uterus continued to bleed, on and on, well past the normal period of postpartum lochia discharge. I know now that the effort to suppress my natural grief—grief for my lost visions, and expectations, and dreams of Allison's birth and for my no longer intact spiritual faith—took quite a toll and lots of energy. I believe my uterus "wept" for the vision of labor we, my body and I, never got to experience. It wept for the "safety" I had tried so hard to guarantee and then couldn't find at Allison's birth. It wept for my years of helpless infertility, for my unrespected miscarriage, for all the loss and pain I had tried to hide—and never healed. And the horror of watching one of my children lying so very still, without breath or life, had been a shock I still felt overpowering me. We watched her anxiously, searching for signs that she was truly normal and healthy, that she hadn't been harmed at her birth. I felt myself teetering on the edge of control, trying to calm the shaking terror that seized me as I endlessly replayed in my mind the scene of Allison's birth.

We had come so close to losing her. Life felt so tenuous to me. I was so afraid to unleash my grief, afraid of its intensity, of what it might do to me, especially when all the world judged me so lucky, so blessed. I held the lid on tight.

One night, though, about five months after Allison's birth, that lid was unexpectedly knocked off. I had attended a lecture by Michel Odent, a remarkable French obstetrician who encourages women to labor in pools of warm water. He brought some lovely and dramatic slides showing laboring women soothing and relaxing their bodies in his birthing center's warm, shallow pools. Suddenly, while I was confronted with those peaceful, idyllic images of birth, my memories of Allison's frantic, frightening, jarring birth flooded my mind. I heard a loud, rushing sound in my ears, and I felt as though I were choking, drowning. All those unshed tears rose up to fill my throat and cloud my eyes. Once the lid was off, there was no clamping it back on. My buried grief, and all the unacknowledged and unhealed losses in my life, clasped me in a tight stranglehold, and finally I could do nothing but surrender.

It was six months after Allison's birth, and yet the tears wouldn't stop coming. I blamed myself for what had happened; I blamed God; but I felt no peace, no matter how much I thought about everything I grieved. All the pain of infertility, all the shock of miscarriage, all my doubts about my body's adequacy came flooding back. My faith in myself, in my body, and in God was shattered this time in a way that demanded complete reconstruction. It was an ending, but it was also a beginning, for I couldn't rest until I had once again found peace in my life.

## THE NEED FOR HEALING

Through our personal journeys, we were led to seek healing for ourselves and inspired to create an approach that may be valuable to others who know the footsteps of grief. We asked ourselves: "Could the pain ever be relieved? Could the iron rig of loss lodged around the heart ever be truly dissolved?"

Psychiatrist Elisabeth Kubler-Ross, pioneer and world-renowned authority in the field of death and dying, tells us that grief is a gift. It is a pure, natural emotion—the infinite sadness of missing a loved one or losing something cherished. When grief is unfiltered, it is right and good and healthy. It needs no work or change or therapy. Kubler-Ross says that it heals itself. But when we begin to filter our grief through sieves of guilt, anger, resentment, bitterness or self-pity, then we need to work, to do what psychiatrist and bereavement researcher Erich Lindemann termed our "grief work" (1979). Grief cannot purify these adulterations (Kubler-Ross 1980-83).

We, as a culture, have failed to prepare ourselves for the experience of death. This lack of preparation has made these adulterations, for most of us, completely unavoidable. It then becomes our task to transform those sieves, in order that our grief may come to healing.

In a lecture given in Boston in 1983, Kubler-Ross stated that she would want to title her next book "I'm Not Okay, You're Not Okay; But That's Okay." What a lovely, hopeful thought. Even though most of us will confront our basest humanity when we deal with loss, we can hope to grow, to patch up our sieves and to let our grief run pure.

We believe that grief is a gift, that healing is not only a possibilty but a vital necessity, and that transformation can supersede human suffering. When football pro Roosevelt (Rosie) Grier sang "It's all right to cry" on the Marlo Thomas television production *Free To Be You and Me,* many women and some men sighed with relief and felt freer to acknowledge, express, and work through their grief. Tears and pain went public, and more attempts at healing and resolution came forth.

Parents and professionals offer us many works today on pregnancy losses. It is a relief to see the many possible readings on the subject. However, no attempt at genuine healing is complete unless the approach supports the healing of the entire body—body, mind, heart and soul. The process of grieving will affect these four aspects of who we are, what Kubler-Ross calls our four "quadrants."

Holistic health care strives to treat the entire being, knowing that all parts are always interdependent. *Ended Beginnings* is a holistic approach to grieving and healing. It explores all four aspects of childbearing loss: the physical, the emotional, the mental, and the spiritual. It offers a model for holistic healing, including visualization and guided imagery exercises we have used successfully in our parents-in grief workshops, as well as in individual counseling. Our approach supports each bereaved parent in finding his or her own best way to feel whole once again. Our book is written for those who believe the process of healing emanates from within the resource system innate in our very beings.

*Ended Beginnings* takes those who join us beyond presentations of what loss is, how it feels, and what is normal and offers a unique healing program designed to transform loss.

It is true that we mourning parents do need to know that we are sane, that our overwhelming feelings are indeed normal, but we need far more. We need confidence to trust ourselves, and we need non-judgmental guidance to find our own way.

It is true that we need the opportunity to release feelings, to express and share our pain, but we need more than willing ears. We need information and support to aid in our physical recovery process. We need a system for release that allows for ultimate resolution without unnecessary suffering and clinical diagnostic judgment. We need some tools for spiritual reconciliation and acknowledgment of information and intuition not documented in traditional scientific terms.

Our personal journeys and yours led all of us to the pages in this book. Let us walk together a path toward genuine restoration and healing. Let us look to our spouses, relatives, friends, and physicians for genuine emotional support. But let us look ultimately to ourselves, to our own inner wisdom. This inner focus can transform pain so that we may be free to turn outward again.

# TWO

# THE MILLIONS IN MOURNING

Who are the mourners? They are ourselves; they are our mothers, fathers, sisters, aunts, grandparents, friends, and neighbors. Literally millions of women and men are touched annually by some form of pregnancy loss. These experiences may vary in intensity and impact, but all are painful and some are devastating.

Webster's defines mourning as "the act of sorrowing," "a period of time in which signs of grief are shown" (Ninth New Collegiate Dictionary 1983). We have all felt sorrow for some loss, if only for the loss of our own hopes and dreams. Pregnancy losses are indeed the loss of hopes, dreams, faith in ourselves, and—most painful of all—our own children.

We believe it is crucial to view pregnancy losses in the largest possible sense for two important reasons. First, many families have suffered multiple losses and must mourn each and all of them in some sense. For example, many women who have experienced a stillbirth may also have been surgically delivered in a medical attempt to save the dying child. The loss of the child is so all-consuming that grieving the loss of vaginal delivery (a common grief experience for many) may not come to parents until later, until they are pregnant again, perhaps.

Often, then, that unacknowledged grief over surgical birth may burden a future birth experience with bottled-up fear, anger, and sorrow—feelings that had been overshadowed by grief for the lost child.

It is not uncommon for families to have experienced more than one pregnancy-related loss over the childbearing years. A woman may have had an abortion in late adolescence or early adult life that seems adequately resolved until she miscarries ten years later and discovers she is confronted with grief for both losses simultaneously. All too often she may suffer in silence, afraid of telling even her husband of the abortion she has kept so secretly in her heart for fear of being judged.

There is a second reason why we consider childbearing loss in the widest possible sense. In this age of constantly changing views of childbearing, may of us feel confused, uncertain, afraid, and very alone as we face choices and decisions about our own and our children's futures. This is a time when forming supportive relationships is very important. Therefore, we need to take an approach to healing that will support our similarities as we grieve rather than compare and compete in our differences. Although the experience of loss is unique to each individual and influenced by the external events, the inner resolution requires some very similar attention physically, emotionally, mentally and spiritually.

It is our hope that by beginning the task of healing with greater awareness of our similarities we will be better able to support one another as women, men and as parents and perhaps avoid the additional pain caused by alienation and separateness. It seems almost our human nature to think in comparative terms: which loss is more serious, who hurts the most, or who has the most indisputable right to grieve. In this system of thought, we all live in the illusion of emotional scarcity, believing that only the one who hurts the most will receive the necessary care. But we can change this way of thinking and living.

In order to heal ourselves, we must abandon such fear-ridden beliefs; we must seek for ourselves the abundant support available when we accept our human similarities and are open to emotional resolution. In this spirit of brotherhood and sisterhood, we can truly heal.

With that goal in mind, we will discuss in this chapter the experiences of miscarriage, ectopic pregnancy, stillbirth, neonatal death, sudden infant death syndrome, infertility and abortion. In Chapter 3, we will cover the additional losses common to normal birthing and postpartum recovery, surgical and other traumatic births, premature delivery, and release to adoption. Through this broad-based approach, we shall begin to know the millions in mourning.

## MISCARRIAGE

Each year in the United States alone approximately six to eight hundred thousand women miscarry. These figures don't account for unreported fetal losses. Miscarriage is probably the least acknowledged and the most misunderstood of all pregnancy- and birth-related deaths, yet it ends as many as 20 percent of all conceptions.

Even in the 1980's many women who miscarry will be unconsciously insulted by their family, friends, and physicians who still remain unaware of the inevitable biological bonding between mother and child. Studies of bonding have clearly demonstrated that a tender and loving bond exists between mother and child long before an infant is born, a kind of biological bonding that may even occur as early as conception (Kennell, Slyter, and Klaus 1970). Yet we have so easily bought the "nonattachment" syndrome, the illusion that women who miscarry are not connected to their children.

We are also often unaware of the physical effects of miscarriage. Many women who miscarry will undergo a procedural D&C (dilation and curettage) to insure that the uterus has been cleared. Anesthetized, medicated for pain and possible infection, they will incur all the physical violations necessary or at least inherent in surgical procedures. Yet very little, if any, attention will be paid to the effects of these physical stresses alone.

Sociologists Peppers and Knapp (1980) have recorded the grief reactions of many women to various perinatal losses. They found that women who miscarried demonstrated grief reactions equal in intensity to those of women grieving over fetal and infant death and different only in duration. They also found that women who miscarried were often unable to resolve their mental questions and concerns about what actually happened.

Unresolved questions are often the basis of long-term guilt and self-punishment. Palinski and Pizer (1980) write: "Undoubtedly the strongest emotional response after a miscarriage is guilt. Without exception, every woman we talked with had experienced or was still experiencing feelings of guilt. They looked back for months seeking a probable cause in their own behavior just prior to the miscarriage."

All too often questions turn into mental guilt monsters that fail to support the inner pain of loss. The "pick yourself up, dust yourself off, and go get pregnant again" theme totally discounts the enormity of the experience. Miscarriage is death. It demands respect, not a jocular wink and an admonition to "go home and make a date with your husband."

Miscarriage may create inner feelings of failure and shame, loss of faith in the physical body, and outer conflicts in marriage and family relationships. Culturally, we feel so much shame associated with miscarriage that we have a tradition of not sharing the news of our pregnancies even with our close loved ones until the first trimester has passed and the possibility of miscarriage has lessened.

Some studies indicate a serious increase in marital conflict after a miscarriage. Peppers and Knapp (1980) attribute some of this difficulty to what they term as ''incongruent bonding,'' where the mother has had the biological bonding experience of carrying her child while the father's process has been on a mental, intellectual plane. Perhaps, as in all conflicting situations, the opportunity for marital breakdown after miscarriage increases, but so too does the opportunity for increased support and intimacy.

Cultural permission supports the emotionality of women while men are more heavily trained in cognitive development. We don't, for instance, always expect women to balance a checkbook or change a tire, nor do we fully support men crying in public. This emotional cognitive difference resulting from sex-role programming, combined with the incongruent bonding process inherent in miscarriage, can become a chasm as the mourning mother grieves the loss of a child her male partner has not yet known.

Lacking a physical image to grieve over, cultural permission to be honest, and marital support for feelings, each woman who miscarries in our Western society will all too often mourn alone. There will be no funeral, few condolences, and little compassion for her loss. A great number of women who miscarry will get pregnant again. However, too many will never acknowledge, or be supported in acknowledging, the physical stress of miscarriage and its accompanying emotional loss. Some will experience sexual difficulties and not understand the relationship between these difficulties and the loss. Some will experience secondary infertility perhaps due to physical lack of healing, blocked emotional hurt, or both. Yet somehow most of these 600,000 or more women will find a way to go on with their lives, grieving, perhaps, in silent anguish.

## ECTOPIC PREGNANCY

Many women attending our counseling sessions while trying to recover from ectopic pregnancy had very little or no prior knowledge that such a condition exists. Yet approximately one in every hundred pregnancies in the United States results in a tubal pregnancy, the most common form of ectopic pregnancy. Ectopic pregnancy refers to any condition where the fertilized egg implants itself outside the uterus.

In recent years, ectopic pregnancies have risen in numbers at a dramatically rapid pace. In a recent study, Sally Faith Dorfman (1983), a gynecologist from Mount Sinai Medical Center in New York City, reported that in 1970 there were eighteen thousand cases of ectopic pregnancy but in 1978 the number had grown to forty-two thousand and in 1981 to sixty-one thousand. This rather alarming rise has been attributed to the increase of sexually transmitted diseases, the possible influence of DES (a drug given to women in the 1940s and 1950s to prevent miscarriage but now known to cause cancer and infertility) and perhaps the pelvic inflammatory disease associated with the birth control use of IUD, the intrauterine device (Grady 1983).

The loss resulting from an ectopic pregnancy can produce a complicated grieving process for the mother, who is grateful to be alive even as she mourns her lost baby. Between 1970 and 1978, ectopic pregnancies accounted for 437 maternal deaths, so this condition does indeed threaten life. The deaths are often caused by undiagnosed ruptures that result in internal hermorrhage (Grady 1983).

For the woman who survives, the impact of the loss is often delayed. Rochelle Friedman, M.D., and Bonnie Gradstein, M.P.H. (1982), write that "During the aftermath, you will probably go through times of vulnerability, bewilderment, anger, guilt, jealousy, and grief if you are like the women we counseled." The simultaneous mourning of both the physical loss of faith in the body and the emotional loss of the child can prolong the healing process. Further loss may be incurred by women who are unable to conceive again or who conceive and experience a second ectopic.

According to Friedman and Gradstein (1983), "Only 50% of women conceive after having an ectopic pregnancy. In addition, there is an increased chance that there will be something wrong with your remaining tube. . . . Subsequently, the woman who has suffered one ectopic pregnancy has an increased risk, 7%-12%, depending on the study, of having a second."

So for the parents mourning ectopic pregnancy loss, the grief may not stop at a lost child, but may become an ongoing grieving process calling for continuous resolution physically, emotionally, mentally, and spiritually.

## STILLBIRTH

More than 195,000 women carry their babies to term or near term every year only to lose them before or at birth. This means that for eighty live births one will be stillborn. Some labor normally with elation at the expectation that they will soon see and hold their live, healthy infants. Others know in advance that the child within has died and are left to suffer the nightmarish pain of carrying a lifeless baby.

In many cases, women begin to experience the warning signals of pain, bleeding, or absence of fetal movement, and may even have some intuitive sense of danger and death. Both parents may deny these signals in a natural attempt to ward off the impending tragedy and to shield themselves against the enormity of the potential loss. Yet all will begin to mourn, even in these early moments of prospective loss.

The actual known causes of stillbirth include umbilical cord accidents and placental problems, toxemia and chromosomal abnormalities. Too often, however, the causes are unknown, leaving parents to wonder what went wrong, what caused this death. In those cases, it becomes even easier for parents to find themselves in some way to blame, deepening the burdensome task of resolution.

Father Martin, the renowned recovering alcoholic priest and spokesperson for Alcoholics Anonymous, often states in his lectures that if there is one thing we are carrying in common, it is the unavoidable human condition of guilt. He talks about life situations that activate our guilt and cause us to punish ourselves. Giving birth to a lifeless child may be the ultimate example of such a situation.

Guilt often results from misinformation or lack of information. Unfortunately, studies indicate that grieving parents may have difficulty obtaining the information they need. In a study by Peppers and Knapp (1980), parents interviewed a year after their loss were still dissatisfied with the medical explanations they had been given. One might attribute some of this reaction to the normal yearning to uncover all that can be known of their child. However, it has been painfully clear in our counseling practice that all too often emotionally overwrought parents meet with resistence, hostility, and lack of support when trying to obtain data, date often rightfully and legally theirs. Peppers and Knapp attribute such nonsupport in part to the formal medical curricula, so intensely oriented toward the living and the saving of lives that effectiveness in dealing with death is hampered or virtually ignored.

In the initial shock, parents wonder whether to hold, touch, and become in some way acquainted with their lifeless child. Some studies indicate that parents who do make such contact ultimately heal more completely. Dr. Emmanuel Lewis, author of several articles on grieving for a stillborn child, feels that parents are able to grieve more effectively for someone who is more fully known emotionally (1976). He further believes that in cases of visual birth defects parents should not be prevented from making contact, since imagined mental pictures are usually far worse than the actual malformations. In our own grief seminars, this has been confirmed by participants, who seem to make their parent-child contact with the "essence" of the child.

Although Lewis's research may give us some important information in order to more adequately support grieving parents, we believe that no findings should become "policy." Each of us must ultimately answer to our own inner voices. Too often we have met parents who fell guilty for not holding their stillborn children even though they felt unable to do so at the time. Kubler-Ross continually urges us to look at the person, not at textbook stages of grief or specific programs for "correct" mourning.

## NEONATAL DEATH

There are many causes for neonatal death, including premature birth, congenital abnormalities, and brain damage due to lack of oxygen. None of these explanations is adequate for a parent who watches a child breathe for only a few minutes, weeks, or months, and then die. The agonies of these grieving parents include the additional burdens of the physical restraints imposed by potentially life-saving equipment that may prohibit the holding of a child in his or her last few hours or the unconsolable nightmare of hearing a child cry when physical comfort cannot be offered. For some parents, there is the heartache of *not* hearing a baby cry. *Born at Risk* (B.D. Colen 1981) tells the story of the silent pain of the neonatal intensive care unit, where babies' cries cannot be heard because the infants are threaded with intratracheal tubing that prevents normal sound.

Parents who are given a hopeless prognosis often wonder how involved to become as they attempt to manage the anticipatory grief of impending death. As Kennell and Klaus remind us, mothers appear to be already attached and bonded to their babies even before birth—a human condition referred to as biological bonding (Kennell and Klaus

1982). For some parents, it would be heartbreaking not to hold their babies or in some way emotionally connect.

For others, the shock would perhaps be too great. Kubler-Ross believes that facing death can be like looking directly into the bright sun—so stark in its nature that we may need to protect ourselves with dark glasses (Kubler-Ross 1969). We must each find our own depth of vision and honor our varying needs to see, to shield our eyes, or even to look away.

When an infant dies, public response is often awkward silence. Peppers and Knapp identified two factors in the nature of grief reactions. The first was the sudden, unexpected nature of the death, and the second was the way the infant is socially defined. In fact, it is only recently that the public community has begun to regard the infant as a living person. Some religious rituals and beliefs have yet to recognize or fully support the parents' loss. Some traditions, for example, hold that a child is not declared a living soul until thirty days after birth and must therefore be treated as such with an unmarked grave. How difficult for some grieving parents to be faced with an age-old doctrine, to feel themselves apart from it despite devotion to their faith, and then know not what to do.

One woman wrote to us at Offspring and said that she had decided to allow her four children to view their brother, Jonathan, who died twenty-four hours after birth. All of the children were ten and over and had been very well prepared for the funeral service. The undertaker, however, was not and berated the parents for allowing the children's presence, telling the parents they were abusive and their decision inappropriate.

## SUDDEN INFANT DEATH SYNDROME

Each year in the United States some twelve thousand to fifteen thousand babies succumb without warning or symptom to Sudden Infant Death Syndrome. Unlike anticipated, explainable death, SIDS, or "crib death," as it is called, gives parents no time to prepare and brace for death emotionally. Nor does it allow the physical body time to marshal its natural defenses, leaving parents and other family members to feel the full and sudden brunt of the loss.

In some cases, SIDS parents suffer the interrogation and suspicion of uninformed authorities who erroneously perceive potential child abuse. Peppers and Knapp (1980) note that "some have spent time in jail and many have suffered harassment due to the lack of understanding and knowledge about this yet unexplained killer of infants."

Although these children have funerals, public acknowledgment, and identified names and personalities, many parents report a sense of isolation and silence after the funeral—perhaps the product of all of our inner helplessness and awkwardness in response to death. Some parents imagine they were in some way to blame for the death, dwelling on thoughts that "if only I had done something different, perhaps my child might have lived." Harriet Sarnoff Schiff, author of *The Bereaved Parent* (1977), describes this severe inner guilt and shares an example of a woman who turned herself in at the local police station six years after the child's death proclaiming herself a murderer. The case unbelievably proceeded through legal channels all the way to the court, where autopsy results showed the baby a victim of Sudden Infant Death Syndrome and the mother a victim of her own inner guilt and pain.

Today through the advances of modern science, potential SIDS children are screened at birth. The family is counseled and taught the technology of life saving, and an alarm system is attached to the infant so that parents are alerted at the first cessation or irregularity in breath. These parents, although often able to save their children's lives, suffer the loss of normal family life and the inconceivable tension of never knowing when they must rush to act in behalf of their child's life. They lose the simple pleasures of having a baby sitter or of sleeping soundly at night, and some even still lose their children. We can hope that much more will be learned about SIDS and that someday we may prevent it.

Now, though, the parents of SIDS victims need the most unwavering support as they feel the sudden weight of grief and struggle to bear it.

## ABORTION

Some people, especially those who mourn other forms of childbearing loss, may cry that a section on abortion does not belong in this book. Yet, approximately one and a half million women abort each year in the United States, and regardless of our beliefs or positions about abortion, it is important to know that abortion creates emotional reactions that often include very deep grief. At Offspring we have seen grief after abortion similar in expression and intensity to that following miscarriage or stillbirth. Such grief is often overwhelming because it may have been totally unexpected by the woman who chose to abort. In these cases, there is virtually no cultural permission to grieve or to seek support after abortion since it was a choice and not a quirk of fate.

Medical advances have made possible the diagnosis of fetal malformations and birth defects. Amniocentesis and ultrasound (although not without risk) can provide information about the normality of a pregnancy. National Institutes of health statistics report that 95 percent of women who learn through amniocentesis that the fetus is abnormal choose to abort. The decision is often painfully difficult, and the process itself is very stressful physically and emotionally. Women who elect to abort under these conditions grieve not only for their lost children, but also for lost faith in their own bodies, and for their lost dreams of motherhood.

Susan Borg and Judith Lasker write in *When Pregnancy Fails* (1981): "In cases of selective abortion, there is grief for a wanted child, questions about the characteristics of the baby—not usually seen by the parents—worries about future pregnancies, ambivalence about abortion itself, and guilt—terrible guilt.'' Even when parents judge that abortion was the right decision for them, they may still feel shocked, overwhelmed by emotions they didn't expect, and filled with grief. Borg and Lasker share one woman's words: '' 'It was very hard to talk to anyone about it. When I did tell someone, it seemed they were either shocked or else they tried to tell me it was all for the best. No one understands that I miss that baby. He was so much a part of me.' ''

Abortion is a physical violation of the body. It is an abrupt violation and produces a rapid hormonal balancing reaction that is often felt as a sort of postpartum depression.

Although a woman may choose to abort for what she feels are the right reasons, she may also feel the loss of her hopes and visions of motherhood or the loss of the culmination of a relationship with a man. She may feel robbed of her childhood dreams or angry because she is the one physically affected, although her male partner, too, was responsible for the pregnancy.

Mentally and spiritually she may question her religious beliefs and moral values. Although abortions are performed in such great numbers today, most women did not grow up in family or cultural systems that supported abortion. It is likely that abortion was either never discussed or that it was overtly condemned. The abortion issue continues to be at the center of conflict in our culture today.

Regardless of a woman's personal feelings, this familial nonsupport and cultural conflict can trigger feelings of shame, guilt and humiliation that may be harbored for years. These feelings may make it impossible for her to heal whatever natural grief she felt over the abortion, and so the residue of loss may linger on and on.

Many women who choose abortion believe that they deserve to be punished in some way. They fear that they will be unable to get pregnant again, will have long and complicated birth experiences, or will give birth to a physically damaged child. Their stressed bodies, minds, hearts and souls often *do* foster other losses.

We recently counseled a woman, Jan, who had had two abortions. She felt so guilty and deserving of punishment that when her health failed, she was not surprised. She expected (perhaps willed) something to befall her. She developed a dangerous infection in the uterus and surrounding tissues. Despite many treatments with antibiotics, the infection persisted, until finally her physician recommended a complete hysterectomy. Jan sought counseling and went through a psychological process of self-forgiveness and spiritual resolution, and the infection disappeared without surgery.

For some women, abortion may have been an agonized-over, conscientiously made choice, truly made out of love for themselves and their yet unknown children. For others, it is a ready choice made with little forethought or concern. yet, often for many women, unanticipated grief is endlessly fueled by subsequent feelings of guilt and lost spiritual consolation. In order for healing to begin, judging must stop. We are reminded of a priest we know who shared his conviction that God created heaven only and left the creation of hell to us. Forgiveness is the only path to peace for us all.

Abortion produces enough hurt and loss without the additional pain of prolonged suffering and feelings of unforgiven guilt. In a recent study of sixty parents, we discovered that those who had had abortions were more likely to have subsequently had miscarriages and cesarean deliveries. The same indications were shown in a study by Margaret Fox, Ph.D. (1982).

The abortion rate continues to rise; currently, more than one and a half million abortions are done annually in the United States. This number is alarming considering all the possible birth control alternatives available to American couples. We are deeply disturbed to hear young women take the attitude of "Oh, well, if I get pregnant, I can always have an abortion,'' an attitude reflected in our current abortion rate. We are incredulous that so many have come to view abortion as a means of birth control and that in China, for instance, it is promoted as a viable method. Unawareness of the physical violation psychological impact, of all of the loss inherent in abortion, has allowed the use of abortion as birth control rather than as a final option in selective situations of need. This pervading ignorance should be combated with thought, reflection, and examination of our values.

We *must* recognize that abortion can produce the same grief felt by those who miscarry or deliver stillborn children. Just as we often brush aside the impact of miscarriage, we almost totally discount the natural grief felt by many of those who abort. That grief can be all the more staggering because it is often completely unanticipated. When a woman's life feels too unsafe to nurture a child, she may think little of her possible feelings of loss until the abortion is done—or in process. In the words of one woman we counseled: ''When the doctor began the abortion, I started to scream. It's been seven months, and I don't know how to make the screaming stop. It's still going on inside me.'' We must recognize that abortion *is* childbearing loss, and that it too needs healing.

## INFERTILITY

A 1983 study by the National Center for Health Statistics indicated that over three million married American women who are not using birth control and who want to have a baby are unable to conceive. This figure represents as many as two in ten couples, according to RESOLVE, a national organization offering information and support to those experiencing fertility problems.

The causes of infertility are sometimes discernible, sometimes not. Dysfunction may be inherent in either male or female, or in both; female infertility is estimated at some 50-60 percent and male sterility at 30-40 percent. We will not attempt to explore all of the causes of infertility, for we seek to focus on the infertile couple's need for support in their grieving and in their healing.

Infertility has been simply described as "involuntary childlessness" (Harrison 1979). There is "primary infertility," where no children are conceived, and "secondary infertility," where parents have a child or children and are unable to conceive again. Secondary infertility is found in approximately 15 percent of the population. Either kind means loss.

Those who cannot conceive a child they want are surely bereaved. They grieve for the loss of their biological heritage, their physical expectations of their bodies. They grieve for the loss of their love personified in a child, a reality of love that could be seen, touched, and held. They also grieve for the potential loss of themselves, for the finality of their own deaths when no children are left to live on.

Infertility creates losses for the couple as separate individuals and as a couple. Many of the tests involve physical violation inherent in any unnatural manipulation or surgical procedure. Treatment may involve risks and dangers and repercussions that may still be unknown. The results of tests and treatment can leave a couple in despair.

Along with the loss of spontaneity in sexual contacts, couples often suffer a loss of faith in their physical bodies and sometimes even a general feeling that the relationship itself is in some way broken, damaged, or handicapped. Feelings of guilt, inadequacy, and blame are common.

For some there may be a grieving for what feels like the loss of one's sanity as test after test proves negative and no physical causes can be determined. It may be true that emotional factors are influential. A few studies have indicated that conception occurred in previously infertile couples after they had completed, or even begun, adoption proceedings. While heightened stress and anxiety may indeed block conception for some, the glib suggestion that adoption will somehow relieve tension and enable a pregnancy to begin may be not only inaccurate for an individual couple but also disrespectful of their feelings. Like the admonition often given to those who miscarry, that they "go home and get pregnant again," the promotion of adoption as a catalyst for pregnancy in infertile couples is at best insensitive.

Other studies cite increased fertility in people who change partners, with, for example, a woman's medical fertility assessment increasing dramatically once she is secure in a new role in life. Perhaps forming a more healthy relationship as a couple and creating a more solid foundation for a child to be born into can remove inner blocks to natural health and fertility. However, such possibilities should not be used as emotional clubs, for people who have loving and complete relationships may still be unable to conceive a child.

In some cases, there may be emotional links to the problem of infertility that can be resolved and that may influence the physical reproductive system. Susan came for emotional counseling and support after seven years of infertility. She had undergone a number of tests and treatments to no avail. She had one son, aged nine, whom she had easily conceived just after marriage, but then through seven years, she was unable to conceive. Susan's son, Eddie, was born three weeks after she discovered that her mother was terminally ill, with less than a year to live. Susan and her husband grieved through Eddie's birth, somewhat in shock at the news that Susan's mother would soon die.

Susan and her family moved into her mother's house, and Susan spent the first year of her son's life caring for him and for her dying mother at the same time. She had psychologically walled herself off from most of the emotion of this period as her way of surviving and coping with her mother's death and the enormous stresses of her own situation.

In our grief work around her infertility, it became clear that she was really mourning the loss of her own mother. She did the necessary grief work and freed herself of the mental and emotional association of childbearing with profound loss. A year later she was able to conceive—a conception she felt was due in part to the emotional release of some long-term stress.

Susan's story should not be construed as a diagnosis or prescription for all infertility. In fact, the bulk of research indicates no specific differences between the emotional lives of fertile and infertile men and women but rather speaks to the myriad of unknown possible factors that may contribute to any life condition.

Susan's story may only remind us that every loss must be fully mourned and healed lest it lead to another. It is crucial, then, that we recognize infertility for the grief-causing loss that it is, and see couples who never conceive but desperately want to as parents bereaved.


## CONCLUSION

Every year those who have suffered childbearing loss are joined by millions of new mourners: 600,000 to 800,000 who miscarry, 60,000 with ectopic pregnancy, the parents of almost 250,000 victims of perinatal death, 15,000 SIDS parents, 1.5 million women who abort, and over 3 million who cannot conceive. In all of these mourners there is a grieving for what is lost, a grieving that will last in some sense for a limited time but in another for a lifetime of unfilled moments. We mourn for the children who once were and now are gone and for those who never will be. We mourn our dreams of a child's first step, first word, first tooth. We mourn for the sounds of children at play, their voices in the classrooms, the report cards never to be seen.

It is our task to heal ourselves so that these losses and this mourning process can become a rich source of blessings rather than unproductive suffering. We cannot forget, but we can be healed.

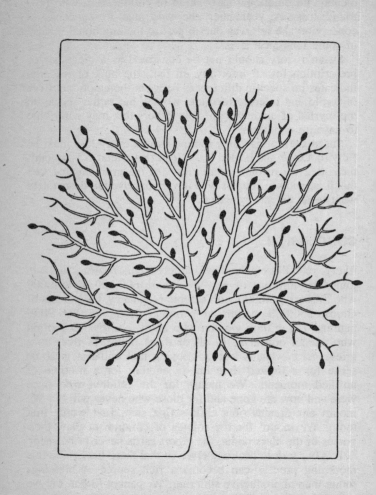

# THREE

# OTHERS WHO GRIEVE

In addition to the millions of parents and family members who mourn lost children, there are millions of others who feel grief over their pregnancy and birth-related experiences. Although childbearing loss may take many forms, the mourning will feel familiar to all aware childbearing women regardless of their differing experiences. This chapter explores the mourning linked to both normal and traumatic birth experiences (including premature delivery and cesarean section) and grief over releasing a child for adoption, as well as the ongoing process of grieving, on some level, over the birthing and rearing of a physically or mentally impaired child.

As we stated in Chapter 2, we have taken this broad-based approach covering many possible pregnancy losses for two important reasons. We restate those reasons now within the context of this chapter.

First, many families suffer multiple pregnancy losses, and

each loss must be acknowledged before healing can be complete. Cesarean section, for example, may precede a stillbirth. The impact of the baby's death will almost surely overshadow whatever loss and stress, both physical and emotional, may be inherent (and felt by the mother) in a surgical delivery.

Women who experience particularly traumatic deliveries may suffer subsequent losses such as secondary infertility, miscarriage, or cesarean section. Until the feelings of grief and perhaps fear over traumatic birth are healed, subsequent pregnancies may be at greater risk of difficulties. Nor is it uncommon for women feeling sad and overwhelmed in postpartum days and weeks to be reminded of prior pregnancy losses—losses that had seemingly been forgotten.

Second, it is helpful to have a frame of reference for an inner experience of loss. This frame of childbearing loss will aid us both in any personal healing process and in our ability to understand and support one another.

We believe that crucial to our collective abilities to heal will be our success in resisting the impulse to isolate and alienate ourselves from one another. When we dwell upon our suffering as greater than that of others or feel that our pain is beyond the scope of others' support or understanding, then we risk further loss: alienating our friends and loved ones. We do not mean to negate the unique grief that each of us may feel; but we do believe that we are capable of recognizing, supporting, and helping to heal each other's pain. All too often we have witnessed grieving parents losing relationships with friends and loved ones—at a time when they have already lost too much.

These broken or damaged relationships are often a result of misunderstanding, lack of communication, unexpressed fear, and overpowering helplessness. By establishing a greater awareness of the similarities in our sorrows, great and small, we hope to bridge these communication gaps.

J.A. Gordon, S.J., wrote: "The tragedy of our lives is the wall we build around our house . . . and the lock we put on our front gate, because they are the symbol of the wall we put around our hearts'' (Sherfan 1971).

We hope that by looking at the many faces of childbearing grief, we may all acknowledge whatever losses—present and past, devastating and seemingly minor—we have known, and then we may come to healing, not alone, but together.

## NORMAL BIRTH AND NATURAL GRIEF

The Tikopia of the Solomon Islands will announce the birth of a child by saying "A *mother* has given birth!" rather than "a baby is born" or "a doctor delivered her" (Raphael 1976). The postpartum Kado woman of Borneo will be massaged, washed, and generally cared for by her kinswomen (Meltzer 1981). The Maya of Mexico will wrap a new mother in swaddling clothes as they will her newborn, feeding her and caring for both (Brazelton 1981).

Yet few American women and men will be appropriately supported and honored. In fact, most parents (especially first-timers) will be shocked by the rapid withdrawal of attention showered on them during pregnancy, by the burdens and overwhelming changes inherent in parenting, by the losses in their relationship as a couple, and perhaps by the isolation and loneliness they may experience. In order for the mother (and father) to be born, the pregnant woman must yield. The body once full with child must become an "empty" vessel, slowly retracting.

Geoffrey Hodson, in his book *he Miracle of Birth* (1981), described the pregnant woman as having a measurable aura or energy that extends several feet beyond the ordinary, nonpregnant human energy field. He further states that as a clairvoyant he could see a white, maternal spirit resembling a guardian angel hovering above the head and back of a woman with child. Although scientific evidence of guardian angels is not available, most people will agree that the pregnant woman radiates a special energy that brings, in many cases, unusual attention from family, friends, and even strangers.

She is likely to be honored at parties and literally showered with gifts. About-to-be grandparents call and write more often. Conflicts with parents are often set aside and new relationships are established.

Men (about to be fathers) may become more attentive, helping with the housework, caring for children, and doing special little things. Men may feel more protective, too. In fact, about-to-be fathers themselves receive more attention. As Bittman and Rosenberg Zalk (1978) write of the expectant father, "Those who love him, will love him more." Pregnant fathers, too, will more likely meet their own parents on more equal terms.

Gas station attendants, bus drivers, supermarket cashiers are all more likely to speak to a pregnant couple, to share a personal story or to give a piece of advice. In fact, pregnant women may be the most well-advised people in our culture!

For some parents, especially women, this attention may help to heal a history of loneliness and lack of affirmation. It may resolve old parent-child conflicts, as the expectant parents meet their own parents on more equal terms. For all its bodily discomforts, the experience of pregnancy may be emotionally satisfying and psychologically healing.

Unfortunately, at birth too many of these benefits may be suddenly and substantially altered. Grandparents may call or visit but will give most of their attention to the newborn child. In fact, they may demonstrate an affection toward their grandchildren that is freer and more accepting than what they gave their own children. In a sense, grandparents' love can be freer, since the burdens of rearing, teaching, and nurturing the children are primarily the parents'.

Friends may seem scarce; lifestyles may change; and personal freedom may be greatly curtailed or seem nonexistent.

The transition from pregnancy to parenthood is very rapid and normally stressful. As Helene Deutsch (1945) notes, "The organism no sooner recovers from the great physiologic shock of delivery than it must assume a new physiologic function, suckling the child.'' This physically stressful period is further compounded by rapid hormonal changes that may greatly influence a woman's inner emotional balance.

However, it must be emphasized that the postpartum period is a psychologically trying time for men and women alike. Studies indicate that fathers, as well as mothers, experience some grief reactions, and these reactions have also been observed in adoptive parents; therefore, their cause cannot be entirely hormonal.

Much of this emotional stress takes place in isolation and loneliness. Many women who are experiencing difficulty do not recognize the overwhelming emotional adjustment necessary and view themselves as inadequate and somehow lacking. Yet in some 250 cultures of the world, the postpartum parent receives more adequate physical and emotional support than in the West.

The Tikopia mother, like new mothers in many cultures, will be assigned a ''doula,'' a woman who will help, counsel, encourage, support, and coddle her throughout her postpartum period. The Western woman, on the other hand, may be supported by her mother (if she lives nearby and is willing or able to help) or by a stranger such as a practical nurse (who receives a paycheck for her work), but probably for no more than a week or two. No wonder the new Western parent is expected to be awkward, nervous, and depressed!

Professor Conrad Arensberg terms the period during which a new mother slowly grows comfortable with her baby and her new role as *matrescence* (Raphael 1976). American mothers are expected to achieve full matrescence sooner than anywhere else in the world. We are often on our own upon leaving the hospital, a few days after giving birth.

Thus confronted with the loss of attention, with cultural abandonment, and with isolation, the childbearing woman is left to mourn her pregnancy while welcoming her newborn child. It should also be noted that she will likely grieve over her unfulfilled hopes of natural childbirth since some 92 percent of American hospital births still involve some medical intervention (Cohen and Estner 1983). Robert Mendelsohn (1981) writes that 10–20 percent of all births are induced; 85–90 percent include a minor surgical procedure (episiotomy); and that in some areas up to 95 percent of births still involve the use of drugs.

Even under what might be considered optimum circumstances, the American childbearing parent has much to grieve over. The thousands of letters in our files and the voices of parents across the land have led us to include normal childbirth as a stressful and perhaps painfully disappointing loss met with inadequate support and attitudes of complete disregard.

Elizabeth Davis (1980) suggests that the cervix opening is a small death and the beginning of several deaths—that of the pregnancy and of the family structure as it once existed. Simply stated, in order for the mother to be born, the pregnant woman must die.

## TRAUMATIC BIRTH

Within the context of Western childbearing practices, traumatic birth and normal birth may at times appear to be the same. Certainly women we've worked with often report it to be so. For our purposes here, we do not attempt to define traumatic birthing by any external standard, since what is traumatic for one may not be felt as so by another. We do seek to honor all our feelings about childbearing, however; and thus if a woman perceives her birth experience as traumatic, then for her it is so.

When birth feels traumatic, women (and men as well) lose more than their visions of what they expected birth to be. They also lose something of themselves, for they often judge themselves as lacking in some way. Women traumatized by birth grieve for their fragmented images of birth and for their own shattered self-images. In their very vulnerable postbirth grief, they may have difficulties adjusting to parenthood. The tender new relationship between mother and infant may suffer. In addition, these women, and their men too, often feel terrified by any prospects of future childbearing.

Two types of birth experiences, cesarean section and premature delivery, may be especially difficult. Since they are, unfortunately, relatively common, we discuss these experiences separately in the following sections.

The experience of traumatic birth demands recognition, for it certainly exists. Far too many women and men hold in their hearts no joyful memories of their children's births, and the sadness of that loss can filter through the years. Birth is always a powerful experience; when it is also traumatic, its impact is enormous.

## CESAREAN SECTION

The status of cesarean section in our country today has become a source of much heated debate. Since the publication of *Silent Knife: Cesarean Prevention and Vaginal Birth After Cesarean*, by Nancy Wainer Cohen and Lois Estner (1983), and other writings focusing on the burgeoning cesarean rate, and because of the grassroots work of the Cesarean Prevention Movement and similar organizations, people are questioning the widespread use of this surgical procedure, which now accounts for more than seven hundred thousand births annually.

The public alarm and accompanying confusion stems, in part, from the fact that only fourteen years ago the cesarean section rate was 5 percent of all births. Today that figure has more than tripled in the national average, with some large teaching hospitals reaching the 50 percent mark. Suzanne Arms (1975) believes that surgical deliveries may become a method of choice in the future, a not implausible suggestion since Brazil's cesarean rate is 60 percent. For many women and children, this surgical procedure has been a life-saving miracle. The controversy over its increasingly widespread use has caused confusion and concern among parents, who are often left to wonder whether the surgery that many of them feel robbed them of their hopes and dreams of birthing was, in fact, a medical necessity. This confusion has further burdened parents by leaving such questions open to guilt-ridden, self-punishing answers. Some parents will never know the answers.

For we often cease to wonder why and simply surrender to the inevitable mourning that accompanies a birth and in particular a surgical delivery. Whether a cesarean is necessary or not, the procedure adds many additional stresses to the childbearing process. Delliquadri and Breckenridge (1978) remind us that the cesarean mother is "not only postpartum and subject to all the natural grief of normal birthing, but she is also 'post-surgical.' " Her body has undergone great pain, stress, and physical invasion, which will require additional physiological attention and emotional resolution.

We certainly do not assume that every parent will be affected in some standardized way but rather remind ourselves that a surgical delivery is always a physical and emotional one. To say "But I had a great cesarean" may mean that the delivery was the best possible with much emotional support and caring.

Much has been accomplished in recent years (through the work of organizations like C/SEC—Cesareans/Support, Education & Concern) to make this procedure more humane, and more family-centered. Linda Meyer, in *Cesarean (R) Evolution* (1979), describes how women now have choices as to medications. Hospital policy rules governing a father's participation and maternal-infant separation have changed and are now changing to support the individual needs of the birthing family.

However, to deny the psychological grief and physical stress of surgical birth is to be painfully and perhaps dangerously unaware. The body's physical system alone is severely stressed and attempts to compensate and heal itself for many weeks.

In addition to the physical stress, cesarean parents may mourn the loss of their hopes and dreams of a peaceful vaginal birth. There is often the lost sense of control, the loss of the teamwork and harmony of partners united in an effort to birth their child, and the loss of the special early moments of intimacy between parents and children.

Since most childbirth preparatory efforts are aimed at normal, vaginal deliveries, cesarean parents are often unprepared, shocked, and overwhelmed. Sadly, our counseling experience and the letters we've received indicate that many parents feel they have somehow "failed" at birth; or worse, they imagine that they have taken the easy way out. How ironic is the latter when you consider the physical stress and emotional impact a cesarean mother is willing to undergo on behalf of her child. She is very much like any brave mother animal, willing to sacrifice herself if she perceives her young is in danger and believing that what is done will save her child. Regardless of the external conditions, most women agree to cesareans because they believe it is the most responsible thing to do at the time.

The highly regarded bonding studies of Kennell and Klaus have identified an instinctive, natural urge in parents to hold and to be close to their newborns. In fact, Kennell and Klaus (1982) believe that biological bonding may occur as early as conception or shortly after for some women. To be separated from a newborn even by some life-threatening emergency, or, inexcusably, by a senseless hospital policy, can be profoundly painful. Our counseling sessions and seminars throughout the country have awakened us to the potential depth of such a loss. We have witnessed women releasing floods of tears as they related painful post-birth separations from their infants. A number of women still report feelings of grief over the postbirth separations they experienced, ten, fifteen, and twenty years ago, when hospital policies commonly dictated a twenty-four-hour special care nursery observation of cesarean-delivered infants.

All too often cesarean parents are discouraged from effectively grieving over their losses by reproofs such as "You have a healthy baby, what more do you want?" For parents who lose their babies to neonatal death, the effects of the cesarean are often forgotten, overshadowed by the impact of death. Yet the surgical delivery may be very much a part of the total picture of birth-related loss; and complete healing must then also include the privilege of mourning the total experience of loss.

Birth by cesarean section means childbearing loss for millions of women. As such, it must be honored. The preface of Nancy Wainer Cohen's and Lois Estner's *Silent Knife* (1983) explains: "We know that many cesarean women are bitter and sorrowful. . . . For many women, becoming pregnant and giving birth are integrally and intricately linked with feeling of self-worth and identity. Is it any wonder so many women in our culture are grieving? To want to give birth in a way that unites us with other women—to all women, to WOMAN—to want to experience each of the cycles of our life, is not insane. It is normal."

## PREMATURE BIRTH AND INFANTS AT RISK

In 1922 the Michael Reese Hospital of Chicago opened the first infant care center for premature babies. In 1983 there were well over five hundred such centers across the land, with primary locations in large, urban teaching hospitals. They are needed, for it is estimated that one out of every seven infants born this year will be born at risk (Colen 1981).

Low birth weight is one indication of an infant at risk. The agreed upon definition of low birth weight is a birth weight of less than five and a half pounds or twenty-five hundred grams. One-half of all low birth weight infants are considered "premature" and the other half are "small for dates" (Kitzinger 1980). All of these children will be at greater risk of suffering such potential difficulties as respiratory distress, lack of body temperature regulation, low blood sugar, and neonatal jaundice. The causes of low birth weights and premature deliveries include mother's cigarette smoking, alcohol or drug use, malnutrition, high blood pressure, placental insufficiency, pre-eclampsia, and some unknown causes (Kitzinger 1980). Poverty will also play its part, with up to one third of the women in nonwhite low income areas birthing at risk (Colen 1981).

Parents of infants born at risk may suffer the emotional shock of an early delivery, fear for the life of their child, and grief for what has already been or could be lost. Many will wonder what went wrong and mentally question or emotionally blame themselves.

The children themselves may be placed in high-risk neonatal intensive care units, where parents will have to sacrifice their innate need to hold and comfort their babies to intrusive yet life-saving miracles of technological medicine. The infants' cries will be muffled by incubators and endotracheal tubes, and the ICU's silence will speak for all.

Parents are rarely prepared for premature birth. Apart from the psychological shock and the dreadful fear for the infant's life, there is the sheer physical unpreparedness. Nothing and no one is ready: no hospital bag packed, no baby clothes washed, no arrangements made for older children. Everyone feels disoriented, worried, anxious, and unprepared—not a strong base for a healthy birth experience.

Before they can begin to adjust to the shock of a premature birth, many parents must face the prognosis, the enormously difficult medical decisions, and the inner question of how "involved" one should allow oneself to become. With the aid of medicine, many children recover and go home to live normal, healthy lives. Some infants, however, go through a long period of hospitalization that for parents may involve both painful separation and travel draining their energy and finances. Such lengthy hospitalization may also cause conflict and confusion for older siblings waiting to meet the new baby.

Many parents will endure weeks, even months, of not knowing whether their child will live or die. They will live in hope and in doubt, tormented by the "unknown" of the future. Finally, there will be those who are told that their babies are too sick, too fragile to survive and the dream of birth becomes the tragedy of death.

All of these parents will mourn their unique losses, losses fraught with the stress of illness and hospitalization. Marriages will be shaken. In fact, research indicates a high divorce rate among parents of premature babies as well as a greater likelihood of difficulties in the parent-child relationship—an indication, perhaps, of the potential stress of premature birth, which is yet another form of pregnancy loss. These circumstances have been expressed so clearly:

> *Those who believe*
> *Place dolls in isolettes*
> *For two pound babies*
> *To play with*
> *And you know*
> *It's a funny thing*
> *The two pound babies*
> *With the dolls in the isolettes*
> *Grow better*
> *The babies of those*
> >   *Who*
> > >   *Believe*

—Rita Harper, M.D., (Colen 1981)

## RELEASE TO ADOPTION

Suzanne Arms in her recently acclaimed book *To Love and Let Go* (1983) spoke to the unique anguish and personal suffering of women who surrender their children for adoption. She addresses the special kind of courage and honesty required of women to admit that they are unready or unwilling to be mothers under present conditions.

Unfortunately this courage and honesty may be met with external attitudes of punishment—a "she deserved what she got" approach. Even worse and more devastating is the silent suffering resulting from inner self-punishment that may take its toll in future pregnancies and births.

One letter to us expressed this suffering:

> When I was seventeen, I gave birth to a little girl. I never even looked at her. I was afraid I would never forget her face. Now, I'm sad that I can't remember her face. I do not know her name or where she lives. I gave her away because I was too young to accept motherhood. I knew I wasn't ready.
>
> Now, I am pregnant. My husband doesn't know about my daughter. I know I must tell him. I feel he will judge me, I guess since I judge myself. I guess I think God might make me lose this baby for giving the first one away. . . .
>
> *Sharon*

Mothers and fathers who surrender their children to adoption are also parents in grief. They may, in fact, be a group most in need of help, support and resolution, for many of them invalidate their own feelings of loss. After all, they have chosen their fates. Death didn't rob them like a thief in the night; they willfully and knowingly released their children. Like the women who experience loss or trauma but deliver healthy babies, they think, 'So why do I have to grieve? It was my choice.'' Their choice, yes, but loss nevertheless. Birthparents do grieve. They grieve for their children, who will grow up apart from them, who will walk and talk and sing and cry beyond their birthparents' vision, outside the circle of their arms. We know that a release to adoption is an act of infinite love for one's child. It springs from that innate need to protect one's child, even at great cost to oneself. The mother deer, without hesitation, sends her young on while she stays to face a mountain lion. We too protect our young by sending them on when our own lives feel unsafe. Yet even in the knowledge of that gift of love and life lives pain and grief.

There are today some 2.5 million adopted children in the United States, about 2 percent of the child population (McNamara 1975). With the increased use of contraceptives and more widespread acceptance of abortion, the number of infants released to adoption annually is declining. There is further an increase in the number of adoptions by relatives rather than nonrelatives.

However, those women who do release their babies to adoption are most often unmarried, unsupported by the child's father, and pregnant during the already stressful adolescent and early adult years. They are likely to be in conflict with religious beliefs, and confused about what is right. Even before birth, the young parent is likely to experience many losses, including the loss of the normal social life and accompanying friendships, and the loss of parental approval (even if only temporarily), as well as separation from school and in some cases from home and family.

At birth, she is confronted with the issues of whether or not to see, to hold, to in any way begin to know or claim the child she will soon surrender. She will find no comfort in any choice. She will likely feel she doesn't belong anywhere since she is a mother without a child. This may be symbolized in even the hospital staff's confusion about where she should recover—the maternity or the surgery ward?

Once she returns home, she must face an empty, hollow abdomen, with no baby to account for her physical "hole." She experiences postpartum change and feelings while confronted with the task of grieving for her lost child and at the same time reintegrating herself into her former lifestyle. She is not acknowledged or supported as a mother and will be very fortunate to find any adequate support for her grief.

It may well be an extremely responsible decision to choose adoption and may truly be "for the best." But the recovering mother under these circumstances is likely to suffer her loss in silent mourning. Somehow, we falsely believe that if you freely choose to give up something or someone you love, then you won't feel very bad when what you love is gone. Our letter files with stories much like the one introducing this section have taught us otherwise.

Unfortunately, the mother who releases her child for adoption is likely to carry her pain for years afterward, sometimes unaware of it herself until a new pregnancy activates the hurt. For many mothers, the new child is an opportunity to grieve over past losses and heal the perhaps unresolved separations. Without such grieving, a mother becomes a more likely candidate for high-risk pregnancy, perhaps precipitated at some emotional level with self-punishing energies.

In Sharon's final letter to us she wrote, "Thanks for your letters. I did need to 'talk' to myself and to my little girl. I've been writing down everything I've wanted to tell her all this time. I know she'll never actually read it, but I feel different for having put all my feelings in words. I feel like a mother."

## BIRTH DEFECTS: THE LOSS OF THE "HEALTHY" CHILD

Of the three and a half million infants born in 1983, over two hundred thousand will manifest some birth defect. Of this figure seventy-five thousand will be significantly serious conditions, resulting in premature death or life-long institutional or family care (March of Dimes Foundation 1975-83).

It is estimated that about 20 percent of these conditions will be a result of a chromosomal disorder. These disorders may be caused by alcohol, cigarettes, drugs, exposure to radiation, environmental chemicals, and other unknown factors. The risk of genetic disorder increases with a mother's age, from 2.5 per one thousand for women aged thirty, up to 13.7 per thousand for women aged forty (Freeman and Pescar 1982).

The other 80 percent of the birth defects will include problems caused by a number of factors. Some of these may be determined before birth, but most of the parents will be shocked at the unexpected results of birthing an unhealthy baby.

As we have been emphasizing, parents so easily feel guilty for anything that even remotely appears to affect their children's lives. Parents of birth-defective children will probably never cease to ask themselves "what did I do wrong," "what could I have done to prevent this?" It's so difficult to remember that in most cases the conditions in their children began and exist out of the parents' control.

In addition to guilt, the parent of a handicapped child faces two levels of grief. The first experience of grief is that associated with birthing a handicapped child. At this level, parents must confront the emotional shock and the far-reaching psychological impact of having the child. They must somehow adjust to the reality of their lives. They may be angry, hurt, enraged, silent, overwhelmed, and unable to give up believing that this baby can be "fixed."

The emotions of brothers, sisters, relatives, and friends must be integrated, as we each learn from the handicapped child a little more about accepting our own imperfections.

Then, when the emotional dust settles, the medical consultations are complete, and the hope of cure abandoned, these parents must face the powerfully painful task of grieving for the thousands of little things that can never be. This second level of grief is the chronic mourning over a child's ceaseless or silent cry, inability to walk, unspoken words. For some parents, it is the mourning for the schooldays and college graduation and first new car that will never happen; the dances never danced; the wedding never celebrated; the grandchildren never to be born. And out of this grief, they must find the courage to carry on their own lives. By some miracle, many do. Helen Featherstone, author of *A Difference in the Family* (1980), has found that path. As a mother of a severely disabled child, she writes of her heartwrenching road to peace through acceptance. She writes: "I know what it is to stand powerless before the gods, to see a child I love hurt by forces I can neither name nor control. The moment we conceive our children we become vulnerable in ways we are often too young and inexperienced to understand. 'Hostages to fortune' is the old phrase. When our children are born disabled, our vulnerability multiplies ten-fold. . . . Through no virtue of our own, we are larger people than we were."

## CONCLUSION

And so childbearing loss takes many forms, and the grief we feel is reflected all across our land. Acknowledging what we have lost is but a beginning, yet it is an important beginning. Now we can set out on the road to healing— together shouldering our collective pain so that for each of us the burden may feel a little bit less.

# FOUR

# THE VOICE OF GRIEF

Letters and calls from those suffering childbearing loss have flooded Offspring for years now—flooded because of their sheer numbers and flooded because we who receive them are washed in our own tears of empathy and caring. The parents who reach us are crying for help: for relief from their pain, for guidance in healing, and for recognition of their children who so briefly graced their lives. Many of them send us pictures: "This was my baby at two weeks—wasn't she beautiful?" They ache for validation, for someone to say, "Yes, your daughter existed, and she was truly lovely." Those left without pictures seek validation of their memories, and these too are real, meaningful, painful, and beautiful.

Ours is a death-denying culture. In denying death we often deny the needs of those who are touched by death and sometimes even the existence of those who were so briefly with us and then died. We are so afraid to confront loss and one another's pain. We look the other way, thinking to protect ourselves from the grief of others and being unwilling to tolerate the infinite helplessness we feel in their presence. Elisabeth Kubler-Ross (1975) states that common attempts to "help"—to distract and shield ourselves and others from grief and pain, to make bodies look "natural," to hasten a return to normal—are really destructive.

What is genuinely helpful, we believe, is our willingness *to participate* in another's grief, another's loss. Not to restore life, for that is not in our power, but to live with our helplessness and to live with death. Here then are the stories the mourners have to tell. As we are each willing to share one another's grief, may we each feel the healing strength of our united caring.

## INFERTILITY

### *Martha*

Martha told us, "I am in the middle of my second round of fertility tests. The first gynecologist didn't find anything conclusive, but we've been trying to conceive for three years. I ache to be pregnant; I dream of babies, babies all the time.

"My sister-in-law recently got pregnant. It wasn't a planned pregnancy, and she is very unhappy. All she does is complain about morning sickness, backaches, weight gain, the inconvenience of it all. It's *so* hard for me to be with her. I feel like I'm going crazy; I'm so obsessed with getting pregnant. I can't even think of anything else. I cry so easily these days. Why is this happening? I pray and pray and nothing changes. Why aren't I, who so wants to be, pregnant, and why isn't my sister-in-law, who professes to dislike children, infertile instead? Wouldn't that make more sense? God just blew it, that's all. This situation is crazy and all wrong. I want to be pregnant! I feel that something vital is missing from my life, and I have to search and search until I find it.''

## Joan

Joan wrote: ''I learned a lot about myself during the four plus years of infertility. I was totally consumed by grief, pain and frustration—nothing could help except my becoming pregnant—I wanted to feel a baby kick inside me, I wanted to grow so everyone could see I was pregnant. I wanted to be able to tell my sisters and mother that I was pregnant. It took me a long time to realize that the reason I did not think of adoption was because I was wishing for a pregnancy, probably even more than a baby. Oh, I wanted a baby, so very much, but the thought of a pregnancy was like a fairy tale come true. It was the experience of the pregnancy I wanted, along with the pampering a first-time pregnant woman gets. It's embarrassing to admit that, because it's very selfish, but it's the truth, and I didn't even realize it for a long time. I think it was long after we started the adoption process that I realized it.

''I hated pregnant women! I cried every time Bill Baird was on the news or the news talked about welfare abortion, or commercials came on for diapers or baby food. I absolutely dreaded baby showers or christenings, and got very angry at being invited. I made myself an island, and stayed away from all my friends who were pregnant or had children. It was very difficult because in one year four of my friends were pregnant and all delivered about 1–2 months apart from each other. One of my friends called me and asked me to take care of her the first day she came home from the hospital with her new baby girl. I didn't want to, but I did, because her family lived out of state. She called me weeks later to see why I was avoiding her. I told her it was just too painful for me. She said, 'You have no right to deprive me of your friendship because I can have children and you can't!' I was losing friends and not enjoying anything— every place I turned there were babies or pregnant women. It was like walking daily head on into a wall of pain—pain that would rush at me, griping my throat and kicking me in the stomach.''

> *Miscarriage*
>
> *Open field of snow.*
> *Another Child gone.*
> *Little deaths falling like icy feathers.*
>
> *Gather me and take me*
> *Where snow buries wounds.*
> *We can take pain only for so long.*
>
> —*Julie Leavitt*

## Elana

Elana's letter stated: "My first pregnancy ended in miscarriage at five months. According to the doctor, the fetus didn't develop. Somehow my baby stopped growing, and I drive myself crazy trying to figure it out. Do you have any information on medical reasons for miscarriage? I don't take any drugs, and I try to eat well. Do you think it could have been caused by the glass or two of wine I had one night before I knew I was pregnant?''

## Lynn

Lynn wrote: "I've just had my fifth miscarriage. No children. This time I got a little further than before, into my fifth month. I feel like a boxer in the ring—keep getting knocked down and keep getting up, staggering on. I'm beginning to wonder when that knockout punch will come, and I'll never get up again.''

## Chris

Chris called to say that she had miscarried at four months. It was her fifth pregnancy, first miscarriage. ''If one more person points out how lucky I am to already have four children, I think I'll start screaming and never, ever stop. One neighbor actually implied that the miscarriage had been a blessing in disguise, given the costs of raising children. It's been so unacknowledged, this miscarriage. As though this baby didn't count, wasn't really a person. Nobody understands or even cares to. It's been three weeks since it happened, and everyone expects me to be back to normal already. Back to mothering my other children, who are supposed to negate the loss of this one. This baby was my child, my fifth child, *but still my child*. My four living children can't erase the death of this one.''

## Barbara

Barbara wrote: ''I've had two miscarriages before. They were both in the second month. Recently I miscarried again, this time in the fifth month. I had begun spotting and cramping, and the doctor felt that a miscarriage was beginning, so he sent me home to rest in bed. My husband had to leave for a while, so I was alone when I actually expelled the fetus. It happened in the bathroom toilet. I was overcome with the horror of it all and then by waves of dizziness. I made it back to bed and collapsed there. I kept wanting to get up and go back to pick up what I had lost, but I just couldn't do it. When my husband got back, I asked him to do it. Now, I feel tortured by guilt. I let my little baby's dead body sit *in the toilet* for an hour or so because I wasn't strong enough to pick it up and give it the respect and honor I think it deserved. I feel underserving of motherhood, and I so wish I had it to do over again. I wish I had called someone to help me instead of waiting for my husband. I keep seeing that scene before my eyes—me all alone and shrinking away from the bathroom. I wish I had been stronger then; if I had, maybe I could sleep more now. The nights are endless.''

### *Jenny*

Jenny's letter explained: ''I had a miscarriage in April at four and one-half months. I had been sick for the whole term. When I began bleeding, somewhere around four months, I visited the doctor who told me to rest as much as possible. Not easy with a hyperactive two-year-old. As I was leaving his examining room, I overheard him tell the nurse to remove me from the OB list, that I wouldn't be carrying to term. I felt sick to my stomach and hurt that he hadn't said anything to me. After a few weeks the bleeding got heavier—he told me the same. Four times I called telling him I knew I was losing the baby. He told me to relax and stay in bed. The fifth and last call I told him I was going to the hospital. He told me it wasn't necessary yet. I lost the baby in the hospital bathroom while changing into my johnny. I was enraged and turned it all inward. I've spent the last three months in depression not talking to anyone.''

## *Dianne*

---

After her miscarriage, Dianne wrote: "I spoke to my OB/GYN's nurse about the results of the pathology report. All she would tell me was there were 'products of conception' in the placenta. I wanted to vomit—how could someone call my baby a mere product of conception! Why is it so hard for people to say 'baby' and 'your baby died'?"

## ABORTION

### *Rosemary*

---

Rosemary called for help after her second abortion. "I'd already had one abortion, and while it certainly wasn't pleasant, I came through it okay. I felt that I couldn't mother a child; my life was just too shaky and insecure. This second time I got pregnant, I still wasn't ready. If anything, my life was in worse straits. So I scheduled the abortion, and I calmly discussed it with the preabortion counselor at the clinic. I never considered any other choice; I felt composed and sure of myself. But then, when I was lying on the table with my feet in those awful stirrups, and the doctor turned on the vacuum extractor, I started to scream. He had already begun, and it was too late to stop. I couldn't stop either—the screaming, I mean. It's still going on inside me."

### *Margaret*

---

A letter from Margaret: "I have read some of what you say about forgiving yourself, and I hope you can tell me how to do it. I had an abortion years ago. Since them, I've had two children, both delivered by cesarean section. My cervix just wouldn't open each time I was in labor.

"I now think that perhaps I wouldn't *let* it open— that I was punishing myself for letting those others open my cervix to do the abortion. I'd like another child, and this time I'd like to be able to open my cervix myself. But I guess I have to forgive myself first, and I don't know if I can. . . ."

## Diana

Diana called in great emotional distress after the cesarean delivery of her first child. "The labor began normally but then it just didn't progress. I couldn't seem to get past three centimeters. I was trying to focus on the labor, but suddenly I was 'seeing' before my eyes the scene of the abortion I had several years ago. From somewhere deep inside me a pain rose up that I had never felt before. I had thought that the abortion was the right choice at the time, and that I had adjusted and handled it well. I never even cried then, just felt mildly depressed. But suddenly, in labor, I felt swamped with pain and grief at what I had lost. I kept wondering what that labor and that baby would have been like. I felt overwhelmed, beaten, spiritless. Finally, as I lay weeping on the operating table, the doctor took this baby from me. Maybe I didn't think I deserved to give birth, or maybe I just couldn't do it for this child when I hadn't for the other."

## Ellen

Ellen sought counseling when her postpartum depression threatened to affect her newborn baby's well-being. "I just can't cope," she sobbed. "I'm so tired, and the baby won't sleep, and there's no one to help us. Even if the baby does sleep, *I* can't. My dreams are horrible—I keep reliving the abortion I had three years ago. I was fine at the time, so I don't understand why it seems so unbearable now. Whenever I look at my baby, I remember the abortion, and I cry."

## STILLBIRTH

### *GRIEF*

*There is no mother here*
*and no child.*
*Only a shapelessness*
*that torn feelings swim about in.*
　　　　—Julie Leavitt

### *Anne*

Anne wrote: "Our son died while in utero. I was 37 weeks pregnant. I was totally drugged for the delivery. The day I found out he died, the grief and hurt were unbearable: I couldn't sleep. I cried, it seemed, like forever. I remember getting up at 5:30 in the morning and pulling apart the entire nursery as sort of a way of saying goodbye. His nursery was very special, something I had worked very hard at making special.

"The delivery was cold and traumatic, the nurses seemed very uncaring, almost cruel. I never saw my son; my husband spent 20 minutes with him. He was buried 3 days later. The funeral was hard; I wanted so much to open the little coffin and see him, hold him and say goodbye.

"After my son was stillborn, we did attend a high-risk clinic for my next pregnancy, which began 4 months after my son died.

"That was a big mistake! Medical intervention—drugs, tests—pressure! 'We only want to give you a healthy baby, and we can't if you don't trust us.'

"Toward the end of my pregnancy Christina failed to settle into a head-down position and was lying in a transverse (horizontal) position. I had what they call polyhydramnios and one day received a threatening phone call from the hospital saying they worried about my baby not making it if I went into labor. They scheduled an amniocentesis and took her by cesarean section the next day.

"I woke up in recovery to amazing pain and a doctor saying my daughter was very sick and probably wouldn't make it through the night. I was devastated. My husband had gone with her—the Children's Hospital and Medical Center are connected by a tunnel. John was treated like dirt and was very hurt.

"He says they wouldn't even let him touch her and he felt that what she needed most, was to know we loved her and cared. He was very angry. I went to see her 5 hours after my cesarean section—she herself had just returned from surgery. It was amazing how much I fell in love with her when I saw her.

"My one thought was 'no matter what little girl, I will never leave your side until God takes you home.'

"I was true to my word. From day two until day sixty-seven when she died I camped out by her side, much to the consternation of doctors and nurses. I didn't care. My eyes were opened wide, too. I couldn't believe how inhuman our society is. These poor babies had no rights at all, or us parents. No one would listen to our convictions, even when we were right.

"I have nurse's training—never letting on to the nurses

and doctors until near the end of our daughter's life. I was shocked sick. I continually prayed for God to heal my baby or take her home. I cried unashamedly. I took pictures of her. I bathed her myself—changed her, changed her bed, sang to her.

"It turned out whenever my husband and I wanted to confront issues, like 'loud' acid rock music being played in the nursery 24 hours a day, that the nurses had more rights than we or our child did. They would never allow that in an adult ICU.

"I wanted to hold my baby but people would refuse because it was 'too much work' to place her in my arms, even though when it was allowed she'd do 100 percent better.

"Finally she was transferred to another hospital 300 miles away for more extensive tests, which really turned into extensive surgery. After surgery she died in that hospital—because of neglect and poor medical management. They had allowed a baby they suspected to have chicken pox in the ICU instead of isolating her. She did have chicken pox and so the whole unit was exposed. Because of this our daughter couldn't be transferred back home and later they innoculated her for it, which six months later I found out was wrong because she was a respiratory patient. She died two days later with a very high blood count and the respirator couldn't even help her breathe.

"She was placed in my arms and died there. My husband was home at the time.

"I did bathe her myself and removed all her tubes. I dressed her for the first time and held her for six hours until my husband arrived. We took her back home ourselves. I prepared her for burial myself. We put her in her bassinet and took pictures. My husband did her funeral service and we have a photo album of her life at home called 'God's Masterpiece.'"

## *Elizabeth*

Elizabeth wrote this letter to her sister's daughter Joy, who was stillborn. Elizabeth had been present at Joy's birth.

"Oh, Joy, why did you leave us? We wanted you to stay . . . we wanted to hold your warm body, not a cold empty one. Where did you go? And you were nearly here! You almost made it. But out you came, and you would not breathe, or move, or cry. 'Come on baby, it's time to breathe. *Breathe,* baby. Come on, you can do it. It's not so hard. And you can make noise; crying's not so bad. It's okay, baby. You can wake up now, and everything will be all right.'

"We want to take you home. You can warm up in your family's great big bed. You'll be safe there. The girls can come and see you and stay awhile. You'll have so many kisses and hugs; they'll sing you a song.

"But the hospital says *No.* They say you belong to them. How ridiculous. How crazy. You are our baby. Why can't we take you home?

"Must I cry forever? I've spilled tears enough to water my garden. I love your mother and father, and I want to give them Joy—but I can't, for you are gone. Joy, sometimes I want to die and be with you. But first I have to live."

## *Cicely*

Cicely's baby was stillborn at term after a seemingly normal twelve-hour labor. "I couldn't believe what they were telling me. What did they mean, no heartbeat? I felt Joshua *move* inside me. He moved, he *lived.* Dead? I just couldn't take it in. Something happened to me then; I felt numb to everything but the searing pain of his death. I didn't care about anything else. Friends brought meals. I knew they were worried about me, that they cared. But *I* didn't care. I ate, but I didn't *care* if I ever ate. I used to be a fanatical housekeeper, but I no longer cared if the laundry was done, the dishes were washed, or the floor vacuumed. Before, I would have been mortified if friends dropped by and my home wasn't spotless, but I didn't care any more.

"My father was partially crippled with arthritis, and I *knew* he was in pain, but I couldn't *care*. I couldn't *feel*. I was filled to the breaking point with such pain that there was no room for anything else."

## *David*

David felt shock and sorrow when his son was stillborn at term. "I never actually cried, but I did feel tears filling my eyes and throat several times after the baby died. My wife Mandy was completely grief-stricken, though, so I became even more concerned for her than I was for the loss of our son. I couldn't really do anything, or say anything, that helped her. I hated feeling so helpless. I threw myself into work.

"Mandy continued to feel deeply depressed. She was exhausted all the time, and not eating or sleeping well. I was worried and at the same time impatient for her to get over this. I started having trouble with some respiratory allergies that hadn't bothered me since I was a kid. My sinuses were so inflamed and throbbing, I couldn't even concentrate at work. Life was the pits. Mandy suggested we attend a Parents-in-Grief seminar at Offspring, and I agreed if she thought it would help her.

"I listened to descriptions of grief and reactions to loss, and suddenly out of nowhere this blanket of sadness descended on me. I started to cry. Mandy held me, and I cried and cried. Another man put a hand on my shoulder. I cried more. When we finally left to go home, my head ached, and so did my whole body, but the throbbing in my sinuses was gone.''

### *Karen*

Karen's first letter read: "We gave birth to our stillborn baby girl at twenty-eight weeks—at home with our midwife friends. We already knew our baby was dead, and we had a noisy grieving of the death as well as a celebration of the birth; both of which were easier to do at home, that's for sure, at least for us. Afterwards I felt very strong within myself and felt positive about my body. . . .''

But her second letter reflected a loss of positive feelings: "When I first wrote to you, soon after the baby died, I was in a more positive place—now I feel that the last year was a nightmare.I find it so much more difficult now (4½ months since the baby died) than the first few months . . . now no matter what I do—or express—there just seems to be an endless amount of pain and suffering involved in grieving—at least for me.''

## INFANT DEATH

*TO SAY GOODBYE A YEAR LATER*

*Is to seal the final death certificate.*
*Nothing you've done this year      no act*
*of denial or patient grief will*

*bring him back.*
*I feel the lunatic's hopelessness*
*gazing nightly at the slippery moon*

*praying to be carried away in an ark, and*

*not a common death like her son, her grandfather*
*not a common, but a fantastic one,*
*swept upon a glowing arc.*


*No, it is the common death we all must give ourselves*
*to:*
*eyes wide open, softening,*
*body folding into heart,*

*last breath a song gasped and mistaken for pain.*

*There is no resolve that does not meet death, no*
*denial that turns its terrified face eternally away*
*looking for corners on our spherical planet.*

*Are we like Earth?*
*Dense and saline, covered with gardens and deserts,*
*mountains and rocky oceans, billions of animals.*

*Who is to say humanity renews itself?*
*Or that the flickering of stars*
*are souls arrived.*

*—Julie Leavitt*

Bill Henderson sent us these paragraphs, entitled ''Words
for Malcolm,'' which he had written as a memorial to his
son who died at six weeks of age during heart surgery:

> *I wanted to speak about Malcolm because many*
> *of you never had the chance to know him.*
> *He would have liked this place, this beautiful*
> *chapel, because he loved to look at anything un-*
> *usual. He had very bright, almost penetrating eyes,*
> *and was fascinated by what he could see. When he*
> *was only a week old he had spotted himself in the*
> *mirror. Whether this was precociousness or vanity I*
> *can't be sure.*

*But everyone around him remarked on a certain acute awareness he seemed to have that was uncanny for a baby so young.*

*He was very popular in the intensive-care units where he stayed. The nurses would request to be assigned to him. One of them told me she had dreams about Malcolm. He had a presence, a sort of princely air about him that drew attention to him in a graceful way. One of the doctors nicknamed him "Hollywood Henderson" because of this little star-quality that he had.*

*He seemed often to be solemn or wise, like there was an old man inside his little body, a wise old spirit who had come to earth just to look around for a while before moving on.*

*He often looked with fascination over our shoulders at something we couldn't see. We would try to follow his look, but it led nowhere . . . or somewhere our gazes couldn't penetrate.*

*Sometimes he would smile—and that was like a shower of gold.*

*He was too young to feel sorry for himself— although he hated to be sick, clearly. He was a fighter—and one day, shortly before he died, he did rage uncontrollably, in a way we had never seen— knowing (as we feel he did) that the health he experienced briefly, after his first operation, was draining away and he was dying.*

*His last morning was very peaceful. He held onto our fingers and when he did go to the operating room, it was with his characteristic fascination with the sights of the world he had lived in such a short time.*

*We felt, and everyone who knew him did too, that he had enormous potential. His intelligence was clear. Physically, he was beautiful. He had a lanky, well-formed body, with big feet that might someday have carried him down a cinder track, like his grandfather. And aside from his fatal defect, he was tough and resistant. . . . And this is very hard: that the life he would have grown into is now only speculation and mystery.*

*But there's another way we choose to look at Malcolm's coming and going; not merely as a loss, a baby lost forever, but as a complete life, lived as fully as possible. He did have a taste of the world. He came home for a while. He watched the trees outside his window. We walked him. We talked to him and played music for him. Carol danced around the house with him. He was a little man who was born, lived, fought, suffered and died. And what more do any of us experience but an elaboration of this basic pattern?*

*In his own way he was a little existential hero, in that each hour, each day, was brand new to him: he took things as they came . . . when he could be happy he was, when he had to struggle he simply got on with it.*

*What is left is this: he has changed our lives. Malcolm has changed us; made us sadder, immeasurably, but increased our capacity for happiness; given us new clarity, a new sureness of purpose—and a new image of each other: when I look in the mirror, I see Malcolm in my face . . . I see him in Carol's face.*

*He has inspired us with his exemplary little life, the life of one, in Carol's words, "who sought the world with eagerness and joy, who suffered without self-pity, loved without judgment, and died in peace and grace."*

### *Kathleen*

Kathleen wrote: "Our son was born at home on a rainy October morning. It was incredibly smooth, seemingly under my control, and beautiful . . . beyond even all my expectations and visualizations. He was my second child. Where my daughter's birth had felt very primitive, hot, and red, his birth was more refined, more ethereal and had a blue aura to it. He was a healthy babe, though never lusty or aggressive. He was coaxed to begin nursing and enjoyed sleeping to anything. Our most powerful contacts were oiling, bath, massage times. We all felt very much in love and the time was peaceful and fulfilling.

"He developed a small snuffly cold around 3½ weeks. This progressed within 2 days from some nasal congestion to full double pneumonia. The second day as he was refusing to nurse, growing limper and paler and slipping away, I was sinking deeper into my own severe cold and depression. My body and emotions were reacting, where my intellect was not. By late afternoon we took him to emergency. As soon as we entered the hospital almost, he stopped breathing. Within a couple of hours his life was solely in control of machines, and a nightmare of a night followed. I remember feeling quite calm and very positive that night, although it was hardest to deal with later, in my memory of it. Fear did not overtake me at the time. Just before dawn, he stabilized for the first time all night and we made very strong contact through the deep blue haze of dawn. He hung on for a farewell to the day and to his father and sister who arrived about a half hour before his death. It was I who pronounced his death, as if it had been I who lifted him from my body and had first seen his new body. It was impossible to believe he had died, yet I also accepted it immediately. We held him and wept, Lila kissed him goodbye, and told us that he flew away. That day dawned clear and sharp blue, the first day with winter chill undisturbed by the sunny stillness. It felt like a tribute to him.

"Driving home, leaving a part of us behind, we went to a friend's and rested, unable to go straight home. When we did, friends had been there, cleaning and smoking out the house, bringing the last flowers from gardens, filling our home with a love and support so strong, it was like a tangible thing to lean against and be bathed in. More and more accepting the mystery and power of life and death. It was the most painful, most open, most spiritual, most ecstatic day of my life. Over the next few days the love of family and friends continued to pour in and cleanse our home.

"It felt very important to reveal all the feelings, experiences and insights with many people. A lot of what has to be dealt with is other people's grief and emotions about their own lives as they come to you opened and pouring out their love. We learned to accept the love and try to drop some of the other emotions. We held a ceremony four days later at our home with about 60 people, families from our community and farther away, his grandparents and lots of children. We planted a tree over his ashes, dedicated to him, sang songs and all felt a tremendous communion under the aura of his spirit.

"I feel that we have gained as much or more than we lost, not to diminish the loss of our beautiful son. It was the beginning of a profound opening for me, I've learned and appreciated so much more since. I've watched our family grow, both individually and as a unit from this experience. The help of our community was tremendous and we have a body of people who know and understand the pain, the acceptance and the beauty of it all. This little spirit was just passing through, no mistakes, no resentments, no bitterness, only pain and LOVE. It's OK Baby, we love you too!

"Lila accepted his death as his birth, with the total acceptance of a two-year-old. Nice gift to the subconscious, to carry for life, and a wonderful lesson and strength for us. I feel very thankful for his birth and for the completeness of the whole experience. It was a perfect life for him and a perfect part of our lives, I only wish I cold continue to always find that perfection, when things don't go as I had planned or wished. I'm working on it. As I write this there are crocuses blooming around his tree and I am pregnant again, dealing of course with a lot of emotions and some fears. My concept of the perfect birth has changed to . . . whatever this one needs.''

### *Susan*

Susan wrote, ''I've heard that you can help people adjust to loss, and I don't know where else to turn, so I hope you can help me. I'm afraid if you don't, I'll just go crazy. As it is, some people think I should sign myself into a mental hospital. Maybe they're right.

''Six months ago my third child was born. She was our first daughter, and she seemed fine at birth. But then she had trouble keeping down feedings, so they started some tests. The tests showed that she had cancer in her stomach. At first I couldn't even believe what the doctors were telling me, and some days I still don't believe it all happened. The doctors would come in and be all cheerful and enthusiastic about how they could help her. They kept saying that with this surgery and that medication, she could possibly live a normal life. I *wanted* to believe that; I couldn't face anything else. I never really noticed (except now when I remember) that they *never* looked me in the eyes. They never came very lose to me either. They just breezed in and breezed out. Well, I listened to them, and I believed them, and I let them operate on Jennifer. They operated three times. She never came home. She died when she was three weeks old.

"Now I barely get through every day. I've cried so much I don't know where the tears are coming from. I miss her so much. I'm so angry with those doctors for giving me any hope at all. I don't think there ever really was any hope. If I had known that then, I never would have consented to the surgery, to letting them cut open her little body. I would have brought her home to be with her family. I would have been holding her when she died. *I wasn't holding her when she died!* I keep seeing her, hooked up to all those useless tubes and machines, and dying alone. She never even came home, she never had a home. I never brought her home. Please can you help me?"

### Neal

"Joanne and I are Christian Scientists," Neal explained. "We have a belief in the power of faith to heal and a trust that whatever happens is meant to happen. When our second child was born with severe birth defects affecting his spinal column and nervous system, the doctors gave us a choice of scheduling surgery or not. The prognosis for success with surgery was very poor. We decided to bring Robert home without the surgery. He died eighteen days later. Although our faith was great comfort, it couldn't take away the pain of losing him. Nor could it completely banish our agonizing doubts as to whether or not we had made the right decision. . . ."

### Carolyn

Carolyn's first son, Matthew, was born by cesarean section after a long labor. Matthew appeared healthy at birth and scored an Apgar of 9 (a health assessment scale for newborns ranging from 1-10). Within a few days, though, he began to fail and was diagnosed as having a serious and life-threatening heart defect. Matthew lived six weeks and died during his second heart surgery. Carolyn shared with us a dream she had had during early pregnancy.

"I dreamed that I gave birth to a beautiful little boy and that I held him with awe and wonder and joy. Suddenly before my eyes he began to age—he aged without growing, until he appeared to be a tiny, wise old man, and then he gracefully and peacefully died. I didn't understand my dream at all, and I even forgot it. But then, later, when Matthew was in intensive care, all the nurses remarked on his 'unearthliness.' They said that he seemed so wise, wise beyond his age, almost as though there were a wise old spirit in his newborn body. The dream came back, and I felt that he was dying. Maybe I really knew all along, but I loved him so much that I didn't want to consciously know. I now believe that Matthew's birth was the way it was because of that knowledge. My cervix refused to dilate, and I think that my body was protecting him, trying to hold him inside, knowing of his fatally weak heart. The doctors finally had to pluck him from me through cesarean section. I didn't understand all this then, but now I think I begin to see. When Matthew died, and I felt the full depth of my love for him, I realized what my inner body and my spirit knew all along. I loved him fiercely, protectively, completely. I wasn't able to release him with the same grace with which he let go. Yet, now I think of that dream, and I reflect on his aura of wisdom, and I am comforted."

## Maryanne

Maryanne's son Gregory was born with serious birth defects; he lived only two weeks in neonatal intensive care and then died. Maryanne shared with us a dream she had

had the night before she went into labor. "In my dream I was in the hospital about to give birth. The baby was born, a boy, and he was beautiful. Everyone was smiling and offering congratulations. A beaming nurse took the baby and placed him in one of those isolettes. Suddenly, four red lights appeared on each corner of the isolette. The lights were flashing. Then a large red DANGER sign appeared on the wall behind the isolette. I was so terrified that I woke up, shaking.

"The next day I went into labor, and Gregory was born. His problems were not apparent right away. We were overjoyed. He was absolutely beautiful, and I almost forgot about my dream, except that he looked exactly like that baby. Later on I realized that the dream *was* real. How had I known? Does God give you warning so you can prepare, do you think? Have other women had experiences like this?"

## *Jessica*

Jessica's daughter, Heather, was born with an irreparable heart defect. Heather lived in an intensive care unit for six days and then died. Jessica's mother was the only family member, apart from Jessica and her husband, Steve, who saw and held Heather.

"It absolutely drove me crazy," wrote Jessica, "that no one else in my life ever knew Heather. It was almost as though she never, ever existed. I just couldn't stand that. She was alive, for such a little time, and she was so beautiful. She was my *daughter*. No one else ever celebrated her birth or her brief life, and she deserved that. She deserved that people be happy she was born. After a while I began to pick up my life. When I was out shopping, local salespeople would notice that I was no longer pregnant and ask me what I had had—a boy or a girl.

"I just couldn't bear any more sadness for her, any more feeling that she had never existed, so I would answer only that I'd had a little girl. Then I would accept congratulations and leave. My husband thought I was losing my grip on sanity when I told him this, and he wanted me to see a psychiatrist. But I knew I was not insane, just filled with grief at losing my beautiful little daughter, and wanting her to know, somewhere, wherever she was, that people were glad she had been born. I wanted her to have not just mourning, but some celebration too. Steve didn't really understand, but I needed to do that anyway. I loved her that much. . . ."

## Mary

Mary's second child, a son, appeared to be fine at birth. Within days, though, his parents knew something was wrong. Medical tests indicated that the baby was suffering from acute leukemia and that his chances of survival were slim. When he died at three weeks, Mary felt her natural buoyancy and joy in living die with him. "You can't imagine," she says, "the pain, the horror, the deadness inside . . . I couldn't understand *why* . . . my innocent little baby was gone, and I was sure I would never be *happy* again.

"I had a husband and a little boy, so there was never any question of my going on; but I was sure I'd never laugh again. Someone gave me this verse, and even though I didn't really believe it all at the time, I clung to those words as though they were a lifeline. I read it over and over and over, *countless* times each day. Somehow, even in my pain and disbelief, it helped. . . ."

*In this sad world of ours sorrow comes to all and it*
*often comes with bitter agony.*
*Perfect relief is not possible except with time.*
*You cannot believe that you will ever feel better but*
*this is not true.*
*You are sure to be happy again. Knowing this, truly*
*believing it, will make you less miserable now.*

## *Peggi*

Peggi wrote: "I'm starting to see the beginning of the end of my deep, blinding grief. It's been five years since my daughter Kim died but I suppressed my grief for the first four years. Not until this last year, through the support of my husband, my therapist and her co-workers (now friends), was I able to realize what was lost that evening in January.

"There was no time to grieve for Kim that first year. Kim's death in January was followed by my unexpectedly becoming pregnant in April. Because of prior infertility problems, finding myself pregnant was a shock. Friends and co-workers were thrilled for me. 'It's just what you need.' 'Have another child right away, it will help you to forget.' Replacing one child with another was not what I needed. It's also an impossible task. You can never replace another human being. I needed time to grieve for Kim but I was on shaky emotional ground and thought 'they' know what's best. That, coupled with the guilt of having been able to conceive so quickly when other women with infertility problems were struggling to become pregnant for the first time, kept my grief buried inside me.

"This pregnancy was also a possible chance to lift my mother's spirits. After Kim died my mother's remission from cancer started to falter. Just maybe this promise of another grandchild, a new life, would renew her will to live.

As I grew more and more pregnant, my mother became weaker and more resigned to what was happening to her body. Because of family pressure—'You'll take away her hope'—coupled with my own fear of death and my mother's fear of speaking with her now pregnant daughter about death, we never discussed her impending death or our feelings for each other.

"When I was five months pregnant, she died. Again it was socially acceptable for me to grieve openly. Instead I kept myself fairly well pulled together. I felt that my husband and our friends had already been through hell and back. I wasn't going to make this any harder. My life revolved on proving to everyone how strong I was. A lot of my time was spent being the comforter of people who had known my mother and daughter but hadn't known of their deaths. I've since learned that my mother died because it was her time and was in no way my fault. My other lesson has been to let people love and care for me when I need it. It's not always easy and many times I have to bite my tongue but I'm getting there.

"Four months later my second daughter, Sarah, was born. What should have been a time of joy was an emotional nightmare. Convinced I was having a son, the shock of delivering another daughter was all encompassing. Ninety-five percent of me screamed NO. Memories of Kim flooded back, haunting me, breaking down my very carefully constructed facade of calm and control. Through sheer will this reaction, outwardly, only lasted a few minutes. I was again 'under control' and smiling. Inwardly, the terror raged on causing various serious complications during my hospital stay. The other 5 percent was berating me. 'You selfish bitch, other women have stillborns, deformed children or can't get pregnant at all. You have a healthy baby, grow up.' The 5 percent won and I was smiling and seemingly happy for the next three years.

"It wasn't until after I had my son, one year ago

now—four years after Kim's death—that the facade cracked and came tumbling down around me.

"Brian was born by cesarean section, as were my daughters, after thirty-six hours of intense back labor. What I initially thought was grief over my inability to deliver any of my children vaginally was that—but it was much more. Deep inside I still felt a bottomless, blinding grief for Kim. Luckily, through friends, I found a loving, caring and sometimes unwelcomingly truthful therapist, Claudia. I've spent the last year accepting and yielding to the feelings of intense grief and guilt of Kim's death that had been held inside for four years. A lot of the past year has been spent crying not always at the most opportune times for myself or the people around me. But it was something that was needed to be done. I repeatedly would say to Claudia, 'I'm tired of crying and feeling like this, when is it going to end?' Her answer always loving but truthful, 'When the time is right, you're not ready yet.' How I hated those words! If only she would tell me when it would be over I could plan my life. The fear that the grieving would last forever was very real to me.

"It's been a long, hard and frequently very painful year but I can now see that it was needed. I've not finished with all the grieving but it's mellower now and a little easier to deal with."

## SUDDEN INFANT DEATH SYNDROME

### *Cynthia*

Cynthia's first child, her daughter Amy, was a beautiful and robust little girl. Her early social smiles at four weeks delighted her young parents. They proudly marked off on a calendar Amy's growth and each developmental step she mastered. One day, when Amy was five months old, Cynthia found her motionless in her crib, a victim of sudden infant death syndrome.

"The most painful reminder of my child," wrote Cynthia, "was that long after she died, my breast milk still flowed. They gave me pills to dry it up, but nothing really worked. My heart was bursting with pain, and my breasts throbbed too. It almost seemed as though the milk dripping out was my body crying . . . I continued to see milk for months, and every drop was like a stab of fiery pain. That was Amy's milk, her nourishment, it would have made her body grow and become ever stronger. I wanted to cross over to wherever she was and give it to her. Nursing was such a comfort to her while she was alive, and I kept wondering what was comforting her now, and wishing she could have taken me with her. Nursing had been my gift to her, and now I could no longer give it.

"I think now that my body just wouldn't give up, wouldn't stop making milk, because I couldn't bear to let her go."

### Maureen

Maureen shared her story: "Almost thirty years ago I gave birth to my third child. Jean-Marie was a wonderful baby! My first two children were not as peaceful and content as she was, and she slept much better than they had as infants. I was grateful to have such a good baby, because my older two were two and a half and four, and they kept me busy. Sometimes I felt guilty for not holding her as much as I had her sister and brother, but she just didn't demand that as they had. She was never fussy. One day—it was summertime—I put her in her carriage for a nap. She was just six months old. I remember that she slept longer than usual, and I used the time to make a birthday cake for my son.

Finally, I decided to wake her. When I picked her up, she was limp and not breathing. I phoned frantically for an ambulance, but it was too late. I know now that she was a victim of SIDS, and I've read every word published on it since then. But at the time, there was little information. Every infant death was judged suspect. Not many people knew of SIDS at all—it didn't even have that name then. My husband and I were ordered to appear at a court inquest. It was one of the most excruciating experiences of our lives, second only to the moment when I knew Jean-Marie was dead.

"The questions were unbearably painful. Were we certain that we did not neglect our child? Had I placed the carriage in the direct sun or covered her with a heavy blanket? Could she have moved her head, or would I have heard her, if she were smothering? Did we have insurance on her life? What had I given her to eat that day? Did we respond to her needs? Had she demonstrated any illness, any physical disability?

"Thirty years later, the scene still haunts me. I drove myself crazy with doubts and with guilt. *Had* I neglected her? Had I deserved to be her mother?

"I now believe that I judged myself in some way responsible for her death. I was only in my twenties, but within months after Jean-Marie died, I began to have problems with my menstrual cycle. The doctor called it premature menopause and scheduled a hysterectomy. I think that I didn't feel deserving of more children. I still wish I could hold Jean-Marie one more time, hold her even if she wasn't crying to be held, and tell her how much I love her. I'll carry that love to my grave."

# BIRTH DEFECTS

## *Lydia*

Lydia's son was born with Down's syndrome. "Someone gave me this poem by Ted Farrell," she wrote. "I read it so often that the words now live in my heart. Here are my favorite verses:"

> *MY BROKEN DOLL*
>
> *A broken doll was sent to me,*
> *From heaven up above.*
> *A broken doll to have and hold,*
> *A broken doll to love.*
>
> *My joy was turned to sadness,*
> *My life I thought was done.*
> *I'd hoped the doll I would receive*
> *Would be a perfect one.*
>
> *It's strange how that which seemed so sad*
> *Should be a joy and fun.*
> *I thank God for this priceless gift,*
> *My broken doll, my son.*

## *Sister Jean*

Sister Jean, a Roman Catholic nun, wrote: "Recently I had to help a patient who had given birth to an encephalitic baby. This was her second baby, first girl. Your workshop certainly gave me some insight into what the parents, especially the mother, felt. Thank you and God bless you in your work."

## *Rosie*

---

Rosie wrote: "I gave birth to Jonathan on June 17, 1965, and he lived for about two hours. I was in a small hospital in Maine. My husband was not with me, as he was stationed in the Air Force in Europe. Not only was I in pain from losing my baby, but the care I received was rotten.

"I was *totally unprepared* for the pain of labor. I was so drugged up that I felt totally out of control. Being out of control scared me so badly that I started screaming—they gave me more drugs. I honestly thought I was dying. Then I had a saddle block. It hurt like hell. They told me to relax because if I moved, the saddle block might 'take' wrong, and I would be paralyzed from the waist down. Nice. Then they gave me more drugs, and I was out during the delivery. When I came to I heard them discussing setting up a spot where they could 'give the news' to my Dad. (My parents were at the hospital.) They were afraid Dad would have a heart attack. I secretly wondered if I was dead and could only hear all this through some freak of nature.

"I asked about the baby several times before they responded; then they told me 'we will discuss it later.' The doctor and my parents came to my room. I was so worried about Dad that when the doctor told me Jonathan had died, I simply said, 'Why?'

"He told me he was a Down's syndrome baby and never would have been 'right.' I said, 'Oh, okay.' I guess I should have screamed or something because the doctor thought I had lost my mind and told the nurses to watch me very closely. When I walked down to the nursery to see my girlfriend's baby, they went berserk. They all but screamed 'what are you doing??' I said I was going to look at the baby. Before I could explain further, they said 'There is no baby, come back to your room.'

"My mom called to find out the date of my release, and the nurse said I was being transferred to the state mental hospital. My mom didn't buy that story and I was released the next day. At this point my husband was home on emergency leave. He was in complete agreement with my going to a mental hospital. I have often thought about what would have happened to me if my folks hadn't acted in my behalf. My relationship with my first husband started falling apart at that point. I felt cut adrift from him and the gap got wider. We were divorced five years later.

"I do want to say one more thing about Jonathan. I have since seen movies about children with Down's syndrome and I loved the retarded people. I saw them as warm and loving with so much to give. It infuriates me to hear anyone tell me I was 'lucky' that he died. During counseling last summer I cleaned up my feelings and I do not still feel any aching, continuous sadness over his death—but I *never* feel like it was a lucky break that he died."

### *Melanie*

Melanie's letter poured out her sadness at having given birth to a son with a cleft palate. "Poor little guy. I just hold him and cry and cry. That's all he does, too, cry. I can't blame him though. He's got a rough road ahead, facing surgery when he's a little older and stronger. I never got to nurse him. I feel so sad for what we lost—he and I—in those first days after birth. We should have been cuddling together, learning how to breastfeed, and feeling joyous. Instead, we failed at breastfeeding because he couldn't suck properly, and we both felt frustrated and sad and miserable.

"I've tried to find answers as to why this happened. I keep going over everything I ate or did or didn't do when I was pregnant. I had wanted at least two children, but now I think I'd be too afraid to try again."

## *Jackie*

Jackie and Mark's second child was born with Down's syndrome. Although they were given the diagnosis within days of Justin's birth, they told no one. "I couldn't bear that anyone know," Jackie told us. "Although the doctors couldn't give us definite reasons, I felt so responsible. I felt so guilty. I felt such anger—why me? Why Justin? We acted so cool on the surface, but inside we were in torment. Finally, when Justin was seven months old, I just couldn't cope any longer. I felt wrung out, and I began to feel ill as well. Medical tests turned up a bleeding ulcer in my stomach. I had thought the pain I was feeling was anguish over Justin. Even now that I know, the pain all feels the same."

## *Pat*

Pat's son was born with a purple-red birthmark extending from one eye down over his cheek. The doctors assured Pat and Joe that the mark would fade in color with time, but that it might not disappear completely. 'I hated seeing it," wrote Pat. "I felt that somehow I had produced an imperfect child, that it was my fault. And that Kevin would be stuck with that blemish because of me! I had so dreamed of this perfect child, *my* child, who would be more beautiful than any other baby in the nursery. And then when Kevin was born, I had to look away from his face. I feel so horribly guilty for having done that, for having looked away from my son. I don't like what I've seen inside myself. And I feel so very sad, so deeply disappointed that I didn't give my son the body he deserved. This sadness is always with me, for my son is the center of my life. I do love him so, and I grieve for the love he may miss because of his unlovely face.''

## Nancy

Nancy wrote: ''In January our second child, Edward, was born and was unable to live outside my uterus due to chromosome abnormalities. He died within thirty minutes. He had a double cleft lip and cleft palate. I chose not to hold him because of the facial abnormalities, but even though that seemed best at the time, I now wish I had held him.''

## CESAREAN SECTION

### Heather

Heather's letter: ''I was surprised and upset when told I needed an emergency cesarean. My body was covered with poison ivy, so I had to be knocked out rather than receive a spinal. I was overdosed with sodium pentothal and didn't wake up for eight hours. Then I was only allowed to see my twin boys briefly—all I got to do was touch their feet. When they were taken away again, I felt like my legs were cut off. Now, eight years later, I'm still haunted by 'missing' their birth.''

### Lee

Lee wrote: ''It took me twelve years and four c-sections to believe that birth is not necessarily a horror. This last birth, although surgical, was a positive birth experience. What a difference from my three previous births. Each one with a different hospital, and each one a new nightmare and an even stronger feeling of failure for me. I was lied to, mistreated, butchered and almost lost my third child because of negligence. When other women were joyous about their births, I was only miserable.''

## Jane

Jane's letter was a plea for help: ''I am pregnant a little sooner than I wanted to be with my second child. I am still not completely 'over' my first birth experience, which was a c-section. It was *awful!* I'm terrified of having another section, afraid of the hospital, mistrustful of my doctor. That birth stripped away all my confidence in myself—and, since my baby was premature, I am also insecure about my ability to carry this pregnancy to term. I feel like a bundle of nerves, and I just can't cope with this. Can you help me please?''

## Penny

Penny's letter told a similar story: ''I had a cesarean after planning a home birth and I sure could use some healing. I read about you in the cesarean awareness newsletter and forgiving yourself does seem to be the key. I had a 40-hour labor and it was difficult to relax since my midwife, whom I had counted on to take control, was asked to leave in order for me to have a photographer stay. My husband had trained to coach me in relaxing exercises but became too emotionally involved. There were variables involved but I feel if I had squatted like I wanted and had relaxed I possibly could have given birth vaginally. It was all so crazy when we reached the hospital, I was in transition after 'failure to progress.' Our doctor literally broke my water against our will, my husband reached to stop him and couldn't, this made me regress back to 6 centimeters. Why?

"Next time it's got to be different, there is such a void to push for 3 hours and then have a cesarean and not have your baby right away. My son is near twelve months now and the pain is like it was yesterday."

### Bonnie

Bonnie called after her daughter's delivery by cesarean section: "As you know, we were planning a home birth. We had so wanted our older children and some dear friends present. We had decorated our bedroom as the birth room— even brought in my grandmother's rocking chair to remind me of her and give me strength. The children were *so* excited about seeing 'their' new baby born. We all felt so close to one another. But then, when I went into labor, I began to bleed a bit. We went right to the hospital and learned that my placenta might be separating too soon (this was confirmed after the birth). We consented to an immediate cesarean section. The baby was in respiratory distress at first but improved over the next few days. We think she will be okay, but only time will tell for sure. We do feel the section was necessary, and in our case, life-saving. Yet we and our children feel intensely sad. I've researched what happened to me and find that it's a very, very rare occurrence in healthy, well-nourished women. Why me? Why us? I have no answers, only great sadness.

"Anyway, I'm wondering if you know anyone who could use our box of home birthing supplies. I hate to throw them away when we had purchased them with such excitement, such hope, but I can't bear to look at the box these days.''

## *Shelly*

Shelley wrote: "Do you have any counseling programs for couples who've had an unexpected cesarean section? Bob and I are in need of help, and since our friends and our doctor don't understand, we don't know where to turn. We prepared extensively for our first birth: we read books, we exercised together (so Bob could support me), we improved our diet, we attended classes. When labor began, we were ready. Or so we thought. The doctor had promised not to insist on a monitor, but then, when I was in labor, he just didn't come through. When I mentioned studies, etc., and fears, he said, 'Although I have to respect your right to your own opinion, I'm not impressed with your research.' It was a battle every inch of the way—not just with the labor but with the doctor and the hospital staff. The doctor said, 'Look, when problems develop with the baby's heart, the monitor tells us right away, so we can react.' When problems develop . . . that's where *our* problems began with that awful machine.

"Bob and I relented, and I was strapped on. I couldn't move at all, because the belt kept slipping. The contractions got more painful. I got more and more exhausted. I won't give you all the details, but after an IV, artificially ruptured membranes, some pitocin, no food or drink, the doctor came in and said, 'I can only give you another hour—really I should say less—and then we'll have to do a cesarean.' Needless to say, that's what happened.

"Bob and I were bewildered. We couldn't understand how all our plans had been so smashed. The baby had some breathing difficulties at first, so I never got to hold him until the next day. I hardly even saw him when he was born. When they finally brought him in, the pain in my incision was so great that I couldn't even hold him.

"I feel like such a failure. Why couldn't I do it? I miss the birth we had so hoped for. I try to explain the depth of my pain and sorrow, but I guess I'm not explaining it very well, because few people understand. I feel so lonely. I know I have a baby and I should be grateful, and I am, but I'm also so very sad. I hope you can help me, because my unhappiness and depression are hard on my husband and baby—and on me too."


## TRAUMATIC BIRTH

### Macey

A letter from Macey: "Please send me whatever information you have on the subject of 'positive birthing.' Please send it very soon, as I have an urgent need to start healing after a traumatic birth experience."


### Dorothy

Dorothy's letter poured our her shock and sadness over her traumatic birth experience: "My husband was not allowed into the labor room. I was totally alone. And scared. Pitocin was given to speed up my contractions, even though my labor was progressing beautifully. I was forced to lie down, which caused a great deal of discomfort. I pushed before the proper time and ended up with third degree lacerations of the cervix, hemorrhaging, shock and oxygen. The birth was horrible. I didn't see my baby for two days. My inability to communicate all my feelings of shock, pain and sadness to my husband damaged our relationship a lot; in fact, the birth just about finished it. We are struggling with the pieces. . . ."

## *Lennie*

Lennie shared her experience of traumatic birth: "My labor was traumatic. It was long and agonizing. There was so much pain that I thought my spinal column was literally disintegrating. By the end I no longer knew I was having a baby. My husband and the nurse on the last shift tried to help me. but my obstetrician so violated me that I pushed that betrayal out of my mind at delivery and did not allow myself to own it until well over a year later. He artificially ruptured my membranes. He augmented an already difficult labor with pitocin. He discontinued medication in a 'continuous' epidural [a type of spinal anesthesia] for the last three hours of labor. Finally he delivered our daughter, Julia, with forceps. He did not acknowledge medical problems I developed as a result of the delivery.

"As I discovered later, I was left anemic and with a prolapsed uterus and a herniated bladder. In addition, my strength was depleted to such an extent that I suffered from biochemical depression for two years.

"The depression started immediately. I remember thinking in the recovery room that it had all been too much: the pain and even the overwhelming love for Julia. I was fragmented. I felt that my connectedness to the outside world had somehow been severed. I had night terrors and was unable to sleep well for months, even after Julia did sleep through the night. When I thought of anything troubling I would become obsessed by it. I had a lot of fear for my daughter, too, because of the violence of her birth and because I was afraid that she might be affected by the way I felt. As time passed I improved my situation.

"Yet because I'd been depressed so long, the wounds connected with the delivery and that period of my life were very deep. I searched Los Angeles for someone who would help me deal with that specific trauma. Through a c-sec support group I was referred to Offspring. Cathy Romeo answered my plea for help with a very long letter suggesting a healing visualization strategy. Even more healing were the acceptance and compassion she expressed. Thanks to her and to all of you."

### *Lauri*

Laurie wrote: "I hope you can help me. I gave birth to a beautiful little girl last month, and yet I can't seem to find the joy I should be feeling. Her birth was very unlike my first birth (her brother's), unlike anything I ever expected. Labor was only 90 minutes long, incredibly intense and overwhelming. I think I just screamed my way through. After Rebecca was born, I hemorrhaged. Apparently, the placenta had not emerged intact, but that problem was undetected by the doctor or the hospital staff. The hemorrhage was slow but steady after birth, and I just attributed the woozy feeling to my rapid labor. The nurses were stretched pretty thin, and the hemorrhage wasn't detected until it was a very dangerous situation. The doctor felt he had to do an emergency hysterectomy to save my life. I lived, but some days I'm not even grateful. My husband and I had so wanted a large family, and now all those dreams have been cut out of my body."

## ADOPTION

### *Leslie*

Leslie made arrangements to release her unplanned baby for adoption right after birth. Very young and unmarried, she believed her child would have greater security and more stability with a couple who were emotionally, physically, mentally, and spiritually ready to parent. Never questioning the rightness of her decision, she nevertheless felt deep grief over her conscious release of her baby.

As she recalled, "When Christina was born, I held her as much as I could for those two days we were together in the hospital. We were only apart for visiting hours, and every other minute she was in my arms. I drank her in, pressing her image on my heart and soul. It wasn't enough. I really want more time with her. When I said good-bye to her, I felt choked with grief and pain. I loved her so much, and I wanted her to have the best, but I really wanted her to have the best *and* me at the same time. Not many people understood how I felt. I wanted to scream that I was grieving, aching inside, but hardly anyone was around to hear. Most people assumed that I must be glad to be 'rid of' (in one friend's words) the baby. It was my choice to release her, but *not* to be rid or her. God, how I hate those words!

"I missed her every minute those first days and weeks, and most minutes these days. The pain *is* getting less, but not my love for her. I'll carry *that* with me always."

### *Judi*

Judi wrote: "I had an illegitimate child; I was 21 at the time—young enough that I feel now that giving up that time was best. I did suffer terribly as I kept it from my parents, family, friends and have carried that guilt for a lot of years. I still have guilty feelings but also feel that I have cleaned a lot of it up. All in all, there will *always* be some sadness for me, and I'll *never* forget him.''

## POSTPARTUM DEPRESSION

### *Jack*

Jack called with anxious concern for his wife, Jessica, and their six-week-old son, Gregory. ''The trouble started about four days after Gregory's birth. We were home from the hospital and trying to adjust to being new parents. It was pretty overwhelming, and our families are far away. Jessica was having trouble with breastfeeding—bleeding nipples and engorgement I think it's called—and Gregory would scream. We couldn't calm him down. This situation went on chronically, sometimes better, often worse, for days. When Gregory cried, Jessica grew more and more distraught. She was also very uncomfortable physically, and disappointed emotionally, because of Gregory's forceps delivery. People would invariably drop by or telephone just as she was getting Gregory to sleep. Jessica became more and more exhausted. She kept trying to keep up with everything—to care for Gregory, to cook nourishing meals, to keep the house clean, and to be a gracious hostess to people who stopped by to see the baby. I worried about her, and I tried to help, but I was pretty beat too.

''At Gregory's first checkup, the pediatrician found that he hadn't-gained any weight. That seemed to be the final blow; Jessica's been deeply depressed for the last week now. She doesn't get dressed, she doesn't eat, she doesn't even seem to care about Gregory. Her doctor is suggesting a mental care hospital. Can you help us in any way?''

## *Jim*

---

Jim called Offspring looking for a postpartum support group. "My wife Irene has been hospitalized for severe postpartum depression. The doctor will release her to go home if we can find an ongoing support group. Our birth experience was so *good,* so exciting, that the depression took us by surprise. Irene had a forty-four-hour labor. I was so proud of her. She wouldn't give up, she kept working with the labor. Finally, after four hours of pushing, Brenda was born. It was the most incredible 'high' of our lives! I finally went home about five hours later and got some sleep. But Irene couldn't wind down, couldn't sleep. She began to get jittery, and then weepy. The sleeping pill they gave her wouldn't work. When we came home, I thought that would help, but it made things worse. Irene was so worried and tense about the baby that she couldn't settle down. She looked like a zombie, and I didn't know what to do. I was pretty nervous around the baby myself. A few days later she completely fell apart. We just hadn't been prepared at all for being parents. Our childbirth classes helped us through the birth, but then we just didn't know what to do."

## *Emily*

---

Emily wrote: "The most helpful thing for me personally was your renaming postpartum depression—postpartum *expression* fits so much better what I experienced in the days after my first child was born.

"At first the feelings of euphoria were anything but depression. Next, according to my mother's and Dave's description (I have little memory of the subsequent days), I crashed or sky-rocketed or something. I vaguely remember that I couldn't seem to comfort the baby, or know what to do with him when he was crying, or get *any* sleep at all. I began acting delirious, with violent chills, almost convulsions, and eyes rolling.

"We were all terrified, and so I was hospitalized—in a mental health unit. I've always felt that if only they'd let me *express* all the 'crazy' things I *felt* and did and said when I first went into the hospital, I'd have been much better off. Instead, I was given 40 mg/day of the anti-psychotic drug Haldol, which completely *suppressed* all those feelings, besides having horrible side effects (I couldn't see clearly, swallow, or speak for days, and it set up a humiliating speech defect that didn't completely disappear for a couple of years).

"I think the reason I left the hospital as early as eighteen days later ('against medical advice'—Dave and I signed me out) was that I took myself off the Haldol by just pretending to take the pills. (I just slipped them in my knitting bag. . .). Not having them for a couple of days gave me back enough of myself to know what they were doing was not good for me. Even so, I remember that it took me another full ten days to even be able to cry.

"Andy was eleven months old before I began to feel consistently happy again. Writing in a diary and having Dave and my parents tell me all that went on in the hospital helped me enormously. When Glen was born two years later, I experienced a happy postpartum period. And the latest thing to help ease the memory of that first painful postpartum experience has been your renaming it postpartum *expression*. Thank you!"

## LOST DREAMS OF PARENTHOOD

*Joyce*

Joyce experienced two ectopic pregnancies, followed by the premature stillbirth of her daughter, Rachel. Four months after Rachel's stillbirth, she and her husband adopted their second child. Because of the grief she felt over her daughter's stillbirth, Joyce felt she lost much of her adopted son's infancy.

"I had always had dreams of a pregnancy in which I ate the best foods for the health of my baby, exercised and felt an inner peace and joy as each day of my baby's growth passed. I had visions of a childbirth not full of labor 'pains' but one in which my contractions were a bond between us: I was stimulating and hugging my child and receiving back 'vibrations' or love and bonding. I dreamed of breasts full of milk that I could offer my child—I can now even feel the desire for them to 'hurt' so that my baby could be nourished. So, much of today's grief is for a pregnancy of my dreams that will never exist.

"Additionally, some of my grief now (much less as days go by and our relationship grows) was for my relationship with B.J. Beej was born one day before Rachel was supposed to be born (although we didn't find out about him until four days later). Although I had done my 'grieving' 4 months earlier when Rachel was actually stillborn, my due date was a very emotional day. When 3 days later we found out about the chance to adopt Beej—well, here was the body we had expected anyway—even though it had a penis instead of a vagina. For the first 22 months of his life I really didn't recognize my true feelings until the day of the conference.

"All the emotions, feelings, reactions, etc. that were described as a part of grief and loss felt very real to me—but I hardly thought of Rachel that day . . . I couldn't stop thinking about B.J. I felt sad and empty because suddenly I realized that I had spent this time working on my grief for Rachel—thank goodness I feel as though I have effectively filed its rough edges down—but in the process B.J.'s first all-important months were 'lost.'

"I am now trying to work out the grief I feel for the loss of my relationship with his infancy. I do feel hopeful about

its outcome—I think that hope comes from having gone
through it for Rachel and the tubal pregnancies and the
'never gonna be' pregnancy/childbirth. I suppose that knowing that the pain does not have to feel so painful, that, with
time and openness and honesty, I can feel an inner peace,
then I can accept the road it takes to get to that inner
peace.''

# FIVE

# THE PHYSICAL IMPACT OF CHILDBEARING LOSS

If your heart, your mind, and your spirit are reeling from the impact of your loss, know that your body is staggering too. Loss is physical stress of the highest order. The impact of loss often shows up in our bodies, in illnesses as mild as colds, or as threatening as cancer; in patterns as debilitating as nausea, or as frustrating as insomnia. Our holistic approach to healing pregnancy loss begins with a most important focus on the distressed body.

In order to respond to physical needs, we must understand the integrated relationship between the body, mind, heart, and soul. In the most simple sense, what we sow in the mind (or heart or soul), we reap in the body. When the psychic pain of pregnancy loss assaults the consciousness, the body *absorbs* and may even *store* the loss. Understanding this important relationship is crucial to beginning an appropriate and adequate physical care response for yourself or for anyone else.

Biofeedback pioneers Elmer and Alyce Green of the renowned Menninger Clinic in Kansas tell us that "every change in the mental emotional state, conscious or unconscious, is accompanied by an appropriate change in the psychological state." In other words, mind, emotions, and body (and, we believe, spirit as well) are a unified system; if one is affected, so are the others.

Childbearing loss is a devastating "change" in the consciousness; its parallel physiological effects are equally great. The resulting physical condition may be one of cellular overload, or what we commonly refer to as stress. The degree of stress on the physical body is directly correlated with the impact of loss on the consciousness, not necessarily with the actual external events. Regardless of degree, the stressed body is predisposed to "dis-ease."

Childbearing losses produce physical stress for parents *and* for other family members. The resulting physical symptoms are all too often misunderstood and mistreated medically, and (without a more holistic response) may even become the forerunners of long-term illnesses and premature death.

Let us examine some of the evidence so that we may more fully understand how crucial is the need for a direct and immediate response to our grieving physical beings. That response may possibly prevent some of the physiological results of loss discussed in the following pages.

## GRIEF REACTIONS

Psychiatrist Erich Lindemann's landmark studies in the 1940s of grief reactions were the first widely reported papers offering evidence that loss can be related to medical disease. Lindemann (1979) writes that "loss of security, especially the loss of another person of emotional significance, is frequently encountered as the crisis in human relationships which preceded the onset of illness." He particularly observed high incidences of ulcerative colitis, rheumatoid arthritis, and asthma, as well as loss of appetite, excessive fatigue, and respiratory abnormalities in grieving individuals.

More recently, cancer researchers and direct care providers Stephanie and Carl Simonton (1978) observed a high incidence of serious loss experienced by their cancer patients six to eighteen months before the onset of the disease. Their mind/body integration approach for the treatment of cancer patients has been phenomenally successful; they report a survival rate of twice the national norm and, in many cases, dramatic remissions or total cures.

The Simontons view emotional stress as a giant trigger, setting off a physiological response that suppresses the body's natural defenses. They believe that there is such a clear link between stress and illness that it is even possible to predict illness based on the degree of stress in one's life.

Endocrinologist Hans Selye (1956) was among the first to call attention to the physical effects of chronic stress on the body. His description of bodily reactions to stress has been supported by more recent researchers.

Psychologist Lyle Miller (1983), director of the Stress management Clinic at the Biobehavioral Sciences Division of Boston University's School of Medicine, described the known physical effects of prolonged stress (and loss is clearly prolonged stress) as follows:

> In the skeleto-muscular system, stress can produce lower back pain and tension headaches.
>
> In the parasympathetic nervous system, stress can trigger ulcerative colitis, irritable bowel syndrome, ulcers, constipation, and diarrhea.
>
> In the sympathetic nervous system, stress effects include hypertension, too-rapid heartbeat, irregular cardiac rhythms, and migraine headaches.
>
> In the endocrine or hormone system, stress-

> related problems include some forms of infertility, menstrual and breastfeeding problems, and growth deficiencies in children.
>
> In the immune system, stress appears to reduce the number and power of infection-fighting white blood cells, leading to immune system problems that may predispose to serious illness such as cancer.

Studies indicate that the most stressful events in human life are loss-related experiences. Psychiatrist Thomas Holmes (1967), and psychologist Richard Rahe, and their associates at the University of Washington School of Medicine statistically validated the effects of stress, noting that the most stressful events, clearly topping the scale, were all related to loss.

According to two recent reports on the effects of stress (the *Boston Globe,* May 30, 1983, and *Time,* June 6, 1983), increasing numbers of medical researchers implicate not stress alone, but also the *integration* of stress as a crucial factor undermining health. The Simontons concur. While they recognize the general stress of loss as significantly increasing susceptibility to illness, they describe how one's emotional/mental reaction to loss (how one copes, whether resolution seems possible) will further determine one's physical response to it. Researchers can assess reaction to loss by examining one's store of coping mechanisms.

In other words, loss may predispose one to illness or poor health, and how one integrates or copes with the loss may lessen—or intensify—that effect. We believe that parents in grief, then, are at particularly high risk of bodily illness, for they commonly express feeling totally transfixed by their loss, feeling that life has no meaning, feeling that little support is evident, feeling unable to uncover within themselves any meaningful coping mechanisms, and feeling that no resolution is possible.

In their study of survivors and bereaved relatives of a

1977 rail disaster, psychiatrists Sing and Raphael (1981) reported significant loss of good health among those grieving. They studied the relationship between disease and bereavement and assigned a morbidity rating (a rating of ill health) to those they studied. *Mothers who had lost children scored the highest morbidity, meaning they suffered the worst health.*

In an Australian study of recently widowed persons (aged twenty-five to sixty-five), R. W. Bathrop (1977) and his associates at the University of New South Wales described how bereavement physically lowers the body's immune response. They found that the lymphocyte function, a critical measure of the potency of the body's immune system, was significantly depressed. Bathrop thus documented a significant loss of power in the physical immune system when death closes a chapter in one's life.

## SPECIFIC EFFECTS OF PREGNANCY LOSS

### *Perinatal Death*

Childbearing loss devastatingly and, most often, unexpectedly closes a chapter in a parent's life. Sociologists Larry Peppers and Ronald Knapp focused on perinatal death as their primary area of research during the years 1976-79. Through numerous interviews, letters and questionnaires that explored with women themselves the effects of their infants' deaths, Peppers and Knapp reported the common physical effects of infant loss. The grief reactions they documented include exhaustion, loss of appetite, sleep disturbances, lack of strength, weight loss, headache, blurred vision, breathlessness, and palpitations.

Apart from Peppers and Knapp, very few researchers have examined the physical reactions of those suffering *childbearing* loss. What of those diagnosed as infertile, who have lost their hopes to conceive? How do their bodies process their grief? Or those who have delivered their children surgically and lost their eagerly anticipated and carefully planned vaginal births? Or those who experienced severe postpartum depression and lost their earlier expectations of contented family life?

In the absence of documented studies, we turned to several authorities in their various fields.

## *Infertility*

Couples who never conceive but desperately want to are bereaved. They grieve for what never was, what never will be. They grieve for the loss of their biological heritage and for the future ending of their own lives with no perpetuation in children. They grieve for the loss of their love personified, made real enough to see and touch.

RESOLVE is a national organization offering information, referral, and support to those experiencing fertility problems and/or pregnancy loss. Merle Bombardieri (1983), its clinical director, confirmed the presence of physical grief reactions in countless women who contacted RESOLVE for help. "The most common physical effects include exhaustion, insomnia, nausea or other forms of nutritional stress, respiratory abnormalities such as breathlessness, and severely reduced immunities," she explained. "The physical health of these women, and of some of their partners as well, seems in many cases to be jeopardized."

## *Abortion/Miscarriage*

Laurea Nugent (1983) is a nurse practitioner who works at a busy obstetrical/gynecological office. She particularly notes changes in the physical appearance of women who have undergone abortions or who have experienced miscarriage. "Their color seems drained; their complexions are sallow; and their overall demeanor speaks of physiological depression. I see such physical signs so often that I can usually pick those women out of a full waiting room. They are so obviously in need of appropriate physical care for their bodies."

Abortion and sudden miscarriage both create *rapid* hormonal changes, effects which stun the body physiologically. There is no period of gradual internal change; it happens abruptly. Such a physiological jolt demands an adequate physical care response.

## Cesarean Section

Nancy Wainer Cohen (1983), pioneer and nationally recognized leader of the BVAC (Vaginal Birth After Cesarean) movement and co-author of *Silent Knife: Cesarean Prevention and Vaginal Birth After Cesarean*, talks about the thousands of women who write to her of their feelings after cesarean section: "They feel intensely sad, having lost—or been deprived of—one of the cycles of their lives: the experience of giving *birth*. They write of the pain in their hearts as a result of the pain in their surgically violated bodies."

"The physical and emotional pain they feel often lingers far longer than the normal postoperative healing period. Many, many women report varying degrees of discomfort, tenderness, or pain in the area of their incisions. Some have described incisions that refused to heal, or incisions that began 'pulsing' whenever they contemplated a future pregnancy. Many report an overwhelming exhaustion that continues for months, even years; pounding headaches; severely reduced immunities and continual colds, viruses and infections; dietary difficulties; or sexual dysfunction. Surely these women are experiencing physical bereavement reactions. Even with healthy babies, they, too, are parents in grief, and their physical bodies suffer.''

Cesarean section is major surgery, and as such it requires a period of physical recovery and care. Many sectioned women who are grieving the loss of a baby or the loss of their expectations of normal vaginal birth are so shrouded by their grief that they pay poor attention to their recovering bodies' physical needs. Whether a section is necessary and life-saving or not, it is *always* a major violation to the body. Surgery first of all requires anesthesia, in and of itself a frightening and potentially dangerous intrusion into the body's normal functioning. Then the surgical cutting, tugging, and pulling, and the exposure of vulnerable inner organs to external toxins severely violate the body.

Some postcesarean women report that their bodies become very sensitive to further disturbance, so that a slight cut or even a stubbed toe may feel very painful. Others say that their bodies seem to ''toughen'' in an attempt, perhaps, to ward off any further violations or pain. One sad effect of that protective self-shielding, though, is that many women then have difficulty receiving physical affection, returning to sexual intercourse and reaching orgasm, and expressing any natural physical desires.

Occasionally we've worked with women who have so totally ignored their physical needs after cesarean section that their incisions could not heal. While complete physical healing always depends on the healing of the *whole* being (if the mind, heart and spirit aren't healed, neither will the body be), nevertheless, appropriate physical care is essential to even begin that process.

## Postpartum Depression

Nutritionist and dietary consultant Ellia Manners, M.S., of Newton, Massachusetts, often sees postpartum women and men who are experiencing the same physical grief reactions cited by Lindemann (1979) and Peppers and Knapp (1980). "These clients describe parenthood as much more difficult or demanding than they had anticipated," she explains. "Some call it overwhelming. They complain of physical problems that have included insomnia, exhaustion, reduced immunities and frequent illnesses, loss of appetite and irregular eating habits. They make no connection between their lost visions of parenthood and the reality they are living, but I certainly do."

## INADEQUATE MEDICAL SUPPORT

Barbara Dill, M.S.N. (Master of Science in Nursing), C.S. (Certified Nurse Specialist), who is associate program director of the Pain Management Program at Shaughnessey Hospital in Salem, Massachusetts, offers these comments on the physical effects of childbearing loss: "We don't really need to document scientifically that pregnancy-related loss creates *intense* physical stress. This we know. If, however, documenting this scientifically would prod physicians into dealing with physical 'dis-ease' on a new level—earlier, *before* pathology is created—then someone should do it! Currently, the existing science of medicine is not geared to diagnose the chemical changes that occur when a person is under severe stress. Physicians rely on laboratory tests for the diagnosis of disease, yet routine testing can only pinpoint existing damage, existing pathology, *not* the predisposition to pathology that loss creates. This system is so woefully inadequate! My hope is that more and more physicians and other health care providers will become aware of the very great danger to physical health that childbearing loss presents. Perhaps then they can more closely monitor the health of bereaved parents, and make suggestions and recommendations aimed at preventing disease'' (Dill 1983).

## OUR CASE RECORDS

We have worked with clients recovering from every manner of childbearing loss. In these bereaved parents we have observed *a universal tendency toward poorer health*. The most extreme manifestations of bodily disease have even included cancer. Rosemary's story offers sad testimony.

### *Rosemary*

In late 1980, Rosemary, a thirty-two-year-old woman, sought counseling services for severe headaches, which she related to an unresolved miscarriage that had occurred six months previously. At the time of her miscarriage she had been five months pregnant. She and her husband had joyously embraced their pregnancy, for it ended a five-year history of infertility. The miscarriage was devastating.

Rosemary described her life as without meaning, her mind as totally preoccupied with thoughts of her lost child, much like the Simontons' portrayal of the classic high-risk client who cannot uncover adequate coping mechanisms and therefore believes no resolution is possible.

At the time of Rosemary's initial visit, she was complaining of severe headaches coupled with periods of blanking out into some state of unconsciousness. She repeatedly stated that she couldn't get her baby ''out of her head'' or ''off her mind.''

She was encouraged to seek medical diagnosis for her physical symptoms. During her second visit she divulged that she had named her baby and placed a small tree in her backyard as a memorial to her child. Although Rosemary said she was feeling foolish for engaging in such rituals over a miscarriage, she noticed a sense of relief in finally acknowledging the depth of her loss. However, she still described herself as very depressed and "unable to live with the loss." She also shared that her physician could find no difficulties that would cause her headaches but had ordered some further testing.

Rosemary never came for her third appointment. She called to tell us she was a patient at a major teaching hospital in Boston and was undergoing extensive tests for her still undiagnosed headaches. After several weeks of testing and medical consultation, the horrifying results were in: Rosemary had a brain tumor and was given six months to live.

The diagnosis seemed to push Rosemary into a psychic state of alienation and even into surrender to her own death. Six weeks later, Rosemary died. Some would judge that her illness came first and caused her miscarriage. Those who knew her well would not agree.

All of us were left to wonder whether Rosemary could have lived—if miscarriage were recognized as the loss it can be for some women, if her infertility history had been emotionally as well as physically treated, if she had received proper nutrition/physical counseling after her loss, and if her medical care providers had encouraged her to seek psychological support for her miscarriage instead of dusting her off and sending her home to get pregnant again.

In *Creative Visualization,* Shakti Gawain (1978) writes, "People get sick because they believe on an inner level that illness is an appropriate or inevitable response to some situation or circumstance, because in some way it seems to solve a problem for them or get them something they need, or as a *desperate solution to some unresolved and unbearable inner conflict* [emphasis ours]." Rosemary's response to her miscarriage may have been just such a desperate solution.

## *Other Reactions*

We have observed other serious physical manifestations of loss; they have included heart disease, back problems, pneumonia, and ulcers. We've seen these conditions in both men and women clients, but they more often show up in those clients who have attempted to withhold or repress their emotional responses to loss over a long period of time. Repressing an emotion can cause it to ''somatize,'' to manifest instead in the physical body. Our most deeply felt emotions always do appear somehow, somewhere. The most common examples of somatized emotion we see are headaches, backaches, and ulcers.

A recent study indicated a particular tendency toward heart disease in fathers who had lost children. Such a tendency may speak to the painful cultural programming that demands men ''be strong,'' ''manly,'' and ''in control.'' All of this male scripting may well produce hardy football players who don't mind being physically abused in the name of sport; however, it may also be killing grieving fathers, whose bodies are bursting with the unexpressed sorrow of a parent without his child.

Medical researchers Mandell, McAnulty, and Reece (1980) from the Massachusetts Sudden Infant Death Center reported on paternal response to sudden infant death. The bereaved fathers they studied offered a reflection of cultural subtyping: ''that men should be tough and stoic, and that one need not be concerned with reactions or general well-being of the fathers. These paternal behaviors, which emerge at a time of crises and which obstruct full expression of grief, may unwittingly be promoted by medical and health care providers who are anxious to help fathers fulfill societal expectations of masculine strength.''

Women, on the other hand, have more cultural permission to express themselves emotionally (though often at the risk of being judged hysterical) and are therefore more likely to seek a grief-support group or some form of counseling. We have noted that several fathers we've known through their wives developed serious physical problems within a month of the time their female partners completed counseling. In these cases, the women tended to express the emotions for the relationship. As long as the women were expressing these emotions, their male partners experienced some relief. When the women completed counseling and grief work, their male partners were left to their own unresolved emotions, which in several cases became seriously somatized, or manifested in the physical body.

## Jack and Patricia

Jack and Patricia's case illustrates this point. Their second child, Ann, had been stillborn. Almost a year after Ann's death, Pat believed that she and Jack were still suffering and unable to communicate the depth of loss each was feeling. However, when she suggested that they seek counseling, Jack rejected the idea. Pat nevertheless attended sessions, and in a few months she reported a sense of healing. She had lost the final twenty pounds she had gained during pregnancy, had begun an exercise program, felt ready to look for a job, and demonstrated a renewed sense of purpose and direction.

Once Pat completed counseling, Jack gained eighteen pounds in two weeks, and then was suddenly struck with such severe back pain that he was unable to move for six weeks. He later reported that he had spent that time lying in bed crying to himself and feeling a desperate sense of depression. Medical treatment involved pain medications and tranquilizers, which further depressed Jack, and strict orders not to get out of bed.

Jack agreed to some bedside counseling, during which he

shared the sorrow and guilt he felt over Ann's death—feelings he had not shared with anyone even though he had lost his daughter almost two years before. In two weeks Jack was able to walk; in four weeks, he returned to work.

## Anemia a Risk

We've noticed that grieving parents, especially women, often exhibit a tendency toward anemia. The anemic conditions may be a result of poor diet, blood losses related to pregnancy, the emotional stress of grief, or all three.

Every woman who has suffered pregnancy loss has also, to one degree or another, lost blood. While blood loss may be greater in some situations such as surgical deliveries or traumatic births, it is a recognized factor in all pregnancy-related losses. Too often this blood depletion is not adequately treated or even understood as a source of emotional depletion as well. Anemia *causes* emotional depression even without the impact of pregnancy loss; it *must* be adequately treated in order that depression may begin to lift.

Women who have suffered childbearing loss and who have not adequately responded to their physical needs are at greater risk during a subsequent pregnancy. We've seen numerous clients who come to us after multiple pregnancy losses. Hardly ever have these women done enough to bolster their strength, replenish their depleted nutritional reserves, exercise their taut muscles, or repair the physical damage to their bodies. None of them received adequate direction or instruction on physical needs from their medical care givers, and the haze of grief just didn't allow them to see for themselves.

Finally, all the grieving parents we've seen professionally have reported at least some of the symptoms documented by Peppers and Knapp, including appetite abnormalities, exhaustion, headaches, insomnia, blurred vision, tightness in the throat, palpitations, and trembling.

We particularly note a high incidence of colds and sore throats that may well be interpreted as unshed tears (colds) or unspoken words (sore throats). When bereaved parents allow themselves the free and full expression of all that they are trying to contain in their bodies, symptoms such as these are usually relieved.

Often we've recommended a good, sad movie to grieving parents with continual colds. *E.T.* may have cured or alleviated more colds than any antihistamine on the market. We need more exposure to strength like that of football pro Roosevelt Grier, who was "man enough" to sing "It's All Right to Cry" to a nationwide television audience.

## THE BODY'S NEEDS

The physical body thus, without a doubt, is profoundly affected by loss. It is not possible to discuss healing in any positive, meaningful sense without adequately attending to physical needs. A malnourished, distressed body simply cannot supply the emotional, mental, and spiritual energy necessary for complete healing. Worse than that, it may foster subsequent pregnancy losses that will only perpetuate the pain, the grief, the illness, and the despair.

It is not always possible to avoid physical symptoms. In fact, each symptom can lead us to further recovery by letting us know what we need to do to feel better. Without his back pain, Jack might never have released his grief for Ann, and he might never have felt peace. However, it may well be possible to avoid serious physical illness and a number of the grief reactions we've documented, especially a long-term body depression, a chronically reduced immune system, and subsequent pregnancy losses caused by physical ill health.

Neglected bodies simply cannot support effective grief

work. The following two chapters offer specific health care responses to the grieving body.

We recognize that even with optimum support, adequate physical care may be difficult to achieve. We understand how very difficult it is to eat well when your stomach is twisted in knots of grief, to exercise when your body feels so crushed, and to reach out for help when your arms ache only to hold your lost child. Yet we know that strengthened physical health may shorten the period of emotional pain and can aid in building the best possible base for restructuring a life.

# SIX

# RESTORING PHYSICAL HEALTH

We hope the evidence presented in the preceding chapter has convinced you that improving your physical health is vital. Apart from preventing illness, optimum physical health will better support your efforts at overall grief work and perhaps shorten your road to healing. The following pages present specific ideas, techniques, and programs you can choose to follow or adapt as you respond to your body's physical needs. Take observant and truthful stock of how you feel physically. You may not even feel a desire to improve. Somewhere in each of us, there is an urge to live even when it coexists with an urge to die.

## EXHAUSTION

After her miscarriage, Carolyn wrote to us. "Everything is such a monumental effort—getting up in the morning, preparing breakfast, picking up the house, *living*. I feel the way I did when I had mononucleosis in college, only worse. *Then* I knew my energy would come back some day. . . .''

There are ways to feel better and to restore some energy to your grieving body. One way is a commitment to excellent nutrition; eating well and appropriately when under the stress of loss is so important to your well-being that the next chapter is entirely devoted to that subject.

Another way to feel better, to feel less exhausted, is to exercise. ''Impossible!'' you say, and we really do understand how you feel. There are days when we both recall barely being able to get ourselves out of bed. In fact, there were days we couldn't. Yet exercise *restores* energy; it is an energizing experience for the body. Exercising can actually reduce the terrible fatigue that parents in grief feel.

Dr. Lawrence Friedman (1976), medical director of the Institute for the Crippled and Disabled, Research and Rehabilitation Center in New York City, describes how inadequate muscle activity can produce fatigue as real as fatigue from excessive labor. Inactivity results in inadequate circulation, a poor exchange of nutrients and waste products in the tissues, and a weaker heartbeat—and then greater fatigue. Exercise, on the other hand, contracts and then relaxes muscles, and consumes more energy, speeding up the food oxidation and excretion process, which in turn stimulates the nervous, respiratory, and circulatory systems. As the breathing rate is increased, more oxygen is taken in. A more ''alive'' feeling results. Exercise can, then, in Friedman's words, ''do much to overcome tired, dragged-out feelings.''

Any exercise that appreciably (but safely) raises your pulse rate for twenty minutes is beneficial. Walking briskly, running, bicycling, or swimming all seem to offer special benefits to those suffering loss. Walking, running, or bicycling can bring you closer to the soul-nourishing effects of nature. Swimming provides a muffled quiet, and the water has a massaging effect on muscles and connective tissue taut with stress. An ongoing study at Western Illinois University has documented these bodily changes among participants in a swimming program:

1. Reduced blood pressure and lowered risk of heart disease.
2. Lower resting pulse rate; less heart strain.
3. Improved breathing capacity.
4. Improved oxygen uptake, increased oxygen delivered to muscles and organs.
5. Reduced percentage of body fat.
6. Improved cholesterol level.
7. Greater blood volumn—healthier tissues.
8. Increased hemoglobin level (protein in red blood cells).
9. Higher hematocrit (percentage of red blood cells).
10. Greater functional ability (efficiency) of the heart.

Other studies of the body's responses to exercise have compiled similar results. A number of the physical effects of bereavement noted by Lindemann (1979) and Peppers and Knapp (1980)—palpitations, fatigue, respiratory abnormalities, anemia, insomnia, headaches—could thus, based on the preceding study, be alleviated by the physiologic changes exercise induces. With a body strengthened through exercise, grief work can be more effective and complete, and healing may come sooner.

Exercise time may also be reflective, a space of "quiet" in the day. While exercise is helping your body, exercising time provides you the opportunity to "check in" with yourself, to stay with your grief-working process. One father of a stillborn commented that until he began exercising regularly, he just hadn't had time to work through his grief. His job was demanding and hectic, and at home he felt his family needed his constant support. "Working out" gave him a way to focus on the daughter he had lost by giving him time to get in touch with his feelings about her.

Exercise is a way of loving your body; it is something you do for yourself, and also for the people who love you. You may not *feel* like exercising, but you can still choose to do it, and you will almost certainly feel different, perhaps better, if you so choose.

We recognize how very difficult—well nigh impossible— it may seem to begin an exercise program while grieving for a lost child. The body-crushing, gut-wrenching experience of such loss is more physically depleting than any other we know. Yet, as Friedman (1976) demonstrates, inactivity can physiologically produce greater fatigue and then prolong the period of exhaustion; it may be especially damaging to grieving parents with living children who desperately need attention and care.

"OK," you say, "I'm convinced. But *how* do I get this beaten body moving?"

Stephanie and Carl Simonton (1978) recommend using mental imagery to visualize yourself engaging in physical exercise. They believe that using visualization in this way begins to build the expectancy of greater physical ease and also establishes a basic commitment to recognizing the *needs of your body*. Visualization is the art of using mental imagery and affirmation to effect change, produce results, or work healing. It is a technique for releasing blocks to the full mobilization of our inner resources.

We suggest that you settle into a relaxed position and then begin to visualize yourself in some form of exercise— swimming, walking, biking, playing tennis—whatever most appeals to you. Continue to picture yourself exercising for at least ten minutes; "see" the setting in detail and picture how your body is feeling while exercising. Imagine the sensations of your muscles stretching and your heart beating faster. Use this visualization at least three to four times a week; then, when you do feel ready to actually begin exercising, you will be accustomed to setting aside that time for yourself. You're part way there!

If, despite these incentives and suggestions, you still feel overwhelmingly stuck, you might consider an even more gentle, peaceful way to stimulate your physical body. It is massage. Friedman calls massage "passive exercise," and that is truly an apt description. Apart from the psychological benefits of massage, which are powerful indeed, there are physiological benefits as well. Massage can stimulate and contract muscles as palpably as exercise does, so it can produce the same—if less magnified—responses in the nervous, respiratory, and circulatory systems. Light, gentle stroking massage can be applied by anyone and with benefit. A professional massage can be even more helpful. Since it is often difficult to recognize qualified masseurs, we have included in the resource section at the back of the book a reference for finding a certified massage therapist trained in healing massage. Please consider giving yourself the gift of healing massage; you deserve no less than the very best health care.

## INSOMNIA

Exercise may help to reduce exhaustion, but it won't banish it. Some of the fatigue grieving parents feel results from shouldering the mountainous weight of their loss; some of it may be a result of physiologic depression; and some is normal healthy fatigue. Often, however, exhaustion is the result of bereavement insomnia, an inability to sleep at all or to sleep enough even though the body needs rest to repair itself.

"I *want* to sleep," Elaine told us. "Lord knows I need to sleep; I'm exhausted all the time. But when I get into bed at night, my mind starts to play back all those scenes. I see myself going into premature labor that nothing could stop. I see her lifeless little body lying there. And then my mind gallops into runaway gear: Why? Why did my body send her out too soon? She needed *months* more inside me. What went wrong? Why? Trying to fall asleep in the midst of that agony is impossible. So I think, and cry, and try not to think, and finally I fall asleep for a few hours before the alarm goes off. The nights are pretty bloody awful.''

Asking you not to think about your loss is unrealistic. However, as a well-known Biblical passage tells us, ''There is a time to every purpose under the heaven . . . a time to sow and a time to reap.''

Bedtime is not the time to sow seeds of anguish and guilt and pain. Bedtime is a time for sowing relaxation so that your body may reap the very necessary benefit of restful sleep. A light massage from a loved one may help to relax your body and prepare it for sleep. When you're alone, you can *visualize* relaxation in your body until the visualization becomes reality. There are available a number of guided relaxation cassette tapes, in which a soothing voice talks you through progressive relaxation. You can do the same thing for yourself, whenever you need rest or sleep.

Begin by removing distractions; if it's daytime, unplug your phone and tack a ''Do not knock or ring'' note to the door. If music soothes you, play something soft and peaceful— ''Spectrum Suite'' or ''Ancient Echoes'' by Steven Halpern, perhaps, or the ''Pachelbel'' Canon. Then lie down or lean back so that your body is *fully* supported by a bed, couch, or the floor. Use as many pillows as you must to make sure that no body part is resting on any other body part—your whole body is fully, freely supported. First, just observe your breath. Notice each inhalation and exhalation. Marvel at the perfection of your breath; each inhalation brings nourishing, life-giving oxygen to each part of your body, and then each exhalation releases carbon dioxide and any other wastes your body doesn't need.

Then give your body permission to begin to relax. Slow down your breathing; you might try a form of krya yoga, an ancient relaxation breathing pattern we call the ''circle breath.'' Connect your inhalation to your exhalation so that you visualize your breath rolling in, through, and out of your body in a gently flowing, unbroken circle. As you breathe in oxygen, now imagine drawing in peace and relaxation, and then let gravity draw away any tension or anxiety with your exhaled carbon dioxide. Focus on that circle breath for a few moments, and let is soften and soothe your body.

Then bring your attention to your feet—imagine that your breath can focus energy there, bringing sustenance and peace and carrying away tension or tightness. Feel your feet relax a bit. Let your attention drift higher; breathe in life and peace and send this nurturing and relaxation higher in your body, to your legs, your knees, your thighs. Your legs begin to feel loose and limp. Warm and heavy. Feel yourself sinking deeper into the pillows. Then you focus the comforting, soothing energy of your breath higher, into your pelvis, releasing and relaxing. The large psoas muscle that wraps around your pelvis releases its tension, and your pelvis spreads a bit. The relaxation reaches your spine and begins drifting upward, loosening each vertebra. You breathe *in* release and relaxation to your spine; you breath *out* any tension that was there. At the same time your abdomen and then diaphragm begin to relax, to let go. The warmth and heaviness that is spreading through your body via your breath reaches your shoulders and then floods down each arm to your fingers. All is becoming loose and limp, warm and heavy. Now your neck feels warm, and your scalp tingles as though you had just used a hair dryer. The warmth of relaxation smoothes your brow and softens your face. Your jaw slackens; your lips part slightly. Your breath has become deeper, fuller, and yet very relaxed and rhythmic.

Appreciate your ability to restore your body. Affirm your ability to rest when you need to do so. Think: "I listen to my body, and when it needs rest, I respond. I release tension and draw in peace and relaxation."

Now, in your mind, call up scenes of places you love, places where you feel the most peaceful and relaxed. Let these scenes drift through your consciousness, one by one, and admire them. A long sandy beach. A cabin on a majestic mountain. A clearing in a deep and quiet forest. A flower-filled meadow. Your own backyard. Be in those lovely settings, in your mind, and then choose one, or *create* one that doesn't exist, and make it your own personal haven. Shakti Gawain in *Creative Visualization* (1978) calls it your personal sanctuary. This haven belongs only to you—no one may enter without your permission. There only peace and acceptance and understanding and love can exist. Lean into that peace. Visualize your sanctuary in its richest sensory details: its colors, its scents, its sounds, its textures. Drink it all in. Feel surrounded by support, by compassion, by perfect understanding. Remain there as long as you need to—rest there. Return whenever you choose, for the truth is that your lovely sanctuary is your own inner beauty and sensitivity and wisdom manifested—and ever present to you. You need only to turn inward. Appreciate your own beauty, and then sleep.

## RESPIRATORY ABNORMALITIES

Bereaved parents commonly experience respiratory abnormalities, often accompanied by palpitations (heart pounding). Lindemann (1979), Peppers and Knapp (1980), and others describe the tight throat and diaphragm, the uneven breathing, and the "sigh" that accompanies respiration in so many grieving people. Such respiratory abnormalities generally require no medical treatment and will lessen as healing occurs. For some grievers, though, breathing is actually painful. Joyce described the tightness in her throat and chest as feeling like weighty, constrictive bands closing around those parts of her body. "It really hurts," she explained. "Once in a while, I even feel panicky when I think that I might not catch my breath again, that I might choke."

Changes in breathing patterns can be very alarming and frightening, so ragged emotions become even more so, and then centering—finding peace within—seems impossible.

To understand how the breath and the emotions are linked, imagine this scene: You are walking alone at night on an unfamiliar, unlighted country road. There is only a sliver of the moon for illumination. You walk quickly, your footfalls the only sound in the darkness. Suddenly, behind you, you hear the sharp crack of a twig! What happens to your breath? Most people report that they gasp inward and hold their breath, that their heart pounds, that their breathing becomes ragged. Grief is a *prolonged* emotional shock—so, often, the breathing response is prolonged too. Yet, just as our emotions affect our breath, so too can we reshape our emotions by altering our breath.

Psychotherapist and thanatologist Richard Boerstler (1982), in his book *Letting Go*, describes a meditative technique that relies on specific breathing patterns. Adapted from Tibetan medicine, this technique can restore even rhythm to respiration and to the heart rate, and it can induce deep muscle relaxation and a more peaceful emotional state as well. Boerstler's book offers these beliefs, and some others not listed here, on which the technique is based:

1. Breath appears to be the pulse of the mind, and thus there is a direct correlation between breathing and thinking.
2. When we experience sudden fear or shock, we feel it in the solar plexus. . . . Our breath or lack of breath tells us all.
3. A most powerful way of centering, especially in acute anxiety conditions, is through the use of breath.

Perhaps we *can* bring some peace into our bodies, then, through our breath. We will describe an adaptation of Boerstler's meditation technique; you may wish to see his original version described in *Letting Go*.

Although you can certainly choose to follow this technique alone, Boerstler's recommendation is that those in a deep state of grief or anxiety choose to *co-meditate*, to be with a chosen other who will act as guide. Your guide need only be a friend who is willing to share some peaceful moments with you. The two of you may sit in a room that is comfortably warm, with dim light, and with uninterrupted quiet for at least thirty minutes. The guide may first offer some general suggestions for inducing physical relaxation. ("Imagine a pool of warmth gathering at your feet and then drifting upward, slowly, soothingly, in your body.") When some relaxation is evident, the guide can begin to lead an audible breath-in-unison respiration (described by Boerstler as the *sound* of letting go). You might imagine that with every exhalation, you *let go* of tightness, tension, anxiety, or pain. If breathing in unison seems difficult, or if you're alone and have trouble modulating your breath, try exhaling to a count ("1,2,3, . . .10"). When respiration feels steady, go on to voicing a mantra on the out breath. "Mantra" is a Sanskrit term signifying a sacred word, verse, or symbol that invokes some specific and meaningful deity or supernatural energy. A guide must never choose a mantra for someone else, for mantras must come from within each of us, out of our own personal beliefs. Try looking within and choosing a belief you've held since childhood or some new concept you hold of spiritual power. Express that belief in a word or phrase. Some suggestions might be: "The Kingdom of Heaven is within me" or "I will be with you until the end of time" from the New Testament; or from the Jewish tradition, "Hear, oh Israel, the Lord our God, the Lord is one"; or the Buddhist "Om Mani Padme Hum"; or any poem or prayer or single word ("peace") that brings comfort. Then while you continue to breathe rhythmically, voice your chosen mantra as you exhale. You can just *think* the mantra, but verbalizing it will add power to the thought *and* bring more evenness and peace to your breath.

When Lydia's son was born with Down's syndrome, she felt consumed with grief, and then anger, and then depression. "I couldn't even talk clearly," she explained. "My voice kept breaking down into deep sighs or moans. My friends were of course concerned. One of them gave me this poem that ended with the line, 'My broken doll, my son.' For some reason, it comforted. Whenever I felt my depression overwhelm me and my breathing become labored, I would say that last line, over and over again. Somehow, it helped, and I would begin breathing normally again."

Lydia had never understood or used meditation or a mantra; yet she instinctively practiced both without even knowing that she was doing so. She followed her own inner guides.

However you choose to use breathing patterns and meditation, or whether or not you decide to try them, we pray that you *will* let go of your pain, while holding on to your peace. Let your breath teach you how.

## DIFFICULTIES WITH SEXUAL INTIMACY

"Some studies estimate that as high as 90% of all bereaved couples are in serious marital difficulty within months after the death of a child," Harriet Sarnoff Schiff points out in *The Bereaved Parent* (1977).

Touch is a powerful healer. Resisting touch can even delay healing, or be a sign of blocked resolution. Yet bereaved parents—former lovers—may be painfully unable to touch each other in sexual intimacy. Some may shy away from lovemaking in order to avoid intercourse and the memory of their dead child's conception. Others may be terribly fearful of another pregnancy too soon, and be unwilling to trust contraception. Still others might be able to *receive* lovemaking but be unable to summon enough energy to *give* it. And then others might judge themselves guilty of too rapid forgetfulness of their dead child if they allowed the pleasure of lovemaking.

Some parents view any form of pleasure or fleeting happiness as the deepest disloyalty to their lost children. Mariah wrote us that when she and her husband made love, it was always with conscious thought of her stillborn son in her mind. "If for just a few seconds I didn't think of him," she explained, "I would feel just *awful*, even panic-stricken, and I would whisper to him in my mind that I hadn't forgotten him . . . and then sometimes I would feel angry with my husband for not understanding and for needing me too. I had such a terrible fear of abandoning my son."

Schiff writes, "I kept feeling that by laughing I had left Robby alone 'out there.' It was as if my grief served as an umbilical cord to keep him close to me. A part of me. My laughter brought about a sense of 'letting go' and I was by no means ready to let go of him. My sorrow, in effect, kept Robby and me wrapped together. . . ."

If you are a parent paralyzed by that fear of letting go, you might try this exercise. Before lovemaking, visualize your lost child. Call her before you in your mind's eye and then visualize creating a peaceful haven for her. Create it as being completely safe and protective, as well as sensorily beautiful and peaceful. Then ask her to stay in that sanctuary, perfectly safe, while you are with your spouse or partner. If you feel the need, visualize calling another dead loved one to be with your child. A grandparent, perhaps, or a favorite aunt. Promise to return to your child later; and then "leave" with her blessing in your heart.

Heather told us that when she used this exercise, she visualized a perfect, beautiful, lavender orchid as a sanctuary for her infant. She pictured her little baby cradled within its center, surrounded by softness, beauty, and delicate scent. "It felt so much better to picture her there," she said. "I could allow my focus to 'leave' her and turn to my husband. I saw those lovely petals curving protectively around her, around my thoughts and memories of her, and then I could really let go for a while."

For those parents who are fearful of intercourse and thus tense and anxious, we suggest a very gentle and slow return to lovemaking. Begin by releasing all thought of performance and all goals of orgasmic completion. Plan to refrain from intercourse for a while and agree on that commitment. Initially, your return to lovemaking might merely be an exchange of tender backrubs. You might then desire intimate caresses and physical closeness, still with no goal of completing intercourse or reaching orgasm. You might even chose to extend your joint commitment of no intercourse or anything else that doesn't yet feel right for you. Talking about sexual lovemaking is difficult for many couples, but agreeing ahead of time on what your needs are would free your lovemaking from hidden fears and constraints. "Hidden agendas"—unexpressed thoughts, feelings, or issues—never remain hidden for long. They show up in our faces and in our bodies; they manifest in our touch and in the way we receive touch. Discussing your fears and needs can release you from their hidden grasp, so that you may fully enjoy the pleasure of intimate physical contact. When you do feel ready for intercourse again, you might choose to change or supplement whatever birth control method—if any—you were using. For example, some couples temporarily use condoms in addition to a diaphragm for added security. Some couples *need* the knowledge of that extra protection from conception in order to feel relaxed enough to resume intercourse. Thoughts of another pregnancy can be terrifying when a loss hasn't yet been resolved.

Finally, for those feeling so drained by grief that there is no energy to give in lovemaking, we ask that you hold compassion for each other. Refer to the other sections on physical healing, and perhaps utilize some of the suggestions for bolstering your health and energy. Then be patient and accepting with each other. Be tender and gentle. One day your arms will reach out again.

## ILLNESS

You may already be suffering some physical ailment or manifestation of your loss. There *is* something you can do for yourself, to heal this specific problem, while you work on healing your whole being. We have had remarkable results with visualization therapy, and it is a process you can do yourself. There are several excellent books on effective use of visualization, such as *Getting Well Again* by Stephanie and Carl Simonton; *Creative Visualization* by Shakti Gawain; and the *Llewellyn Practical Guide to Creative Visualization* by Melita Denning and Osborne Phillips. Also, *Silent Knife* by Nancy Wainer Cohen and Lois Estner and *Birthing Normally* by Gayle Peterson both offer testimony to and samples of visualization exercises.

As the Simontons have demonstrated, our bodies have virtually unlimited potential to heal themselves. We only need to believe that and we will be able to open the door marked ''can't'' and then to ''see'' the healing accomplished. It is a perfectly safe but potentially powerful technique for healing. Although we have described a visualization exercise earlier in this chapter, the following version is specifically adapted for healing physical body ailments.

Find a very comfortable, relaxing position, either sitting or lying down. Allow your body to be fully supported, no body part resting on any other part. Use plenty of pillows, if they help. Then just observe your breath for a moment, appreciating its life-sustaining power in your body. Recognize that your breath draws in the oxygen that your body requires and that it carries out the carbon dioxide and other toxins that your body doesn't need and can't use. Picture your breath bringing in *good,* and releasing anything *bad.* Then give your body permission to relax, to let go, to release any tension, anxiety, or unhealthy forces. Allow your breath to work this process for you. Begin by slowing down your breathing rhythms a bit. Breathe lightly, rhythmically, slowly. Try visualizing that you can focus your breath and send it specifically to any part of your body, to bring in sustenance and goodness, and to carry away tension or toxins.

Begin, perhaps, with your feet; focus the power of your breath there. Gradually, allow your attention and the healing of your breath to rise higher in your body. Feel tension being smoothed away; let your exhalation take any released tightness and dissipate it harmlessly into the atmosphere. Begin to feel an enveloping peace, a restful relaxation. Imagine that you are lying on a beautiful sandy beach basking in the hot July sun. Or that you are lying in a soft and downy nest of pillows before a crackling, snapping fire. Or that you are floating on a puffy, white cloud. Let yourself feel your way through several peaceful, relaxing scenes of sensory comfort and delight. When you feel deeply relaxed, imagine that a healing white or golden light begins to glow above your head and that it magnifies and spreads itself until it surrounds your whole body. Let its glow radiate out and radiate in, too, bathing every part of your body with soothing, nourishing, healing energy. Just allow yourself to be there, suffused with healing light and energy. Picture your body drinking it in, absorbing it into every cell.

Next, let your attention go to any part of your body that has been ill or in pain. Ask if there is anything that specific part of you needs to communicate, to let you know, or to help you understand. Wait patiently for an answer. Our bodies always have full inner knowledge; if we are open, we can often consciously learn what our inner wisdom already knows. If an answer comes and you need more direction, ask for that. You might need to learn whether there is something you should do or change. If you don't intuitively receive an answer, leave the open question in your consciousness; an answer may come at another time or in another way. Then implant support in your consciousness: willingness to support whatever your body needs for healing.

Then visualize healing for your body; for the part in pain or distress first, and then for your whole self. Radiate the healing energy again; raise the energy level a bit, until it glows with pure healing power. Take time to fully encompass the part of your body in pain or suffering illness. Fill it, surround it, suffuse it with healing. *See it as healed.*

Then see your whole body as completely healed, in

perfect and vibrant health. Relish that state of perfect health, appreciate it, and affirm it. Think: "My body is now filled with the vitality of perfect health. I feel the energy of excellent health pulsating through my entire body. I feel radiant and energized with natural good health." Add any affirmations of health that occur to you and end your visualization with thoughts of love and appreciation for yourself.

If some of the images suggested in this visualization don't seem relevant to you, let your own creative forces suggest your own personal images. One bereaved parent we know of chronically and continually suffered from respiratory illnesses—bronchitis, pneumonia, racking coughs. She began to visualize her illness-attacking white blood cells as an army of rapidly multiplying rabbits. Her little white bunnies simply overran any invading negative organisms, which faded helplessly away in the face of so much hopping, playful energy. Susan laughed about her visualization. "I felt so silly picturing those white rabbits hopping around in my body; even when I tried to be serious, it made me laugh a little. The funniest thing of all, though, was that it *worked*. I felt taken care of by those silly little guys, and I'm really proud of myself for bolstering my body's own healing power!"

Elisabeth Kubler-Ross (1980-83) tells the story of the cancer victim who was a Quaker. His beliefs against violence and killing were so strong that they blocked the "killing" (as he saw it) effect of the chemotherapy he took. Finally, he began to imagine that the medications were catalysts that released into his bloodstream a hoard of gentle little gnomes who carried off all the cancerous cells and released them outside his body where they could do no harm. The Simontons, in *Getting Well Again* (1978), describe a myriad of visualization images devised by their patients to successfully overcome illness. Your body's potential to heal itself is unlimited—and probably untapped. Look inward; see the healing power that is there; strengthen it by calling on any power meaningful to you; and then reach toward radiant good health once again.

# SEVEN

# NUTRITIONAL NEEDS

*by Peter Janney, Ed. D.*

The experience of grieving may possibly feel debilitating, exhausting, and physically depressing. Whether we are recuperating from the loss of a child, loved one, cesarean section, abortion, or the birth experience itself, we are apt to feel at certain times that there is no end to our pain and anguish. We may encounter moments of acute sadness and depression that seem to drag into endless hours, days, or even months, with no sign of our former vitality. For some there may be also times when we feel like giving up, ever questioning our will to live and our commitment to ourselves. But as most of this book has already implied, the healing that takes place as a result of our wounds may be unexpectedly beneficial; our crises can give us opportunities, perhaps with a new-found spirit, to begin a new life in a way that we could not before.

If there is a time when we need to be handled delicately, with utmost care and respect, it is in the midst of our grief and healing. This chapter will give the perspective of understanding physical needs in a time of crisis as well as information on overall health. For any and all efforts at nutritional care can aid in emotional recovery and healing, alleviating the painful distress of prolonged depression and general fatigue.

Why do mourners need stepped-up nutritional care? In simple terms, grieving is a *physical activity*, much the same as any other activity, like walking, running, or working. Grieving requires that we expend quite a substantial amount of energy, and our bodies will feel that expending of energy as a physical act. Physical acts, including the basic bodily functions, all require energy provided by the consumption of nutrients. Whenever we make greater than normal demands of our body, we then require increased supplies of nutrients, and grieving for a lost child or any other childbearing loss is an excessively demanding and draining physical experience. As such, grieving consumes nutrients at greatly heightened rates. If proper nutrients are not available or only available in small amounts, the organs, glands, and systems in our bodies start to lose their optimal efficiency. They will gradually become depleted and progressively move toward exhaustion. We are likely to experience their internal breakdown outwardly in the form of depression, a lowered resistance to disease and infection, changes in weight or diet, a loss of well-being, or in all these ways. Having lost our physical strength, we are more inclined to feel crippled by grief.

For many of us, a first response in this situation is to seek relief. Our search for relief may take us toward drugs, alcohol, sugar or food, anything to dull the pain or soften the bleakness of our darkened state. We live in a society that, unfortunately, sanctions these fruitless remedies. Though they may temporarily give the illusion of change and cure, drugs and alcohol, in truth, only serve to deplete our bodies further and put our true feelings and souls to sleep. To ignore, through drugs or alcohol, the needs and demands of the physical body is to heighten, increase, and lengthen suffering.

As a culture we pride ourselves on being the most advanced in the industrial world, and yet our ignorance in regard to optimal health and well-being has barely been reduced. Nutritional education is poor not only among the general population, but it is also woefully inadequate in our medical school curriculum. Dr. Robert Mendelsohn wrote in his book *Mal(e)Practice* (1981) that most veterinarians know more about nutrition and the maintenance of health than the physicians we seek out for our health care. This is not to imply a lack of concern but rather a severe gap in training that must be filled by our own resources and those of nutritional experts.

Therefore, in order to care properly for our body we must have a correct understanding of how it works. It is vitally important that bereaved parents, perhaps even more than others, understand some basic concepts of nutrition and health care. Let us first examine some prevalent myths about health care and eating habits.

*Myth 1*   "I get all the nutrition I need by just eating well and watching my diet."

This is perhaps the most dangerous cultural fallacy. We usually don't get the nutrition we need for optimal health from the food we eat. Even if we are nutritionally well-educated, committed macrobiotic vegetarians, or only eat natural foods, we are still likely to come up short. Food in the United States is each year becoming more contaminated with pollutants and pesticides, and thereby provides less and less nutrition. Chemical pesticides and artificial growth stimulators can destroy certain nutrients. Our soil is becoming depleted of its mineral richness, partly through normal use and partly through pollution. Dr. Michael Colgan (1982) recently tested the vitamin content of certain vegetables and fruits; he found that there was a wide variance of nutrient content in similar items tested. Some of the oranges he tested even had no vitamin C content at all.

Our general food supply is depleted of its nutritional "life" and therefore cannot adequately refuel even the most vital physical system. A stressed system is even further burdened by additives and preservatives that require additional body energies just to process unnatural and even toxic substances.

Even our water supply may be weakening our systems. Tap water can be replaced with distilled water and provide a stressed body with the purifying liquids needed for regeneration.

A water filter on your faucet is not necessarily trustworthy (depending on where you live); nor is so called bottled spring water because there are now few, if any, uncontaminated springs what with the arrival of acid rain.

We still must face the fact that the quality of food we eat will not be enough to feed our bodies adequately. Moreover, as Lindeman (1979), the Simontons (1978), Peppers and Knapp (1980), Singh and Raphael (1981), and others have shown, grieving individuals are at a much greater risk than others of succumbing to illness or general poor health. Put quite simply, we are unlikely to get our nutritional needs taken care of just by the food we eat, especially in a time of grief or stress.

_Myth 2_  "We all grow old and lose our youth, vigor, and stamina. It's just a matter of time before I do, so why fight it?" (Bereaved parents might additionally believe that a loss of health during mourning is unavoidable and thus acceptable.)

These are erroneous beliefs that we have accepted, to our detriment. They are also self-fulfilling prophecies, for as we age or react to stress, we program ourselves with these perceptions, and they start to become reality, to the extent that we believe them and live them. But they are not categorical truths, by any means. Theoretically, as we grow older, we could slow the aging process through optimal nutrition, exercise, and the elimination of unhealthy stress. In the same manner, we could reduce the physical ill effects of loss. It is often disease that kills us in old age, disease that may be preventable. This if not to say we can live forever, physically. Our bodies are not fixed structures. They change slowly, but very surely, to match the nutrients we give them. The normal life stress we are subjected to takes a serious toll on the body. This toll may even lead to chronic illness or interruption of future healthy pregnancy and childbirth unless adequately supported through nutritional care.

If our lives are continually stressful, we will accelerate our own aging processes. Of course, it would be difficult to eliminate all stress, and grieving over a loss is recognized as among the most stressful of life's events. Yet properly replenishing the body with nutrients it needs will combat many of the ill effects of stress, including depression, insomnia, digestive disorders, and others.

Exercise, as previously discussed, increases internal movement. Greater movement helps the body feed itself and eliminate water, poisons, and toxins that must be removed.

Our bodies become dynamic expressions of our own life processes; the substances or nutrients we choose to inject and the experiences in which we participate physically, mentally, emotionally, and spiritually. Again, any care given to the body nutritionally can aid not only in the recovery of loss now but also may increase the prospect of future pregnancy and childbirth. Much evidence today indicates major gains in cases of women with multiple miscarriages who become pregnant after altering nutritional and vitamin intake.

_Myth 3_ "I take vitamin supplements, so I know I'm giving my body what it needs."

A great deal of confusion surrounds the question of vitamin-mineral supplementation. Many people wonder how much of which vitamins to take and for how long. Parents in grief may suspect that their bodies do need additional help, but they often don't know how to begin, what is missing, and what could help. To answer these questions correctly is to understand two extremely important principles which form a framework for human nutrition.

The first principle is the concept of biochemical individuality. What this means is that your metabolism, your chemistry, and all your bodily functions and systems are, like you yourself, unique. There is no other you; part of your uniqueness is expressed internally, *inside* your body. No other body works *exactly* like yours.

For example, in his laboratory Dr. Michael Colgan (1982) routinely measured the vitamin C excretion in the urine of patients and athletes. At first he was trying to find out whether supplemental vitamin C was simply excreted from the human body as some chemical scientists have claimed. He demonstrated that this belief was completely inaccurate. Some of his patients could ingest 5,000 mg of vitamin C and excrete almost none at all; all the vitamin C was thus being used in the hundreds of biological functions that vitamin C is known to have. Other patients did excrete the vitamin C but only in a fraction of the amount ingested. The range of usage in different people was significantly variable.

Thus, what your body may need for *optimal* functioning in terms of any single nutrient can be highly variable, especially during a period of great stress. The notion of "minimum daily requirements" seems to make no sense, since what may sustain borderline good health for some may allow the development of illness in others. The principle of minimum daily requirement levels of supplementation is misleading at best; certainly this principle does not support the possibility of attaining an optimal nutrition input for our bodies.

The second principle, in this framework of human nutrition, is the concept of synergy. Individual nutrients (vitamins, C, B complex, etc.) never work independently. They work together and in collaboration with each other. This fact explains why it may not help much to take extra amounts of vitamin C only to combat a cold. Vitamin C alone will probably have little effect unless other necessary nutrients are available in increased amounts as well. Every nutrient needed by the body operates by multiple interaction. For example, a deficiency of the mineral zinc can cause a deficiency of vitamin A, even if adequate amounts of vitamin A are being ingested. Since vitamin A depends on the presence of zinc for proper absorption and utilization, a deficiency of zinc could cause a malabsorption of A (Colgan 1983).

Biochemical individuality and the concept of synergy thus form a framework for establishing the best health maintenance program for ourselves. We must acknowledge these concepts when considering how our nutritional needs are created and what we can do to satisfy them. These two factors support a customized approach to nutritional care that is best accomplished by seeking a nutritional expert who is experienced in the use of herbal and vitamin supplements as will as the more traditional dietary approach.

Crisis offers us the opportunity to make a new commitment to improved physical health. Though expending any effort at all may feel like a monumental task during mourning, it is important to remember that it is ultimately we who will heal ourselves. Our responsibility in our own healing process is, in the final analysis, what eventually restores a sense of well-being and balance. No one else or anything except ourselves will be able to do it for us.

## IMPROVING OUR NUTRITIONAL AWARENESS

*Step One* Educate yourself. There is a great deal of interest and material on human nutrition. Dr. Thomas Brewer, founder of the Society for the Protection of The Unborn Through Nutrition stated in an interview that he frankly knew of "nothing" specifically written for the grieving mother on the subject of nutrition. Although very little has been applied to childbirth losses and the grieving process, we do know that these events are highly stressful and can cause stress-related illnesses. *Your Personal Vitamin Profile* by Dr. Michael Colgan (1982) is probably the best up-to-date and all-around useful material on the subject. There are several other materials cited in the references. The work by Gail and Thomas Brewer in the field of childbirth offers a variety of dietary suggestions, including some possibilities for simple improvements in current nutrition.

_Step Two_  When you feel ready, seek out a _competent health practitioner,_ who is well versed in nutrition and who understands the stress of loss and the need for proper supplement intake. A practitioner with some knowledge of herbal remedies as well would be even more valuable. Adequate diet/supplemental programs for those in grief should include generous amounts of vitamins A, B complex, C, possibly D, E, pantothenic acid, minerals or herbs, and possibly some specialty products such as raw glandulars if needed. A competent holistic health practitioner knowledgeable in nutrition should be able to assess your individual health needs and then help you fit them into your lifestyle.

If you have difficulty locating a health practitioner with good nutrition knowledge, seek out a whole natural foods store that stocks vitamin and mineral supplements. Inquire about the remedies that follow.

## HERBAL AND VITAMIN RESPONSES TO STRESS

_Vitamins_ (daily)

| | |
|---|---|
| C | 1,000—4,000 mg (preferably time release with rose hips) |
| B complex | 200 mg |
| Pantothenic acid | up to 3,000 mg |
| E | 800 units |
| Raw glandulars (adrenal rebalancing) | _note:_ check with local health food store |

| Instant protein powder | *note:* may be mixed with milk or juice to fortify body |

*Herbal Responses:* The following herbal products are manufactured by several reliable companies under various name brands.

| CAC or CA-T | aids in digestion of calcium and may be of value to those craving dairy products or suffering from insomnia |
| EX-STRESS<br>E-Z<br>SP-14 | herbal products that calm the nervous system and may greatly reduce anxiety and insomnia, as well as aid in the regeneration of stressed nervous system |
| Herbal teas | peppermint, chamomile, comfrey aid in soothing digestive system and may soothe stomach and colon |
| Natural Lax #2 | aids in reduction of constipation |
| SP-7C | aids in healing and restoring uterus and other reproductive organs in women |

(McGrath 1977)

• All of the above products are available at health food stores; some chiropractors; and natural, herbal medicine oriented physicians.

• All of the above herbal responses to stress were obtained in study with Dr. George Dillinger, nationally known physician and naturopath.

*Step Three* *Eradicate* as completely as possible those foods or substances from your diet that are *injurious* to your health. Based on widespread evidence, those substances include chemical additives (such as nitrates and colorings), sugar, caffeine, and harmful fats; or foods highly saturated with artificial hormones and chemicals, exemplified in American diets by red meats. In addition, canned and processed foods, white flour and other "refined" products, and a too heavy reliance on dairy products can undermine good health. Optimum nutrition is more likely maintained by a well-balanced diet high in fiber and rich in "live" foods—*whole* grains, *fresh* (and often raw) fruits and vegetables, seeds, nuts, fish, and poultry.

Much of our food supply is not only saturated with additives but may also be generally "lifeless." Think in terms of "live" foods that require no extra effort to digest and that fuel rather than burden the body.

Most of us grew up believing in the need for a "balanced diet," and yet parents in grief are likely to eat a very *un*balanced diet. In times of great loss, feeling wounded and vulnerable, we may unconsciously wish we could revert to childhood, when our parents soothed our hurts and softened many of life's blows. Some of us reach back to our earliest experiences of comfort, when milk and cookies filled our empty hearts. Breast milk is recognized as the most perfect, most complete human food. But cow's milk and other dairy products are not so perfect and in fact induce allergic responses or mild respiratory distress in a high percentage of our population. Our emotional links to milk and milk products are really quite strong, though, and so many people ignore any physical distress that results from overusing milk.

While it may not be at all necessary to eliminate dairy products from your diet (in moderation and in the absence of allergic reaction they may help fill important needs), do be aware of a common American tendency to overindulge in dairy products during times of stress. Count the glasses of milk you drink (and the cookies you consume with it) or the bowls of ice cream you eat. One woman we counseled mentioned that in the weeks after her miscarriage all she wanted to eat was vanilla ice cream. Another bereaved parent consumed bowls of tapioca pudding, like that which her grandmother used to make years before. If you crave occasional glasses of milk or dishes of ice cream or cookies you loved as a child, indulging yourself may help you feel a little better, but unbalanced overindulging may be a sign that what you're really craving is relief from your pain—milk and ice cream and cookies can't provide that.

Even if dairy products are not seen as "comfort" foods, the physical body may be craving calcium, a mineral much needed during stress, and hence the craving for milk, ice cream, etc. One woman in our program showed no calcium in a nutritional workup, yet she was drinking 9-12 large glasses of milk each day. In her case, the calcium she was ingesting was not being absorbed and the milk was causing respiratory difficulties as well.

Good nutrition is vital to good health, and yet we don't need to prepare elaborate and heavy meals in order to eat well. On the contrary, lighter, easily metabolized foods will go further toward restoring health. If you don't feel like cooking, ask friends or relatives for help. Their gift of nourishment for your body is also a special sort of gift you offer them, for filling your need may reduce the terrible helplessness that they, friends and relatives of bereaved parents, feel. It is important that those who support bereaved parents understand the effects of diet. So often, when someone we care about is hurting, we offer a "sweet," perhaps hoping, in vain, to offset the bitterness of loss with the sweetness of sugar.

Sugar and alcohol, although they may provide some quick fuel or immediate relief from depression, ultimately only further depress the body. Much has been written about the "sugar" blues, where blood sugar levels are initially raised with the ingestion of a candy bar but actually drop lower than the original starting point several hours later, only increasing the desire for more quick fuel.

Sugary cakes and desserts only sabotage good health, though, and they further threaten the precarious health of those bereaved. Because of the metabolic "depression" that sugar ultimately induces, bereaved parents can feel even more weighted down by sadness after they eat sugar. Parents in grief must ask for, and we who support them must offer, *real help:* nutritious, healthful foods and meals. In order to illustrate and offer guidance in choosing simple, healthful foods, we include several cookbooks in the resource section.

*Step Four*    Build some sort of *exercise program,* preferably aerobic, into your life. Exercise, as explained in Chapter 6, is especially important during a time of grief or any period of bodily stress. Exercise is also important to the optimum usage of nutrients. Even if it is only a walk on a difficult day, *do it.* You will notice how much better your body makes you feel. Movement aids in digestion, circulation, and general body functioning.

## A HEALING SECRET

Some of us have driven our car when we knew it was badly in need of repair. The car moved but did not run as well as it was designed to carry us. When we took the time to give our auto proper care and treatment, more often than not it ran well and we could depend upon it.

So it is with our bodies. If we do not take the time, care, and love to insure that we are giving our bodies (ourselves) what they truly need, they will eventually break down, either suddenly through illness such as heart disease or acute cancer, or gradually. Fully entrusting our health to chance or to anyone other than ourselves is one of the worst mistakes any of us can make.

John Naisbitt in his celebrated book *Megatrends* (1982) observes that we are on the verge of a major change in our health-care system, for people are learning to make decisions about their own symptoms and to take care of themselves. As he points out, "Personal habits are the key element in the new health paradigm, so personal responsibility is critical." And that represents a real turnabout. In the past we believed our health was the doctor's responsibility—that seems incredible now—and that the insurance company's responsibility was to pay the bills when we got sick.

The essence of Naisbitt's words lies in "personal responsibility," what we are willing or allowing for ourselves. And personal responsibility is basically what John Travis, M.D., who coined the term "well-ness," underscores in his *Wellness Workbook* (1981). Carl Simonton, M.D., and his wife, Stephanie Matthews-Simonton, again and again note the correlation between personal attitudes and cancer in their book *Getting Well Again* (1978). Finally, Norman Cousins in *Anatomy of an Illness* (1979) tells how he became aware of the effects of his attitude and outlook on his own healing process.

What we *choose* to will for ourselves as expressed in our thoughts, attitudes, and actions thus becomes our present state of being. If we continue to hold onto negative thoughts, beliefs, and actions concerning our nutritional needs, then we will continue to live a reality that betrays who we truly are and what we could truly become. If we can fan our innate "spark" for wellness, we will be able, with restored health, to better fuel our quest for full healing.

# EIGHT

# OUR MENTAL ATTITUDES
## The Key to Recovery

Thomas Hamblin, a spiritual leader in England, once wrote in a letter to Isabel Hickey, noted author of *It Is All Right* and lecturer on metaphysics and religion: "You will notice that I do not pray that trouble will be removed in order that you have peace of mind. I pray that you may have peace of mind in spite of the trouble.... When you have reached this point, I know all will be well with you in every way and in the highest and best way of all" (Hickey 1976).

We, too, have begun to cast aside our own illusions that peace of mind is a function of living without conflict. Our work with child-bearing families, in fact, has magnified for us the myriad of stresses and difficulties life has to offer. We observe the agony of lost and handicapped children; of traumatic births and surgical deliveries; of the daily trials that simply adjusting to a child can bring. We know well the parents' plight not only through professional eyes but also through our own losses and our own children's lives. Yet, we believe that our minds can contain our losses and our anguish, that we can work through these tragedies and challenges to feel and to live at peace with ourselves.

Childbearing loss triggers severe mental anguish. "How?" "Why?" "What did I do?" "What *didn't* I do?" "What if?" "If only . . ."

The questions, the doubts, the thoughts of guilt, blame, and bitterness fill our minds until they are reeling with pain. Headaches are a common physical effect of loss, and it's easy to imagine why. Our grieving minds just cannot let go in their search for answers.

We do believe that fact-finding and information-seeking are normal, healthy aspects of the mental resolution of loss. It may be vitally important to learn and understand whatever there is to know about a pregnancy-related loss. Some of our mental anguish can be relieved when we do find explanations.

However, we believe that our search for answers must be undertaken within a mental framework that is based on beliefs in our inherent health and goodness and wisdom. Grounded in those beliefs, we can hope to deal with the guilt in which most bereaved parents are so trapped. Guilt may indeed be universal, but to the bereaved parent it feels like hell on earth. "Was it the wine I drank?" "The time I tripped and fell?" "The tiring business trip I took in my sixth month of pregnancy?" "All the junk food I ate in college?" "If I had agreed to the surgery sooner. . ." "If only I had *heard* him gasping or losing his breath . . ." *"I wasn't with her when she died!"* And on and on and on.

Current mental health systems respond to such normal mental anguish as though pain were a sign of disturbance rather than a normal human condition and an opportunity to learn. For too long now, women, especially, have been treated as hysterical basket cases because they have the courage to feel and to experience openly normal human pain. How can we openly share our guilt, or sorrow, our hurt if we fear that we can so easily be labeled as "disturbed?" How can we express the gamut of irrational feelings common to loss when the mental health system stands ready to render a diagnostic label—"neurotic," "manic-depressive," "hysteric." Grief may cause us to feel we are losing our grip on sanity; we can't have it stripped away by a system that fails to dignify human emotions.

We have seen that once confronted with serious loss we can never be the same. In essence we are left to choose whether we will live in greater pain or in greater peace. Those who live in escalating pain may then lose even more: they may lose their most basic belief in life and living.

This may prove to be ultimately the greatest loss of all—not only to oneself, but also to the surviving children, who can no longer be adequately parented, to the surviving spouse longing for love and intimacy, and to the family as a system, for it may suffer the resulting conflict for years and years to follow. The following passage was written by a man expressing this pain: "I have not lost a child but I am a victim of pregnancy loss. My mother lost one of her twin daughters twenty-nine years ago. On that day I lost my mother. She's been bitter, distant and a victim of life ever since. I'm so sorry she lost my sister, but I'm even sorrier that I lost my mother." In essence, after loss, our minds *are* filled with doubts, with questions, with thoughts of guilt, or anger, or bitterness. These thoughts are normal and common. Yet if we allow them to take up permanent residence, if we do not move on, then we will not come to healing.

We are in no way attempting to put forth some "pie in the sky" approach to mourning that negates the humanity of emotions such as resentment and guilt. We each can recall times when we wished our friends didn't have babies because we were reminded of the ones we wanted for ourselves. We remember, too, seeing an overwrought mother in the supermarket yelling at what seemed to be a perfectly innocent child and judging that she didn't deserve to have him or her—that we would be more loving parents.

Nor do we believe that true spiritual resolution comes from thoughts such as "It was for the best," or "I should be grateful to accept God's will." Such attempts are empty of consolation, dishonoring our very humanity, and insulting the spiritual higher power. It would be foolish to think any of us could lose someone or something of such great importance and initially be glad for the learning or grateful for the opportunity to grow. In the next chapters, we will discuss the gamut and depth of human emotion in grieving that we have ourselves witnessed and believe to be good and right in its nature.

Here, we shall offer a *mental* framework for effective healing. This framework is built on four attitudinal principles that may be essential for relieving mental anguish and restoring peace of mind after childbearing loss.

The four principles for mental resolution that we need to believe in are:

1. Our drive toward psychological and physical health
2. Our goodness within the human condition
3. Our own inner wisdom as the ultimate guide
4. Our ability to accomplish healing

## 1. DRIVE TOWARD HEALTH

We believe that each of us has an innate drive to live in optimum health and to be treated as a healthy individual by all those with whom we interact. We are living in a time when obstetrical practices that treat a normal, healthy childbearing woman as "sick" are being challenged and changed. The laboring woman is in a sense the only "well" patient who may choose a hospital setting not for treatment of disease, but rather in which to birth a child. All too often she is treated as though her body is *not* functioning normal-

ly. She is met with a wheelchair, stripped of her individuality, and dressed in hospital clothes. She may be given routine
IVs, drugs that alter the natural course of labor, and often
the ultimate insult: Unneeded surgery. All of these practices
fail to honor the innate health of the human system and
instead support a giving over of control of one's labor and
birth to a technological system and medical staff that *appear*
so much wiser.

These comments are not in any way a disavowal of the
miracles of technological advances that have saved the lives
of many mothers and children. We hope, rather, to emphasize the prevalent and painfully deceiving attitude that fails
to see our bodies as resourceful, capable systems that can be
our most reliable source of physical and emotional healing.

Doctors are trained to care for the sick. We are grateful
for their dedication to healing. Physicians make many personal sacrifices so that we all may receive necessary medical
care. It is our sorrowing judgment, however, that too many
physicians are not adequately trained to work with those
who are essentially well. Too few physicians see that the
fundamental power of human healing lies within each individual. Physicians are rather trained to feel ultimately responsible for those in their care in a way that causes many
doctors the pain of anxiety, inadequacy, and sheer helplessness
when medical systems fail, patients die, or as in the cases of
most childbearing women, there is simply nothing to do but
be supportive.

Just as obstetrical practices are being challenged, so too
must similar challenges now be mounted in the field of
mental health. None of us, especially childbearing parents
attempting to heal loss, can afford to be entrapped by a
psychological system that does not honor our innate emotional strengths and intuitive drive toward resolution.

Sigmund Freud, "the father of psychoanalysis," recognized the mourning process as a longing for something lost,
and he wrote that the psychical task was one of "detaching
the survivor's memories and hopes from the dead" (Freud

1917). His medical model approach to one's psychological state was based on a perception of the mourner as sick or pathological, requiring long-term psychoanalysis in order to cope.

Some traditional psychological systems view those seeking counseling as "sick" or malfunctioning, rather than as healthy and attempting to function more effectively. A familiar joke among psychotherapy professionals tells the story of the "patient" who can't win with the system, no matter what. When she arrives early, she's an "obsessive"; when she arrives on time, a "compulsive"; when she's late, she's "resistant."

Pregnancy losses cannot be healed if we view ourselves as sick, as anything *less* than healthy at our core. We must rely on our own healthful resources. We must begin to evaluate our behavior in terms of effectiveness and concern ourselves with the basic question: "Is what I'm doing helping right now?"

The following story illustrates how blind our mental health system can be to the basic health innate in each being. The story is true; the events took place in 1982.

## Noreen's Story

Noreen, a thirty-seven-year-old woman, came to our office for counseling several months after the deaths of her premature twin daughters. She was, she said, searching for something to help her go on. She appeared pale, tired, and overwhelmed.

Her daughters died at birth. She carried their picture to every session, and one could clearly see the beauty Noreen beheld in their images. Noreen and her husband had suffered five years of infertility and one miscarriage before this pregnancy. These children were to be the answer to a thousand prayers.

Although Noreen kept herself in bed for a week attempting to prevent a threatened premature labor, her efforts were to no avail. Labor began in earnest at thirty weeks. Noreen and her husband, Gus, labored normally, knowing their babies would probably die. When the twins were stillborn, Noreen and Gus talked to them and honored them with a funeral in spite of family disapproval.

The day of the burial Noreen mentioned feeling that she wanted to die. She told her husband that she felt she had abandoned her babies, that she didn't know where they were, and that she wanted to be with them. Such feelings we at Offspring hear universally expressed by bereaved parents.

She also told a friend, who called the local priest. The priest called Noreen and asked her if she felt like dying, and she responded that she did and explained how she wanted to be able to comfort her daughters. The priest called a psychiatrist. The psychiatrist called Gus and said he (the psychiatrist) had received word that Noreen was suicidal and probably needed to be hospitalized.

Gus told Noreen that the psychiatrist wanted to admit her to a local psychiatric hospital. Noreen, already doubting her sanity, agreed to go, feeling that maybe they all knew something that she didn't know. She was signed in and immediately medicated.

Noreen recalls sleeping in a drugged fashion for a while and then waking up in a room with a teen-age girl who was screaming. Noreen looked for Gus, but the staff had sent him home, telling him that they needed to get to know Noreen without his presence.

Noreen went out into the community room. Other patients and staff began to ask why she had come. Noreen told of her babies' death. Many of them cried and Noreen recalls having to work along with the staff counselor, trying to comfort these patients who could no longer comfort themselves and were severely upset at Noreen's loss.

By late evening, it was clear to Noreen that she did not

belong in a hospital. In fact, she told the staff that she belonged at home, in bed with her husband. They discouraged her and instead offered her more medication, which she flushed down the toilet. She called Gus, and together they left to go home and cry for their daughters.

A few months later she wrote: "If only they had seen that what I was trying to tell them was not so much that I wanted to die but that I wanted my girls to live. They were all so afraid to see the depth of my pain. I guess I was afraid to see it as well. Drugs don't heal, nor does being locked up comfort anyone. I just wanted my babies."

David Hendin in *Death as a Fact of Life* (1973) describes how common it is to feel like dying when you've lost someone you love. John Bowlby in his book *Loss* (1980) writes: "Ideas of suicide, conceived especially as a means of rejoining the dead person, are common during the early months of bereavement." How many of us have felt we wanted to die in times of death, divorce, or separation.

We must never take lightly anyone's suicidal threat, nor do we suggest that taking one's own life is a natural act. Rather, we emphasize the possibility that the maternal instinct to be with, to love, and to protect one's lost children may not constitute genuine danger of suicide but instead may be an expression of a parent's pain and helplessness that should be handled in just that context. The distorted lens of anticipated or presupposed mental illness disallows such a context, causing the outrageous and inappropriate care Noreen received.

In the chapters ahead, we will suggest some possible responses to these feelings that may more adequately dignify the mourning process. Hospitalization should be the very last (if ever used) option for the grieving parent.

## 2. OUR GOODNESS AND HUMANITY

There are religious belief systems in Western society that are built on the notion that human beings are intrinsically evil. Such views cloud our basic goodness and lead us to believe that making human mistakes and expressing human emotion are the inevitable marks of weakness and evil.

In some psychotherapy traditions, we are not only treated as though we are "sick," but also implied in this approach is the judgment that we are destructive and perhaps evil in our natures. Our present diagnostic systems are designed to analyze and criticize our weaknesses. Feelings are over-reasoned, categorized, and slotted into boxes of "appropriate grief" or "inappropriate grief." We are described as "resistant," as bad little children, if we find therapeutic approach ineffective.

R.L. Sutherland, M.D. (1966), describes our Western thought in terms of its dualism, where rigid external systems define good or evil. This duality is translated into the emotional realm of feelings, so that we may have "good" feelings, such as feelings of happiness, peace, joy, and excitement, or "bad" feelings, such as guilt, anger, sorrow, hurt, resentment, and bitterness. This splitting of human nature causes us to run from those feelings we define as "bad," failing to allow ourselves to see that all feelings are actually *neutral* and all require observation and release.

Kubler-Ross (1969) reminds us of this same duality in our cultural dealings with life and death. We view life as good; death as bad, dark, even horrifying. We lie to our children about death's nature and attempt to deny our own death to ourselves.

We attempt to live in ecstacy, failing to accept and profit from life's agonies. Death is seen as out of the normal course of events, yet it is life's only guarantee. Jimenez writes in *The Other Side of Pregnancy* (1982): "To cope, or avoid coping, with death we hide it in hospitals and funeral parlors, concealing the body in ornately engraved boxes made of strong metal. . . . We are a death-denying society."

Thus we Westerners find it easy to view our own feelings as "good" or "evil," and even to view ourselves as "dark" because we have been touched by death or loss. Mourning is a vulnerable state, one that already amplifies one's inner guilt, self-hatred, anger, and fear, and yet we attach external labels that support our own inner confusion.

We cannot hope to release our inner pain if we view our very emotions as bad and death or loss experiences as dark. We are basically and innately good. Leave it to Charlie Brown to remind us of our "Good Grief!" We cannot allow ourselves to be treated in any system that fails to support our basic goodness. The lens of duality leads to inappropriate, debilitating care.

As Sutherland points out, "The being or self. is not so much to be repaired like a faulty structure taken down part by part and rearranged and added on to, as it is to emerge as an ever changing experience by means of sharpened consciousness" (1966).

Again, we refer to a woman's story—a story of someone seen as "bad" by a system that viewed a woman's pain through a negative lens and made recommendations that could well be viewed as primitive rather than curative.

### Wendy's Story

In the fall of 1982, we at Offspring received a phone call from a distressed father who said he was desperate for assistance. Bob told us that he and his wife had given birth to their second child, a boy, Michael, just six weeks before. Since then, his wife, Wendy, had been very upset, tearful, and angry. Now psychiatric hospitalization and placement of their child in a foster home had been recommended. They had sought outpatient psychological assistance for several weeks, but nothing seemed to help. Wendy said she didn't want to be a mother; she didn't feel love, she just felt sad. She had been medicated with Valium, which only seemed to exacerbate the depression. Now the case was being referred to youth services for potential child abuse claims, because she declared verbally her feelings of anger toward Michael.

Bob and Wendy arrived in the office two hours later. We asked Wendy to tell us her story. She explained very lucidly that she herself did not understand her reaction. She thought she wanted this child and could make no sense out of her own withdrawal from Michael. Her body racked with sobs, she whispered that she just didn't know how to be a mother to two children. She begged us not to allow her to be hospitalized. She said that being separated from her child would not help her feel like a mother. We agreed.

We also agreed to work with them without drugs and with their firm commitment to come to daily sessions until the feelings were resolved. We insisted as well on round-the-clock help for Wendy at home. Church members volunteered to help with baby-sitting and cooking. Bob had to work during the day but came in for evening sessions.

Wendy traced her feelings back to her own childhood, where she herself was the second child born to an alcoholic woman who was barely able to care for one child. In the course of counseling and in an atmosphere of safety, Wendy recalled her younger days, when she so wanted to be mothered. Over the weeks, we fed, held, and comforted Wendy in the style of Jacqui Schiff's reparenting principles. (Schiff is a psychotherapist and author of *All My Children.*) In this model, parenting not available during childhood is offered in a structured format in order to heal the emotional holes of the past. We hoped to fill Wendy's cup with responses that would support her mothering of Michael.

Further, we were aware of the postpartum practices of other cultures, where such care of mothers is customary and allows mothers to more fully enjoy their postbirth weeks.

After each session, Wendy would feed, hold, and play with Michael in ways that she had just experienced—and just learned. Healing the losses of her own childhood allowed Wendy to feel whole and capable of mothering her own child. It is our joy to watch Wendy and Michael giggling in our living room at Offspring. We see—and Michael feels—Wendy's health and newfound confidence.

Wendy's cries for help may not have been as neatly packaged as our traditional system would prefer, but when we approach pain believing in the individual's inherent goodness, we are less likely to see evil, in this case, a "child abuser," and more likely to see a healthy but struggling parent.

We do believe that there may be times when parent-child separation could prove useful, but, like psychiatric hospitalization, it should not be explored without first looking at every other possibility and seeing all with a belief in human *goodness*.

## 3. OUR OWN INNER WISDOM

Helena Petrova Blavatsky wrote: "There is a divine power in every man and woman, which is to rule his life" (1888). She was referring to the innate, intuitive wisdom in each of us that can ultimately guide our actions and our behaviors to the most effective resolution of all our conflicts. This intuitive wisdom, although inherent in each of us, may not always be a conscious, accessible guide, for much cultural childhood training has taught us to ignore ourselves, to obey without evaluation, and to view external "cures," advice, and help as more valuable than our own inner sense of what is best.

Earlier in this section, we described how childbearing parents have come to challenge present medical systems. Childbearing women, especially, are seeking to be treated not as sick patients by hospital personnel, but as normal, healthy women. We are weary of practices that treat normal childbearing as an abnormal function.

We are weary, too, of systems that fail to recognize the childbearing parents' emotional and psychological resources. We are questioning the widespread reliance on drugs and other medical interventions that are only appropriate as a last resort but are used in up to 92 percent of all births in most American hospitals (Cohen and Estner 1983). We have seen the results of Thalidomide, DES (DES diethylstilbestrol, a drug used until the early 1970s to prevent miscarriage and now known to be associated with reproductive abnormalities, infertility, and cancer in the children whose mothers took it), and perhaps now Bendectin that have cost us the health of our own bodies, as well as the health, or even the lives, of our children.

We are confronted with the ultimate fear that perhaps "the doctor has not always been right." For many of us the illusion that doctor knows best has been a painful source of false hope. Further, it has burdened medical practitioners with unrealistic expectations of their own performances and has impeded progress by not allowing room for physicians to change, if one way must always be "right."

For some, confronting this illusion has shaken their very core of belief in false magic, in rescuers, and in some "omnipotent force" that will save us all in the end. For others, however, this somewhat frightening, yet perhaps enlightening, conflict has meant a challenge to think more clearly, to act more responsibly, and to claim their own divine power to rule their lives.

This is not to say that we should ever avoid taking necessary medicines or seeking a physician's much needed information in times of health care decision making. Rather, we should examine our attitudes toward using such information. Are we looking for information or parental approval? Are we seeking the best medical care systems or are we looking to be loved by someone in authority? Do we want to take charge of our own lives or would we rather let someone else, some parent figure, do that for us? The latter choice has robbed far too many childbearing families of the right to birth without unneeded intervention and, in some cases, unwanted drugs. Such choices in mental health care can rob us of our long-term psychological health and well-being by shifting the power to heal outside our inner resource system.

We see fewer, but still far too many, people who accept physical or psychological advice *without question*. Recently, Anna, a woman in her late fifties, came for counseling at Offspring. She had had a mastectomy a year before and was burdened with much normal fear and anxiety since then that primarily manifested itself as insomnia. She explained that her cancerous condition was a result of some "change of life" hormones she had been taking for "hot flashes." Her physician had given her no warning when she began using the drug. After her cancer developed, however, he did tell her that the medication had probably had a lot to do with it.

She told this tale in a completely calm, almost emotionless, manner and concluded by saying how grateful she was to her doctor for taking her off the drugs once he knew she had a tumor, and how she felt that he really knew what was best for her.

In spite of the fact that her sister and her dearest friend had urged Anna to question the use and safety of prescribed hormones, Anna would not listen. When confronted in counseling about her trusting acceptance of such treatment, Anna replied, "Doctor knows best."

Again, we are not suggesting that *anyone* should *disregard* medical information, but rather that we use our inner guides to seek trustworthy sources for our health care and never act from blind powerlessness. Today Anna has begun to see the cost of giving over control of her health care to someone other than herself. She has begun a treatment program similar to the one described in *Getting Well Again* by Carl and Stephanie Simonton (1978). As the Simontons' records demonstrate, maximum patient involvement has produced more frequent remissions and longer life spans in their cancer patients, who fully participate in their care, than those cited by general national statistics for cancer victims.

We are also pointing out that loss itself stimulates deep feelings of helplessness. We feel powerless to restore our children to life or health, or to conceive after years of infertility, or to cope at times with "normal" postpartum depression. We doubt ourselves more easily and feel more vulnerable to the opinions and advice of others. We are, at times, desperate for something to alleviate our pain, our hurt, our guilt, and our disappointment. And, feeling this helplessness, this desperation, we seek guidance outside ourselves that can rightfully only come from within.

We may have to do much fruitless searching just to find out that it is ourselves we must trust. Of course, we need support from others, and such support will be discussed in the next chapter. Our point here is that all help, advice, and support must be filtered through our inner intuitive wisdom that can discriminate, evaluate, and determine ultimate effectiveness.

If we are truly to claim power over our lives, we cannot afford to turn over the ultimate authority for our physical or psychological care to anyone but ourselves. We must become responsible not only for our physical care but for our emotional well-being as well. Psychologist and author Claude Steiner once said that a common stance for Western psychotherapists is "I'm okay and you're disturbed" (1975). He was referring again to a psychotherapeutic system built on a medical model that expects physicians to perform the impossible task of *making someone else well*. The mourning parent knows only too well the failure of this system to provide any consolation.

In fact, childbearing parents in grief have more recently moved away from so-called professional care and sought support in groups such as Compassionate Friends or through consumer organizations such as C/SEC (Cesareans/Support, Education & Concern), founded by Nancy Wainer Cohen and Jini Fairley. Such groups rely on self-help through group support. People are seeking a system that can more appropriately respond to their feelings, needs, and genuine desires to feel better—a system that asks each of us to become our own expert, to find our own way.

Eric Berne (1972) wrote that there is a part of each of us that is waiting for Santa Claus: a childlike, innocent part that believes that if she does everything those in authority tell her to do, then she will be rewarded. Many of us have these feelings reactivated each holiday season.

Jim Morningstar (1981) wrote that today's adults were generally reared on parental disapproval syndrome, a style of Western parenting based on the withdrawal of love when the child displeases the parent. Most of us are clearly not used to Carl Rogers's (1961) idea of unconditional positive regard or Berne's idea of unconditional love (Berne 1975).

When a child dies and illusions of Santa Claus and tooth fairies are instantly and painfully shattered, there are also no white knights on charging stallions that can spare us from our hurt. When couples try unsuccessfully for years to conceive, sacrificing their sexual spontaneity and intimacy for the sake of a wanted child, they do not receive the reward they struggle for, the "prize" for being good and decent people. When surgical deliveries (necessary or not) slash a parent's dreams of harmony and peace at birth, there are no magical princes or fairly godmothers who will heal this scar and these wounds.

No, mourning parents, if we are to be restored, each of us must look within. We cannot find resolution for our pain in advice, in pills, or in illusory television portrayals of physicians like Marcus Welby. We must give up thoughts that, if we only are "good," *someone else* will save or restore us. These thoughts would only render us further weakened and debilitated in our task.

John Bowlby (1980) wrote that "to the bereaved, nothing but the return to the lost person can bring true comfort; should what we provide fall short of that, it is felt almost as an insult." For many of us this perception has been true. There really have been days when no consolation seemed forthcoming, or days when attempts at consolation were inadequate, and fell far short. Only when we seek from within will we ever find true comfort and restore our natural power to rule our own lives.

## 4. HEALING CAN BE ACCOMPLISHED

In the *Wizard of Oz*, Dorothy searched and searched for a wizard to bring her home to Kansas, only to find that the transporting system existed in her own belief that returning home was possible. Although we all know that recovering from losses cannot be accomplished by closing our eyes and believing we can be in any other place, we must at least hope that healing is possible.

It is difficult to hope again when everything you've hoped for has died. It is also difficult to believe in healing when we have been so trained in coping and surviving. Some may even say that to seek total healing of any loss is an impossible, unrealistic approach.

We believe that to seek any less may cause parents and other family members serious physical damage through life-threatening diseases, potential long-term inner conflict, and a possible whole lifetime of disturbance and turmoil within the family system. We believe that a loss or a death can help us reveal to ourselves a better, more meaningful way to live. Further, we believe that resolution of body, mind, heart, and soul offers the hope of a future generation who can all begin to grieve in the way Kubler-Ross (1980-83) described—without guilt, resentment, or bitterness but simply experiencing the pure, natural emotion of grief.

Western psychotherapy has taught us to cope under stress and to survive in difficult times so that we may resume a manageable lifestyle. In some situations coping and surviving are much needed goals. In grief work, they are just the beginning.

We cannot afford to simply cope with or survive a loss, to rearrange our psychic systems so that we can somehow tolerate living with pain. Loss, in particular a child's death, requires a much broader, more complete response. For many, a healing response may come through awakening emotional and spiritual resources never known before.

Most Westerners often think in terms of adjusting rather than transforming. As children we often had to adjust to situations that did not honor us. For example, when we were too young to defend ourselves, we may have had to "adjust" to a classroom teacher who treated us badly. In college, we were older and more powerful, more capable of dealing with larger systems, yet many of us still felt that we needed to make the adjustments to those who treated us badly without first seeking other options.

In order to heal physically after an infant's death or after any deeply felt childbearing loss, we may need sustained help—someone to cook for us, to help care for our children, to give *us* physical care as well (a backrub, or a shampoo, or a foot massage, perhaps). But all too often we try to adjust to stress, to cope, to carry on alone without asking for assistance or even believing we deserve such help.

Healing involves believing in our right to be healed, to be cared for, to care for ourselves *without settling* for another adjustment to physical or emotional pain. "Adjusting" causes suffering.

When we speak of "suffering" we are in no way referring to the genuine sorrow, pain, and sadness of the mourning process. We are speaking, rather, of the *unnecessary* self-inflicted hurt caused by attitudes such as false pride and self-pity, or by the belief that healing is impossible. Harriet Schiff (1977) refers to a poignant Chinese proverb when she writes: "You cannot keep the birds of sorrow from flying overhead. But you can keep them from making a nest in your hair."

Suffering is valued in Western society. Our news publications and television commentaries describe the endless world suffering every day. We simply do not place a priority on hearing of the decent, good, pleasant events occurring every day as well.

These cultural standards invite us to become or in some sense to remain consumed with the identity of a mourning mother, the poor infertile couple, or the woman who always has difficult postpartum periods. In some ways, these victim positions offer us attention and cultural acknowledgment or even approval.

However, the cost of a lost identity and a lifetime of suffering may be too great. Since our physical health care system seems at present more geared toward the treatment of disease than toward the prevention of potential illness, suffering may well take a serious physical toll before it is recognized. This toll may even result in further pregnancy losses, ongoing stress illnesses, or more serious conditions that result in death.

Suffering may exact an emotional toll from us in our marriages, unmet intimacy needs, friendships, relationships, with other family members and even with our own children. It may cause us to see the world through discolored lenses that darken even the brightest flowers and the most brilliantly blue sky.

It may cost us mentally by focusing our thoughts on negative painful images, or even on wishes that others would suffer as well. It is not uncommon, indeed, it is human, for a grieving mother to feel bitter or jealous about a friend's child. However, suffering may cause such a thinking pattern to become a way of life. This is a frightening thought if you accept therapist-author Sondra Ray's (1980) premise that everything you think up about someone else is translated by the mind into the first person singular. Thus, we may wish upon ourselves all the pain we wish on others.

Finally, suffering blocks our spiritual growth. When we imprison our souls in suffering, in self-sustained pain and resentment, we *cannot* be open to the healing power of our own spirituality. We believe that God is *not* the punishing, judgmental God many of us believed in as children. God is, rather, more like an inner friend and guide.

Believing that God wants us to suffer or endure pain or

that God has abandoned us in our need can spawn even more bitterness and anger in some of us when we look around the world, see others seemingly not suffering, and wonder why we were so chosen.

Instead, we believe that our inner healing and unconditional love *always* desires peace for us and is *always* available. We only have to be willing to receive it. Suffering blocks reception, however; it isolates and imprisons us in our own self-pity and bitter loneliness. It takes courage to tear down the prideful walls we throw up, to allow ourselves to stand free and needy before God and our fellow humans. Yet, we believe that a willingness to let go of suffering and to accept support from each other is what makes life meaningful. It is what allows healing to happen.

Ultimately, we must all face our God, our spiritual beliefs. Death and loss may help us find our way—not through suffering but rather through our own belief in genuine resolution and healing. Perhaps then, when the birds of sorrow fly overhead, they will be unable to nest in our hair.

# NINE

# THE EMOTIONAL ASPECTS OF MOURNING
## The Grieving Heart

*Blessed are they who mourn, for they shall be comforted.*

For many grieving parents, emotional comfort and resolution may seem light years away. Grieving knows no time schedule, no social appropriateness, no unwavering pattern. Mourning flows and ebbs like the ocean tide, and attempting to bound its energy seems as fruitless as trying to control the sea.

Emotional responses to loss have as many variations as there are mourners. Each of us, no matter how similar the events in our lives, experiences and expresses loss uniquely. These differences in expression *all* deserve to be supported with dignity and respect.

Most works on the grieving process identify various stages of grief, generally based on the original model described by Elisabeth Kubler-Ross in her classic *On Death and Dying* (1969). More recently those studying the experience of grief caution against using such stages as rigid rules or judgmental standards for effective (or ineffective) grieving. Kubler-Ross herself has stated that we might do better to ignore "stages" and simply support the mourner's experience.

However, we do feel that there may be value in discussing some general responses to loss, viewed not necessarily in a specific time sequence, but simply as common emotional experiences. First, we believe that such descriptions may help release grieving parents from doubts that their own responses are "sane" or "normal." Mourning is often such an out-of-control, irrational, and seemingly senseless experience that restoring one's belief in one's sanity is vital. One's grip on life can be strengthened by an inner permission to *be* irrational.

Second, we believe that describing just a few of the myriad of possible responses to loss may further help us to understand the similarities in our human grief. Our approach to healing pregnancy loss is based on our belief that understanding our alikeness with others in grief may assist us in our own inner processes of healing, as well as further expand our capacities to know one another's pain and therefore to offer appropriate, loving support.

Most descriptions of grief include some variation of the five stages described by Dr. Kubler-Ross or the four emotional phases described by Dr. John Bowlby (renowned psychiatrist and researcher) in *Loss* (1981). Kubler-Ross defined the classic stages of death and dying after two and one half years of interviewing dying patients and their families. These stages are:

1. Denial and isolation
2. Anger
3. Bargaining
4. Depression
5. Acceptance

Bowlby's work was written after years of research and direct care of those experiencing losses not only through death, but through other forms of separation as well. The four phases he describes are:

1. Numbing
2. Yearning
3. Disorganization and despair
4. Reorganization

We have culled from and synthesized the observations of Kubler-Ross and Bowlby, as well as those from our own work with bereaved parents at Offspring, to describe the common emotional reactions to loss. There is no single right, true path of grief; yet as we each find our own way, there may be common passages for us all. Here are the ones we see most frequently.

## DISBELIEF, SHOCK

It is painfully obvious to those who have faced death that it is always a shock. Even when we have forewarning that someone we love is dying, the anticipatory grieving in itself is done in shock, and even that experience can never fully block the emotional blow of death itself.

When one is expecting a child to be born, one hardly expects that child to die. The anticipation of life, of health, or birth is a stark contrast to the stillborn child or the infant who dies. When one expects a normal (perhaps not even natural) vaginal childbirth experience, the impact of a traumatic birth, a premature delivery, a sickly child, or a cesarean section may also come as a psychic shock.

Bowlby refers to the first phase of grief as numbness, a sort of shutting down of the system so that reality can be integrated more slowly over a period of time. Kubler-Ross believes that such a reaction is a healthy response because we are emotionally so ill prepared to handle death. She reminds us that we would certainly not expect ourselves to look face on into the bright midday sun without shading or protecting our eyes. Facing the unvarnished pain of death is surely a time when we need psychological "sunglasses" to shield ourselves from the intensity of loss.

Originally, this natural shielding was termed "denial." Since denial often carries the implication that one is not facing something one *should* be facing (in mental health circles denial is considered a form of resistance), this term may be misleading when applied to grief and loss. Rather than being a sign of weakness, denying a loss may be a statement of great psychological health.

Unfortunately, the denial or shock response is often misunderstood, especially by those in helping professions providing direct care services. For example, one woman wrote to us after being accused of possible child abuse. Her child had died of sudden infant death syndrome at the age of four months. The emergency room staff, not understanding the emotional reaction of shock, believed the mother to be cold and unresponsive. This led to a call to the police and a painful and tragically violating inquisition of both parents.

Some bereaved parents may appear to be functioning normally when they are in fact so far removed from their actions that they don't even remember driving home or leaving the deceased child. No matter how they appear to us, parents who have lost a child may be in such deep shock or numbness that they need a great deal of care and help. Because parents in shock may not initially feel up to discussing the events of their loss, medical professionals, relatives, and friends may mistakenly assume that the parents don't *ever* want to talk—so the subject is avoided, or the parents themselves are avoided for periods of time after the death or loss.

Dr. Emmanuel Lewis (1976), a London psychiatrist, found that many parents of stillborns are so deeply shocked that they do not have enough energy or enough of a hold on themselves to ask to touch their children, take a lock of hair, or find someone to take a picture. (Having some memento or physical memory of a child is often very important to bereaved parents as time passes.) Lewis describes one woman, who, *when offered her child*, removed his clothes, walked him, and held him close for hours, and then gently gave him back. Had not someone taken the caring initiative to bring her the baby, that woman might never have had those seemingly precious moments with her infant.

Shock, therefore, seems almost universally common after death or loss. In shock, we may need others to help us think and plan—perhaps to offer the chance of contact with a dead child, to retrieve a memento, or to help with basic tasks like making telephone calls.

The couple who miscarries can also go into shock. Initially, such parents may not feel the full brunt of their loss and may seem to be comforted by the idea that they were not attached to their baby and can get pregnant again soon. Shock cushions that early impact. This cushioning effect may well be crucial physically, so that the woman who has experienced bodily stress (pregnancy, labor, birth) may restore herself somewhat before she deals with the full intensity of her loss.

Interviews with abortion counselors have indicated that many women who seemed "fine" right after their abortions call the clinics back weeks after expressing feelings of depression or emotional upset. Some women are so "numbed" after an abortion that they do not immediately feel any physical effects at all and simply return to their jobs that very same day. A number of women we have counseled reported doing just that and then days later suddenly feeling physical effects of the abortion: pain or discomfort in the pelvic area or vagina, nausea, an overall weak feeling, or overwhelming fatigue.

Women who describe their grief reactions to surgical deliveries often express a disappointment or sadness or even deep grief that surfaces months after the cesarean took place. (Cohen and Estner 1983). The initial shock of loss may have cushioned the period of postsurgical recovery.

Some parents in shock seek comfort through immediate spiritual acceptance, yet often such acceptance gives way to a painful and serious questioning of faith when the full impact of loss begins to slowly seep into the consciousness.

Grieving parents may sustain a sort of numbness for years. We have witnessed this as a healthy state of being, observing it in women or men who were not feeling emotionally ''safe'' enough to fully grieve at the time of their actual loss. Doris was one such woman we counseled. Doris, a sixty-year-old retired schoolteacher, came to Offspring feeling cut off from her feelings of love and sexuality. She stated that she felt depressed and related her depression to a separation from her youngest son, who six months before had left home and married.

Doris confided that she couldn't seem to get a grip on her life. She said at one point: ''It's as though someone died, and as though *I'm* dead inside too.'' When asked if any of her children *had* died, she very calmly said that the fifth of her six children, Brendan, died shortly after birth some thirty-two years ago.

When recounting the events of her child's death, Doris recalled attending a small family funeral service at church and then going home to care for her other four children, all of whom were under ten. She had spoken very seldom of her lost son from then on and remembered telling herself every day to forget for the sake of her other children. She judged then that she couldn't let herself feel the sorrow because she had too many responsibilities and no support.

Doris never forgot. When encouraged to gently let in the reality of her little boy's death, she cried for two hours. She described an enormous feeling of relief when her sobs were finally released.

Within a few months Doris was no longer depressed. Although she described herself as still mourning, feeling many different emotions, her feelings were at last no longer obscured or stifled—they were once again available to her. Doris began to feel more alive and more complete.

She revealed that she and her husband had not felt sexually close since Brendan's death. They just hadn't been able to recover enough from the shock and the loss to reach out to each other. Yet the more Doris grieved openly for Brendan, the more her emotions, sexual feelings and all others, were awakened. Doris had waited some thirty-two years to feel safe enough to mourn. She raised her children, sent them on their way, and when the time was right, she wept.

## ANGER, FRUSTRATION

''Why me?'' We have all asked ourselves from time to time, ''Why must I suffer when someone else does not?'' Feelings of helplessness and powerlessness over death often leave us vulnerable to anger, frustration, envy, and blame, In these feelings, death has no reason, no explanation. Life is out of control, and sanity may seem out of reach, causing fears of losing one's mind.

Because this is a time when emotions run raw, even small irritations and violations seem piercing. Laurea Nugent, R.N., a practicing obstetrics/gynecology specialist, notes that grieving women are often more physically sensitive during postpartum checkups. She describes them as more often reporting that they feel physical pain during routine examinations and that they may cry easily, out of vulnerability and sadness. Cesarean mothers also often report a physical and emotional vulnerability so that an ordinary irritation like stubbing a toe may be extremely painful. For all grieving parents, even sexual contacts and simple touching may be experienced as violations.

Emotionally, it can be easier to lose control, to burst out in anger. Bowlby (1981) described intense outbursts as part of the numbing phase, when emotions erupt more unpredictably than usual. He also described anger as a result of the unsuccessful search for the lost loved one, the end of the yearning and longing.

Among health professionals, hospital staff nurses are often likely candidates to receive the anger of bereaved parents. Many parents in grief have lashed out in despairing anger at the nearest human target, often the hospital staff nurse. It is difficult not to take that anger personally and to understand it so that the grieving parent will not be slotted as a difficult patient who is to be avoided if at all possible. It is often extremely difficult to remain calm, endure the anger, and *still* offer support. Yet those bereaved parents do know—and remember—what they are offered. Both through Peppers and Knapp's (1980) studies and our own work at Offspring, we have learned that staff nurses who stood by their patients through such distress were remembered and appreciated for years after the loss. A compassionate and supportive attitude on the part of a professional was often described as the only "medicine" that helped.

Kubler-Ross (1969) describes anger toward the deceased as a natural part of grieving. Yet for parents who have lost a child through miscarriage, stillbirth, or infant death, the innocence personified in an infant is hardly provoking or even permitting of anger. Also, we commonly think that if we are angry with someone, then we are somehow not loving that person, and we are terrified of not loving our children enough, or in the right way, or as we are supposed to love them. In reality the people we feel the most angry toward are often the ones we do love the most. But knowing this doesn't necessarily help the bereaved parent, who cannot accept her own human anger toward the child who left her.

One father shared his feelings of anger toward his first-born child, Jonathan, who died at birth because of a prolapse of the umbilical cord (umbilical cord descending before the baby).

Jack had come for several sessions of counseling. He often reported feeling unusually angry toward his wife and his boss. In fact, he was contemplating quitting his job out of what he felt was pure frustration. His wife, Darlene, was shrinking from his unusually irritable emotional state. Several times we suggested to Jack that he try letting Jonathan know how angry he felt toward him for dying. However, Jack would most often reply that "You can't be mad at dead babies."

Jack was a salesman for a computer software company and spent most of his days on the road. On one long-distance trip, Jack suddenly felt more fully overwhelmed than ever before by the loss of his son. Without forethought, Jack picked up the tape recorder microphone he often used to record business information, and began speaking—to his son:

> Jonathan, right now I need you to be sitting in the back seat of this car. The good thing about talking to someone in a car is that they can't go anywhere on you—they just have to sit and listen like you're doing right now. Jonathan, I know your body is small, but I think your soul is big—so you should listen with your soul.
>
> I'm angry—goddamn angry that you checked out on us. I wanted you. I wanted a son. I wanted to be a real father who could see his son, hold him, play ball with him. I don't want to clear out your room. All those beautiful things . . . I worked so goddamn hard to get your room ready.
>
> Who do you think you are—I was going to be a good father to you. Where the hell did you go?? You never gave me a chance.

Jack stopped speaking then and pulled off the road to cry out his anger and his grief. Jack says that he still occasionally feels a need to share something with Jonathan, and when he does, he takes him out for a ride again—somehow in the privacy of his car, Jack can talk to his son.

## YEARNING, LONGING, SEARCHING

Feelings of longing, of searching, as Bowlby described, for someone or something lost are familiar in some form to us all. Surely, we can all recall a time when a favorite possession was lost or broken and how we longed to find it or fix it.

Losing a loved one or even a dream fills us with yearning for what we have lost. We long to recover that which is lost and to restore some sense of normalcy to our lives. This yearning may take the form of information seeking, a desire to know all we can about the child who died or about the circumstances surrounding the loss. The search may include gathering medical records, speaking to medical experts in the field, and reading everything pertinent to the loss.

This longing to understand as fully as possible may also be a healthy and resourceful way to deal with thoughts bonded in guilt, the guilt that seems almost universal to all bereaved parents. Thoughts of guilt are probably impossible to avoid, since most Western parents feel guilty for *something* and many for everything in their relationships with their children. We feel guilty for what we eat or don't eat during pregnancy; for whether we exercise or don't; for the very air (if it's impure) we breathe; for not bonding ''properly'' or bonding too late; and for untold incidents that all serve as weapons in our self-punishment. Bereaved parents are even more terribly the victims of guilt.

As the reality and pain of loss takes hold, the mind is filled with questions about what happened and why, with underlying thoughts about what the parent may have had to do with the child's death, or the surgical delivery, or any loss that was part of childbearing. Seeking accurate information not only helps us to know our losses more intimately, but may also help to quiet our mind's conflicting and relentless questions.

There is, as well, another form of yearning—an emotional, perhaps spiritual, longing to be connected with the one who has died or with what one has lost. In Parkes's (1970) study of London widows, most of the twenty-two women reported a need to visit old "haunts" and to return to familiar activities once shared with their deceased spouses. Many reported "seeing" their husbands sitting in favorite chairs, or walking out of the house, or "hearing" their spouses coughing at night.

Dr. W. Dewi Rees, a general practitioner, reported that bereaved individuals often suffered from what was termed illusions (visual, auditory, tactile) or a sense of the lost loved one's presence. He found these behaviors and these observations to be far more common than one may have expected (1971).

David Hendin in *Death as a Fact of Life* (1973) reported similar findings. He discusses the reports of a man who felt as though his deceased wife were lying next to him at night. Men and women attending our grief seminars and counseling sessions have also shared their longing to know their children and their experiences with some sense of contact. Many have been awakened at night by what they felt were their babies' cries; others have felt some sense of their children's presence; and some have described it as perhaps a "spiritual awareness."

The clinical explanation of such "illusions" is that they are merely hallucinations. We wish for something so desperately that we can lose touch with reality and imagine that the object of our wishes is near us. However, this explanation implies the possibility of mental health disturbance, and we reject the notion that grieving parents are mentally disturbed.

Another explanation may be the possibility of "soul" connections, spiritual relationships that we don't fully understand because we are so used to relating from one *physical* body to another.

We make no attempts to prove or disprove such reports of communication on a spiritual plane. What we do support—and plead for—is an acceptance of the bereaved's yearning for connection with what is lost as an expression of *absolute health* and acceptance of the premise that some sense of connection *is* possible even without scientific documentation.

Our minds are so trained to want concrete ''proof'' that we may at times lose track of our own intuition and all the knowledge to be gained from experience. In the final analysis, we must each adhere to what we believe to be true for *ourselves* only, and we must honor whatever our own intuitions and feelings tell us.

## DEPRESSION, DISORGANIZATION, DESPAIR

At some point during yearning and longing we will be confronted with a physical reality of loss—some sort of hole—that our searching has not been able to fill. We ultimately will know and feel our loss and how it affects our life.

Mothers must reconcile their breasts full of milk with their empty arms. Mothers with children must somehow surrender to the pain of knowing that the womb once full with child is now an empty space. Infertile parents may have to resolve the pain of their biological children never-to-be. Cesarean parents who hoped and planned for natural births must somehow reconcile their lost dreams with their surgical deliveries. Parents who surrender their children to adoption must say good-bye forever. And in these moments, we all will weep, and nothing will happen to bring back our children or our hopes of life, or our dreams. And so we weep for the emptiness left in our lives.

When hopes of recovering what is lost are abandoned, the yearning, searching, and intense longing give way to the reality of loss. Bereaved parents confront the *now*. The "now" may be a newly decorated nursery splashed with bright colors, or, for the woman who miscarried, a closet full of maternity clothes. It may be a surgical scar that aches with every step. It may be daily trips to a neonatal unit where a tiny infant lives in a glass box fighting for life. It may be, for a teen-age mother, a return to school and social life where friends turn away from her and loneliness prevails. Reality, the aftermath of loss, may feel like life without a future.

Bowlby (1981) refers to the time of confronting reality as characterized by disorganization and despair. Kubler-Ross (1969) describes a stage of depression when the dying person and her loved ones give up hope that a cure is possible.

According to Bowlby, disorganization and despair vary in intensity with the external events and their internal impact. We do see loss almost always creating some degree of confusion and conflict in the lives of those affected. The sudden disintegration of all our plans and dreams can leave us feeling as though we've landed on another planet. Plans and dreams and goals provide us with psychological security, a sense of knowing who we are and what we are about. When these are shattered, we feel vulnerable, emotional, and out of control. At times, we may feel we are losing our grip on sanity.

The interval between the disintegration and the reorganization of our lives may vary. Weeks, months, or even years may pass before we can pick up the pieces and reassemble them in some meaningful way. Meanwhile, we encounter our new reality at the most unexpected times.

Nancy, a woman we counseled, remembered a time about two months after her son's death when she went into a bank to cash a check. As she stood in line to wait for a free teller, she noticed a woman with a two-year-old child. Up to that moment, Nancy had found herself searching, trying to find her son in some way. On that day in the bank, as she looked into the child's face, she thought, "This child doesn't look at all like me," painfully recognizing that here was another woman's baby, and Nancy's own had died.

She was almost in tears when she reached the teller, who asked that Nancy sign her name on the back of the check. Nancy stared at the check, blankly; she could not remember hew own last name. Horrified, she left the bank without claiming her money or her check. For several days after that incident, Nancy wept.

Harriet Schiff (1977) tells a similar story of a mother who, after her child's death, was shopping in a supermarket and couldn't find the peanut butter she had come to buy, and then felt overwhelmed by deep sadness and sorrow——a sorrow that sounds similar to Claudia's sudden sadness when she was unable to locate a familiar municipal parking lot three months after her ectopic pregnancy. In these examples, the unfamiliar child, the hidden peanut butter, and the missing parking lot brought home the stark realities of lost children and opened the emotional floodgates of sorrow.

As our emotional energies flow to the surface, our physical bodies are likely to show signs of stress. As Chapter 5 documents, physical exhaustion, insomnia, headaches, loss of appetite, weight loss, reduced strength, blurred vision, palpitations, and breathing arrhythmia are all natural physiological responses to the reality of loss. One father, a long distance runner, described his loss experience as being like that of a marathon runner "hitting the wall": a physical sense of depleted energy, of a body unable to go on.

Stevenson and Staffon, in *When Your Child Dies* (1981), say that during the confrontation of the reality of loss many of the following may happen:

1. Activities may seem unreal.
2. The world may seem colorless and flat.
3. There may be a physical sense of the dull ache of sorrow. (Many parents have likened this to a headache

or toothache that goes on hurting in spite of steps taken to relieve the pain.)
4. The power of reason may be distorted and confused.
5. The bereaved may say things they don't really mean.
6. Tears may come without warning.

This may be a particularly difficult time emotionally. Earl Grollman (1981) tells us: "Reactions to death are varied and contradictory, appearing in widely contrasting combinations. Many feelings may be expressed in the space of a few moments."

Questions may reappear and answers may seem more empty than ever. Guilt and blame may surface, and marital conflicts erupt. Sexual expression may be blocked, a clue that other energies are probably blocked as well. Peppers and Knapp (1980) found that many couples experienced sexual difficulties that were characterized by fear of pregnancy, loss of faith in the body, disallowing of personal pleasure (a feeling of guilt for enjoying intimacy), and a general diminishing of the sex drive.

All of these symptoms should not be read as abnormal or negative, but simply as signs that the body is hurting, and the emotions need support. We sometimes remind couples that when their baby dies, or some form of pregnancy loss has touched their lives, a common emotional response is a feeling of overwhelming vulnerability—a harkening back to the vulnerability of childhood. That terrified "child" within the bereaved parent may need to be comforted and held not as a lover but as a child would be held by a parent. Sexual intimacy may just be too much for the "child" within. Bereaved couples may need to try other means of physical comfort than sexual intimacy first.

In addition, pregnancy losses often involve physical invasions (such as a D & C, or a forceps delivery) of the external parts of a woman's body. It may take some time and some emotional resolution for women to feel healed and ready for sexual contacts.

Disorientation and despair may be a period of great overall physical and emotional vulnerability. Stubbing a toe or bumping an elbow may cause inordinate physical pain. Carelessly spoken words and ineffective consolations may cause deep emotional hurt. It may be a time when the presence of friends *with* babies may be intolerable.

The following letter was written by a bereaved mother describing her pain when daily confronted with other women and their babies.

> *Dear Mothers of Babies I Don't Have,*
>
> *There are days when I want to walk up to you and say, "I lost my babies. Do you know what that is like?" Of course, you'd think I was crazy, but I have to tell you what it's like. It's a horrible, endless nightmare. It never stops completely. When I go shopping, and I hear your babies crying and gooing, I hate the sounds. I look at my groceries and think, where's my baby. I did all the right things.*
>
> *I read books. I ate well, I rested. Yet, just when I thought I'd made it past the three month mark, I'm done in. I bleed for two days, and then labor a little, and then it's over. Two times in exactly the same way, I lost my babies.*
>
> *Your babies remind me of the hole in my belly, the empty hole. The hole in my heart is probably even bigger. It's so embarrassing to face people who think you've done it, and then you fail. I know my mother wants to see a baby. Look at your mothers—how alive they are when they can be grandmothers. My mother may die just a mother.*
>
> *I hate being at parties where you bring your babies. I feel like a fool. I feel so lost.*
>
> *Some days I hate my body. I wish it worked. It just won't. Mothers, I know I must find a way to forgive myself, and then, maybe, I will stop feeling*

*so angry toward you. After today I think I'm
closer, but I might see you in a grocery store,
tomorrow, and feel mad again. I can't tell you out
loud. So, I'll probably just keep writing. You see,
what I really want you to know is how hurt and
lonely and empty I am. I sure know.*

Kubler-Ross (1969) reminds us that this period is *not* a
time to try to cheer someone up or to attempt to cheer
ourselves. "Try not to think about it," or "I know how you
feel" are painfully discounting responses that too often
become the basis of a lost friendship. Trying not to think
about loss is not only impossible, but also antithetical to
healing; and we can never *know* how another feels—we can
only share how we feel and accept the feelings of others.

A time of despair is a time to weep, to allow ourselves
the privilege of our own sorrow. Grollman (1981) writes:
"Weeping helps to express the depth of despair that follows
the slow realization that the death of your beloved is not just
a bad dream."

The experience of disorganization and despair is very
normal and psychologically healthy, although it may feel as
though happiness shall never be ours again. These may be
difficult times for other family members, particularly children. (In Chapter 11 we discuss the grief process and the
young child in order to offer some tools we have found
helpful in our work with bereaved children.)

Depression, in a certain sense, is a natural part of the
mourning process. Depression is often encountered as a
dread disease, a pathological deviation in our culture. In very
traditional psychological diagnostic systems based on medical models, depression is considered unhealthy and a sign of
sickness.

If depression is treated within this context rather than one
of health and situational *appropriateness*, grieving parents
will not receive adequate care. The following letter came

from a woman in the Midwest, who had sought help at an area mental health clinic:

> *I heard you speak last week in Chicago. My twin daughters were stillborn last year, about this time. I went to therapy three months ago because my friends felt I needed some help. I guess they thought I should be better by now.*
>
> *Anyway, my therapist keeps wanting me to talk about my childhood. She says that I have suppressed anger at my mother for having so many children (six), of which I was the oldest. Maybe she's right. But I think that I need to talk about my daughters more than about my past. I feel a lot worse about my babies than about anything my mother did or didn't do.*
>
> *Thanks for today. I cried about my girls again. I loved the visualization. You helped me feel okay about wanting to still cry. Please let me know anything else I can do.*

We prefer to view depression as a normal response to a stressful situation, somewhat in the terms of Dr. Alexander Lowen's (1972) concept of disappointment. In his framework, depression is a recovery time for the body to rest and sleep, for the mind to relax, and for the emotions to come to the surface.

However, when emotions do churn to the surface and there is no inner, or outer, permission for them to be expressed and released, then a state of blocked emotion can cause further pain. Psychotherapists have long been aware that supporting emotional expression, in tears or anger for example, can break the grip of blocked energy. Prolonged blockages can become a more serious kind of suffering, often termed the depression reaction.

Depression may manifest itself as a lack of motivation or mobility, or as irritation with daily events. It may well have a physiological component, as discussed in Chapters 6 and 7. We cannot overstate how often the physical stress of loss goes unrecognized and untreated.The painful sense of being forever mired in grief is prolonged by the sheer lack of physical stamina necessary to process emotional energy and to heal. Muriel James, author of *Born to Win* (1973), said at a seminar that she herself refuses to work with anyone who feels depressed but is not willing to undergo a complete physical evaluation. She claims that in many instances a checkup showed evidence of physical conditions, treatable with nutritional aids or other physical care. To ignore the physiological repercussions of grief is perhaps to further burden ourselves with thoughts and feelings that we are somehow "failing" at grief work, at a time when we are already in enough physical pain.

Depression may feel like a lack of inner responsiveness or a lack of internal force. Lowen likened depression to the loss of air in a balloon or a tire. Mourning may lead to more serious depression if *expression* is not supported by the mourning parent herself and by those in her environment.

"Expression," wrote Lowen, "is outward moving force." It is the opposite of suppression, which is "the impulse pushed down under the surface of the body." Perhaps much of what we call postpartum depression is really just that, the depressing, or suppressing, of natural, normal postpartum feelings. Perhaps if those suffering from postpartum depression were given full cultural permission, acceptance, and support to *express* rather than suppress their feelings, postpartum adjustments would be much easier.

Expression may take numerous forms: writing, crying, yelling, singing, laughing, indeed any outward movement of energy. The next chapter is devoted to "expression." Here, we will simply say that the energy of grieving must be honored and supported.

## ACCEPTANCE, REORGANIZATION

Beth Jameson in her book *Hold Me Tight* wrote: "Yesterday is not to be forgotten. It is to be cherished and remembered. But tomorrow? Tomorrow is to be created" (1971). Acceptance was described by Kubler-Ross (1969) as a time when the terminally ill patient was no longer angry or depressed by his future and his "fate." For parents attempting to accept the "fate" of their pregnancy losses, though, there will be no tomorrow, only the pain and hurt of today. These losses may feel unacceptable for a very long time—months, even years.

Yet there is a movement from deep, unconsolable sorrow to the reestablishment of daily living. Stevenson and Staffon, in *When Your Child Dies* (1981), say that "Healthy recovery depends not on a denial of tragedy, however, but on the painful separation and acceptance of what cannot be changed." They recommend that mourners "spend time alone" and "take stock of their lives," and realize that they made the assumption that life would go on according to their dreams and plans.

In our counseling work at Offspring, we see that for most bereaved parents letting go of their lost dreams and plans is inordinately painful and difficult. Even as young children, we learn to imagine ourselves as mommies and daddies through our toys and make-believe games. We hold perfect dolls with adorable pink cheeks, bright eyes, and happy smiles. We pretend, in our doll houses, that the world is made up of families very similar to the 1950s television family portrayed in *Leave It to Beaver*. There were no miscarriages, neonatal deaths, infertile couples, abortions, premature deliveries, or mentally handicapped children on such TV productions as *Father Knows Best*. Twenty years ago, children were rarely included in the mourning process. Few of us knew our mothers' pregnancy histories, child-bearing losses, and deep sorrows. Miscarriages were secrets. Abortions were nearly nonexistent, and neonatal deaths were usually explained to children through idealized visions of babies turning into angels. The sadness, the horror, and the grief were almost always hidden in the background.

In our teen-age years, we baby-sat for younger children, practicing our parental skills while perhaps pretending in some secret way that we were caring for our own. Most of our romantic relationships, including our marriages, were built on dreams of future family life: dreams of buying a home, having children, and fulfilling all our childhood fantasies and hopes.

None of those hopes ever included a birth ending in death; a labor ending in surgery; a marriage relationship confronted with the pain of infertility. Our dreams die the hardest death of all and, in the end, may require the most grief work.

Acceptance, then, is not necessarily a happy state at all. It is, more accurately, the end of a long search for peace. Peppers and Knapp (1980) describe acceptance and reorganization as a time of "relief and reestablishment." They observe this as a time of some emotional resolution of the grieving process, a time when "the reminders of loss can be confronted without emotions bubbling to the surface." For many families with pregnancy losses, Peppers and Knapp believe, this relief and reestablishment come with the birth of a subsequent child.

Sherry Lynn Mims Jimenez, in *The Other Side of Pregnancy* (1982), describes reorganization and acceptance as a time when parents begin to make decisions and function more easily overall. It may be the beginning of new life alignments, such as finding a new doctor, changing jobs, buying a new house.

Susan Borg and Judith Lasker, in *When Pregnancy Fails* (1981), remind us of the "rewards" of grief. They write of parents who have reached acceptance: "They have survived. Their emotions, their relationship, their ability to cope, were all tested, and they know, now, that they can get through a crisis and survive. They find strengths they did not know they had and often begin to think of other interests."

We must, ultimately, accept the unacceptable. There is no choice if we are ever to be free of the piercing pain of death. We must know that we have made it and that a new day is dawning. However, it is our belief, after years of counseling families surviving loss, that acceptance is not *enough* if we are to be truly healed. Acceptance is only sufficient for returning to a functioning social, professional, or family life. Acceptance will get us out of bed in the morning a little more easily, but it does not seem to quiet our endless spiritual quest to know and continue to know our children—to find meaning in life and death.

The Reverend David Biebel, author of *Jonathan You Left Too Soon* (1981), describes his experience as a father and pastoral leader when his son died unexpectedly at three and a half years of age. He adds that, "for an unbeliever, the acceptance described here is comparable to the decision to stop banging one's head against that wall, since to continue to do so would simply cause more pain."

We make no claims to be spiritual experts, but we do feel certain that without some attempt at spiritual resolution, our children's lives and deaths will hold less meaning. We will limit our life to survival, having released and rearranged enough of our hurt and pain so that we can pick up and go on, secretly grieving and clinging to our children in our thoughts and dreams, perhaps fearful that others will see into our souls and diagnose us "insane."

Because we believe in the innate sanity, goodness, and wisdom in every human being, we know that the continuing experience of grief is a healthy one, for it can teach rather than burden, and it may offer us a key for making sense out of life.

Rabbi Harold Kushner, in *When Bad Things Happen to Good People* (1981), writes: "Is there an answer to the question of why bad things happen to good people? We can offer learned explanations, but in the end, when we have covered all the squares on the game board and are feeling very proud of our cleverness, the pain, the anguish and the sense of unfairness will still be there. . . . In the final analysis, the question of why bad things happen to good people translates itself into some very different questions, no longer asking ourselves why something happened, but asking how we will respond, and what we intend to do now that it has happened.''

Now that it has happened—now that our childhood dreams of becoming parents have so sadly begun to die—let us not settle for bare acceptance and survival. In the next few chapters, we will share some techniques we've developed for emotional and spiritual healing.

Emotional release may help us in the task of truly letting go, slowly and gently, of the pain and sorrow we so deeply feel. Our years of counseling have shown us the value of emotional release.

Our thoughts on spiritual resolution have also developed through our work as counselors, for we are determined to reach beyond the bounds of traditional psychotherapy to help ourselves and others find a meaning in loss that can improve our lives, rather than debilitate our beings. To do any less costs too much.

Biebel (1981) sums up the need for spiritual resolution as follows: ''For if the sum total of our existence is contained between the day we are born and the day we die, then we are truly poor players on the stage of futility, actors in a cosmic tragicomedy. If the grave is the end, with nothing beyond, then this is all simply absurd.''

**TEN**

# LETTING GO
## Releasing Emotion, Suffering, and Pain

After a loss, churning emotions can overwhelm, frighten, devastate—even cause us to doubt our sanity. Some parents in grief recognize and express their feelings; others leave them unacknowledged or even repressed. As previous chapters explained, we all must find some effective ways of releasing those powerful and painful emotions *before* they wreak further havoc in our own and our families' lives. There are a number of ways to release emotion safely. Good professional counseling can be one avenue for emotional release. We offer the following description of the course that one woman's grief took, within the framework of professional therapy. We tell Anne's story as an illustration of the power and scope of emotional grief, of the necessity for emotional release, and of the healing that comes with letting go.

## ANNE'S STORY: EMOTIONAL RELEASE

On April 5, 1983, the phone rang and was answered, as usual, by the Offspring staff. The voice on the other end said hello, gave her name as Anne Masters, and then managed to explain, "My baby died," before her voice broke and she couldn't continue past the choking sobs in her throat. An appointment was arranged as soon as possible.

### Session 1. About Emily

---

Anne arrived at Offspring looking pale and drawn. She had barely seated herself when she reached into her purse for photographs of her daughter, Emily. Through a stream of tears, Anne told her story: Emily had been her second child, first daughter. The pregnancy had seemed normal in every respect. Even labor began normally, but then progress seemed to halt, and Emily showed signs of distress. Emily was born, by cesarean section, after thirty hours of labor, with no dilation past five centimeters. Anne and her husband, Rob, while deeply disappointed and bewildered by the stalled labor and the surgical delivery, were delighted with Emily. They phoned home, together, to tell their three-year-old son, Steven.

Their joy was short-lived, however, since Emily began to fail, and within a day after delivery, she was undergoing various medical tests. The results indicated that Emily had a cancerous tumor in her tiny stomach. While surgery could be attempted, the prognosis was not good. Anne and Rob did consent to surgery, which was planned in three stages. Emily survived the first two operations, but died before the third, on December 10, 1982, at four weeks of age. Anne concluded her story by saying that her grief had seemed so excruciating at first that she couldn't imagine surviving herself. Like many mourning mothers, she somehow found the courage to continue, and she even began to feel stronger. Then, about a week ago, an overwhelming pain and sadness had seemed to envelope her. Her grief seemed bottomless, and Anne described her life as sliding down the sides of a narrow black pit. She could locate no handholds or footholds, and she felt herself sinking deeper every day. At times, she said, she wanted to stop struggling and just disappear into the pit of despair. But then, at other times, she felt desperate to go on, our of love for her husband and her son. As she spoke, Anne was releasing some of her overwhelming emotion. She was beginning to let go. Anne was then encouraged to share specifics of the photos she had brought. "What day was this?" "Where was it taken?" "Emily's age?" "What was her hair like?' "Did she look at you?" "How did she cry?" "Could you hold her?" As Anne spoke, Emily became a real person with her own appearance and her own personality. We focused, especially, on Emily's interactions with her parents, both before her birth (while she grew within Anne's uterus) and after. Although these moments had been painfully brief, they had existed. Emily had lived. Anne grew calmer as she talked; as the session came to an end, she impulsively reached out to grasp a hand. "Thank you," she said quietly. "I guess I was desperate to talk about her. Everyone else thinks it's all over and done with—she died over four months ago—and hardly anyone else ever even saw her. Only my parents and Rob and Steven. It's almost as though she never existed, and I can't bear that. I really had a daughter, and I loved her so much."

## Session 2. Labor and Delivery: A Mother Protects

At the beginning of Anne's second session, we discussed Offspring's holistic method of grieving and healing and told Anne that we would try to help heal her loss physically, mentally, emotionally, and spiritually. As a first step toward physical healing, Anne was asked to schedule an appointment with our staff nutritionist. We also spoke about exercising, massage, relaxation techniques, and meditation as additional ways to strengthen and support her physical health.

At the same time, Anne was told, we would be recalling all of her relationship with Emily, all of the experiences they had shared. Our goal would be to release any mental anguish or emotional pain, in order to rediscover and redefine the connection Anne still had with Emily, a connection that can endure beyond death.

We began by recalling Anne's labor and delivery of Emily. We used a technique developed at Offspring and termed recall processing. It is designed to place one "in" a scene, in order to release any emotional pain associated with it. Anne was asked to lean back so that her body was fully supported, not needing to be erect or rigid in any way. We followed a progressive relaxation and visualization exercise, and together recalled the events.

Once Anne seemed more peaceful and abler to focus within herself, she was asked to take herself back in time to the end of her pregnancy with Emily, to a day and time when she felt that labor might be beginning. She described a crisp late fall day and how she and her son had made oatmeal cookies together. The contractions began by midafternoon and continued steadily through that night. Anne was clearly "in" the scenes she was describing, she was able to recall details of clothing, room decorations, and others' facial expressions with ease.

When she described how her labor just wouldn't progress, a pained, frustrated expression came across her face. "My cervix won't open!" she cried. "My body is failing my baby!" And, then, "No, I *won't* let my baby out!" And then heartrending sobs. "I *knew*." Anne said softly through her tears, "I knew, somewhere inside me, that she was in trouble, and I wouldn't let her out. How did it happen? Was it something I did? Did my body do something wrong, to let that cancer grow? I must have known she wouldn't make it on her own." Anne was gently guided to complete the recall of Emily's birth, and then she was asked to do an additional process.

"Can you forgive yourself, Anne, and your body, for not letting Emily out, for loving her so very much, that you tried to protect her for as long as you could?"

Anne nodded. Her breath was even and peaceful. "I did know," she said, "and I did try to protect her, I loved her so much. I was so afraid they'd think I was crazy for saying that I knew. It's a relief to say it now."

Then Anne was asked to visualize a symbol of that deep, protective love she had felt for Emily, and had demonstrated at Emily's birth. When Anne spoke, there was a new note of awe in her voice. "I'm seeing an evergreen tree," she explained. "A beautiful, straight blue spruce. It holds on to its needles, through the winter and doesn't let them go when all the maples and oaks and others are dropping their leaves. Some of them do fall, of course, when their time is up, but the tree remains, and it holds on as long as it can."

Anne was asked if there was a way she could make that blue spruce part of her life.

"Why, yes," she said with a gentle excitement, "I could buy a young tree and plant it in our yard. Then, whenever I look at it, I'll remember how fiercely I tried to protect Emily, I'll remember that I loved her that much."

## Session 3. Anger Released

Anne's third session began with a check on her physical well being. She had seen the nutritionist and was incorporating some changes in her diet, as well as adding much-needed vitamin supplements. She had been using some relaxation techniques at bedtime, and so her insomnia was a bit less of a problem.

Satisfied that we were making some progress, physically, we decided to move ahead with the recalling of Emily's life.

After initial relaxation, Anne began to describe the hospital scene, and how a doctor first approached her with news of Emily's poor health. Since recall processing is designed to place one *in* a scene, we ask parents to share their stories in the present tense. "This rather young doctor is coming into my room. Rob had gone home to be with Steven, and Emily is in the nursery. He has heavy black eyebrows and a short, clipped beard. He comes up to my bed and says, 'I'm afraid I have some very bad news. Your baby isn't doing very well.' I couldn't answer for a minute. 'What do you mean?' I ask. 'I mean,' he said harshly, 'that she isn't doing well. She is seriously ill. She might, in fact, die.' Then I start to cry, and he looks more annoyed, or upset. He backs out of the room and tells me that he'll let me know the test results as soon as they are in. He's so afraid. I want him to comfort me, take my hand. He can't! I'm alone."

Anne sobbed out her grief and her shock and her terror, for some minutes. Then, we halted the recall to deal with her feelings toward the young doctor.

"Let's write him a letter, Anne, and tell him how you feel about his professional care. You may decide to send it, or you may not, but we must, somehow, release feelings about him from your body." Anne began to dictate:

> *Dear Dr. B.E.:*
>
> *Where in heaven (is hell more appropriate?) did you do medical training? Don't you know that health care is more than lab tests or surgery, it's also human support and understanding and caring! How dare you burst into my room and tell me my baby is seriously ill, without once saying you're sorry, or do I have any questions, or do I understand the situation, or do I need any help! How*

> *dare you treat me that way! Did you touch my*
> *daughter? I didn't want you to touch her—I only*
> *wanted her touched by kindness, not by damnable*
> *callousness. I can't bear to think of you touching*
> *her! You are a miserable discredit to the health*
> *care field, and I hate you, I* hate *you!!*

As Anne's voice rose to a crescendo of emotion, it as quickly broke and dissolved into tears. After a few moments, Anne was asked if there was anything left to say to the doctor. When she shook her head no, she was asked again to begin to imagine an eager, young medical student who wants, perhaps, to cure the world; who, perhaps, chooses obstetrics because of all the new life pulsing through each day; who toils through years of school learning to cure, to heal, to save, to *do*. And then, being confronted with a situation in which there perhaps may be *nothing* to do. His behavior is surely at fault, but can you, somehow, forgive him? Can you *begin* to forgive, to see his frailty, his fear when he cannot save, his anger when new life doesn't live, his helpless inadequacy in the face of grief? For if not, you run the risk of holding pain in your own body that can hurt *you*, damage *you*. Can you forgive him for telling you that your daughter might die?

Anne sobbed deeply and then gradually returned to even breathing. "Yes, yes I can," she whispered. "It is pretty awful to feel so helpless—I felt it myself. And a part of me *was* blaming him for Emily's death, just because he was the one who told me. He *was* lacking in compassion, maybe he felt it, but it didn't show—but then, so was I. He is responsible for his fear, his poor professional behavior, but I do not want to bear the pain of those, too. I also blamed the messenger for the message, didn't I? I can't hate him for that. It does feel better to view that incident in this way, my chest doesn't hurt so much. One more chunk of pain seems gone."

## *Session 4. Intensive Care*

Anne's fourth session began with the usual focus on her physical health. She had begun to eat a little more, and so she had stopped losing weight. Although she was still quite tired, the bone-crushing exhaustion she had felt was lifting. She had already had a massage, and she was even contemplating beginning an exercise program. "Only contemplating!" she joked. It was a joy to see her smile, even a little.

In this session, we began to recall Emily's stay in the neonatal intensive care unit. Anne felt such agony at being separated from Emily, yet Steven, only three, needed her too. He had been frightened and bewildered by the continuing crisis to save Emily's life. He clearly sensed his parents' anxiety, and so he grew fearful of separation from them.

Taking herself back, Anne sobbed, "It's so unspeakably *awful*. I can't bear to leave her there, lying so helplessly in that little bed with all the tubes sticking out of her body. The nurses are wonderful, but I feel that she wants and needs *me*. And Steven needs me too—he is so scared, and I'm not much comfort. We brought him in to see Emily, of course, but he couldn't hold her, and it frightened him to see her. I am haunted by guilt for all the moments when Emily cried and I wasn't there, and I am haunted by what Steven went through, too. He really lost his mother for a while, and I'm not even all back yet."

We talked, then, about the vital connection, the sheer bond of love, that exists between parent and child—a bond that does not sever, regardless of the external events. Regardless of her physical presence, Anne always had that bond with each of her children, in the same way that their love was always with her.

Anne was asked to close her eyes and visualize each of her children before her. She was asked to tell each of them how very much she loved them, how very much she wanted to meet their needs, but that above all else, her indomitable love was *always* with them, no matter what. Anne's words to her children were intensely moving. Her voice vibrated with love for them, a love that seemed to comfort her even as she spoke. "Somehow, I know that they feel it too," she said.

We then spoke of healing techniques for children (discussed more fully in Chapter 11). Anne decided to try some recall processing with Steven, to help him heal from the loss of his sister and to cement his awareness of his parents' love for him.

## Session 5. A Child Understood

Anne's fifth session began with a report of her progress with Steven. "He loved doing recall processing! Of course, it seemed like a fun game to him, and he had Rob's and my total attention. But it also worked well, he did share a lot of fear and confusion. He still may be somewhat confused, since he's not old enough to have a full command of the language, but he expressed enough so that we could help him. We finished by talking about loving each other, and how much we missed each other when one of us was with Emily in the hospital. I think he understands, just a little, that Emily was lonely and needed us too. When I asked Steven to think of something we could give each other as a reminder of the love we feel, he suggested teddy bears! Isn't that wonderful? We're going to look for two sets of hugging bears—a bear for Steven, Rob, me, and even Emily. We're going to keep Emily's in a special place to remind us of her love for us and ours for her.

"And then if one of us goes away, he or she can bring a bear as a symbol of the love that always goes with each of us. It's been a special lesson for all of us, to understand that our love for each other is *always* with us, even when we're apart.''

## Session 6. Emily in Surgery

When Anne was asked whether she was ready to confront Emily's surgeries, she responded that she was. ''I'm frightened,'' she said, ''but I feel stronger too.''

She went back in time to the diagnosis of Emily's illness and the presentation of the option of surgery. Tears filled her eyes: ''I can't decide,'' she moaned. ''I see her tiny body, and I can't bear to think of her being anesthetized and cut. I want to scoop her up and bring her home where I can cuddle her and hold her all day, without those tubes and wires. The doctors can't really help us decide. The surgery *may* save her, or it may not. Actually, it's more likely that it won't save her. But that one chance . . . oh, no, I have to take that chance. Is it right, the best decision? We tell them to go ahead . . . a nurse came to us with news that the surgery was over. She held our hands for a moment. The doctor came then, he said he was sorry, that there wasn't much hope, but they'd keep trying. And they *did* try. Yet, how I wish we had just brought her home to die! She died alone, apart from us, while we were on our way to see her. I wasn't there, *I wasn't there!*''

Anne's body was racked with sobs. When she had quieted a little, she was asked to visualize her sanctuary or haven (an exercise described in Chapter 6, which Anne had done frequently as a part of relaxation or meditation). Anne was reminded that only support and understanding and acceptance can exist there—never blame or judgment. When she felt in touch with that sense of peace and freedom, she was asked to call an image of Emily before her—to see Emily and herself with only her highest, purest thoughts. She was told she could feel free to just be with Emily in whatever way felt right, to hold her, to speak or not. There is no right or wrong way to feel love.

Then Anne was asked if she could forgive Emily for dying, when Anne so wanted her to live. "Of course," Anne said softly. "She did the best she could, I really believe that." I suggested that she tell Emily that. Anne's face, with her eyes closed, looked lovely and peaceful.

The next suggestion was that Anne "ask" Emily whether Emily could forgive Anne's not being with Emily when she died. Anne did, and then healing tears flowed from her eyes. "I feel that, somehow, she told me there's nothing to forgive, my love was with her when she died, and that was all she needed. She also seemed to say that she, too, knew that I was doing my very best. We both were, and our love for each other sustained us both."

Anne left with a warm hug and a lightened heart.

### Sessions 7–9. Release of Spiritual Pain

When Anne returned for her seventh session, she seemed to have lost a great deal of the peace she had gained.

"I don't know what's happened to me," she said, "but I feel so empty. I keep asking myself, *why*. Why Emily, why me, why us. I prayed so hard for that surgery to work, for some miracle to happen. Emily tried so hard too. We all did—me, Rob, my parents, the doctors and nurses. Where was God? Why didn't he answer our prayers, why didn't he help her? Why did he ignore us when we most needed him? Why did this happen at all? Was I being punished? Why did my body let cancer grow? Where was God? What kind of a God gives a baby cancer?"

"Why don't you tell God how you feel?" So Anne did: she raged, she yelled, she pounded pillows with her fists until she was spent. She poured out all her anger, all her hurt, all her lost hopes that God would "fix" whatever most needed fixing. When she was done, she was asked to whom she'd been speaking. "Why, *God*," she answered. When she was asked to describe God, she hesitated. So we wrote an essay, Anne dictating, entitled "Who Is God?" It was another beginning for Anne, the beginning of the spiritual resolution of her loss.

During the next two session, Anne took long and clear looks at what her spiritual beliefs had been, before Emily's death, and at what they were becoming. The exercise essay about God had given her a telescoped view of her beliefs, and Emily's death challenged most of them. One of Anne's impulses had been to turn away from her God, in anger, to abandon all her spiritual beliefs. Anne expressed a deep loss of faith in herself, in her body, and in all she was brought up to believe. "It's painful and frightening to say these things, but when I do, I feel relieved," Anne said.

During her ninth session, Anne followed a visualization exercise in which she asked Emily for answers as to why she had died. The response that Anne felt within her was that Emily's death had given the whole family an infinitely heightened appreciation of each other and of the love they shared. While doing the exercise, Anne's body seemed to tremble a little, and then she shared her feeling that Emily (or God, she wasn't sure) was also telling her that God's love, too, had been with her, sustaining her, through this terrible time. When Anne opened her eyes, she looked more truly peaceful than she ever had before. "I don't really know why I feel better," she said, "but I do. Somehow I feel that I'm on the right track, and that it will all keep getting clearer. Right now that seems to be enough."

## FREE TO BE

Poet e.e. cummings wrote: "To be nobody, but myself, in a world which is doing its best, night and day, to make me everybody else, means to fight the hardest battle which any human being can fight; and never stop fighting.''

There are stages and phases of loss, and books and studies on mourning. There are descriptions, definitions, and explanations of grief. There are support groups and some nonsupport groups. There are those who advise; those who pretend nothing has happened; those who truly console.

There are therapeutic techniques, words of wisdom, simple poems that express sorrow. There are the stories of those who suffer a broken heart and stories of how to mend it.

Then, finally, there is the despair of our own individual sorrow: each of us struggling to find relief, to express our feelings and needs, to grieve each in our own way and in our own time, without losing any more than has already been lost.

Yet to be oneself in a world that denies death, withholds feelings, and buries emotions is no easy task. To release the pain of lost dreams of childbirth, dreams dashed by cesarean deliveries or traumatic births, is difficult, especially when physicians, family, friends may disapprove and wonder, ''Why all the fuss? After all you have a healthy baby.'' In this world, the tears of a woman who has surrendered her child for adoption are easily discounted by those who judge that her choice was ''for the best.'' The grief of couples who miscarry is swept away in glib suggestions that they conceive another child.

And for the Annes and Robs, whose babies die, there is often only limited permission to express their grief. After a time, usually brief, friends and relatives may be unable to deal with their own helplessness in the face of so much pain. So they withdraw, or the bereaved parents themselves withdraw, or try to repress the feelings that make others so uncomfortable.

Why are our feelings so unacceptable? Why do we try so

hard to run from our emotions, or to lock them safely away? We believe that if we, parents in grief, are to heal ourselves, we must *be* ourselves. We must honor our own feelings, regardless of the opinion of the world. We must find ways to express those feelings, to let go of that which could hurt us if kept locked inside.

Samuels and Bennett (1974) define feelings as "messages from your body and mind, which tell you what to do to achieve ease." They further define ease as "The state in which inborn healing abilities are free to work their best." In order, then, to support our inborn healing abilities, we must *first* honor the messages of our feelings. To do that, we must recognize our feelings, and rather than suppress them we must *express* them.

Expression may take many forms. For Anne, screaming, crying, pounding pillows, writing, talking, and envisioning allowed release and some return to ease. For others, sobbing, laughing, exercising, or even dreaming are also forms of letting go.

The mode of release is best designed by one's own inner guides and within the context of one's feelings of safety. Later, in this chapter, we offer some suggestions as vehicles for release. In addition, we propose the following framework for effective emotional release. It incorporates three basic premises:

1. Assume all feelings are valid and sane.
2. Become a supportable person.
3. Anchor yourself in self-acceptance, and release emotion without suffering.

## *1. Assume All Feelings Are Valid and Sane*

Many grieving parents found their way to Offspring for counseling because they began to doubt their sanity. Their feelings were very real and overpowering to them but were judged abnormal or unhealthy or inappropriate—or even totally discounted—by others in their lives. How confused these parents felt, how despairing of ever again feeling normal! The world's message was often that they ''should'' have been feeling differently, and yet their own emotions told them otherwise. No wonder their sanity felt questionable.

We encourage parents to acknowledge their feelings as *testimony* to their health and sanity. Assume that your feelings *are* valid and sane even if others don't understand or accept you. Find someone who will; and, most of all, accept yourself and your feelings. You are not alone; you are one of millions of others whose feelings cry for recognition and expression.

Aware women, who sensitively feel their own pain and express their grief-stricken emotions, are often perceived as ''hysterical'' rather than as the sane and healthy women they are. Women who feel upset, depressed, and disappointed after their cesarean deliveries or traumatic births are often judged as excessively emotional, or even immature, to be so upset. Women who miscarry and mourn the loss of their children are, all too often, criticized for their mourning by those who judge a miscarriage is best ignored or quickly forgotten. Even those whose babies die, or those whose children are handicapped are not allowed the sanctity of their own feelings. After an initial period of support for their sorrow, most grieving parents are expected to shoulder their losses, dry their tears, and return to normal life again, usually long before they feel ready to do so.

Our culture is so death-denying, so emotion-repressing, that it's no wonder our feelings are often unacceptable to others or even to ourselves. And yet, traumatically birthed women *feel* their losses, and women who miscarry *feel* their grief, and all bereaved parents *feel* their pain, for however long they do. As the Marriage Encounter weekend (a retreat experience for couples seeking close communication, renewal, and growth in their marital relationship) tells us, feelings are neither right nor wrong. They just *are*. And so they deserve to be recognized. *We* deserve to be recognized. So, too, with all our pregnancy and birth-related losses. We must trust in our sanity and claim our right to mourn until we are done.

## 2. Become a Supportable Person

When our children have died, or our dreams have been slashed, we are raw, vulnerable, and hurt. Ordinarily insensitivities, the unconscious words and actions of others, may inflict a piercing pain on an already broken heart. Our tendencies may be to criticize our friends and families, and probably justly so, for their failures to respond more sensitively to our losses. Because of their poor support, we may withdraw—and then *we* may become unsupportable, cutting ourselves off from any help offered.

We live in a world that has failed to teach appropriate, supportive responses to grief or pain. We ourselves have certainly violated others at times through our own clumsiness and lack of skill. We have *all* been insensitive. It is difficult to remember that truth when we are in such pain, but remembering is important. We do need support, despite our tendencies to pull back and try to heal our wounds alone.

One grieving parent told us that she had pushed her best friend from her front step because her friend knocked at the door with flowers and said, "I know how you feel." It's true: no one *knows* how *you* feel. When your dream dies, you want it back, not empty words, flowers, and sympathy.

However, to be at emotional war with a friend is to incur greater loss and more pain. Often, we have to tell our friends what to do. Becoming a supportable person means that we assume responsibility for our needs and feelings. We must ask others to stop when they are hurting us, we must let them know exactly what we do need, and we must give them a chance to respond appropriately. Grief may be uncharted territory not only for us, but for our friends and relatives as well.

Once we are willing to allow others some emotional clumsiness and the pain of their own helplessness, we have a greater chance of receiving the support others can give. We owe ourselves physical touching, nourishing food prepared by others, a friend who will listen, some time alone. We owe ourselves the right to give up the "social acts" and obligations that may only increase pain.

Social acts can be debilitating to parents in grief. Serving as a gracious hostess, carrying on social conversations, or even *smiling* stoically can all require more energy than bereaved parents can muster. We must abandon painful acts such as these and tell the truth about how we feel. Too exhausted to play hostess? Ask friends to sit with you, but ask them to make their own tea and bring their own snacks. Impossible to pull your mind and feelings from your loss? Tell your family and friends that you know how hard your grief is on them, but you really need the freedom to speak what is on your mind and not about community affairs that hold no meaning for you right now. No desire to smile? Ask friends if they can bear your sad expression because it's real; it's you; and you need to know that you can be honest, for that is how your sadness will heal. One couple we worked with placed the following sign on their front door:

> ## GRIEVING FAMILY
> ## ENTER AT YOUR OWN RISK!

Our attempts to become supportable by telling others what we need can often dramatically and positively change our relationships. Sandra and Michael came for counseling after their fifth pregnancy loss—two miscarriges and three stillbirths. They had six pregnancies and only one surviving child. They desperately wanted to have another child. They both came from large families, and while there were many people who could offer support, little was forthcoming. Both families had great difficulty expressing feelings and needs and being open with one another. Sandra and Michael had both grown up observing feelings held on tight reins, and yet they were both finding it harder and harder to do that with their own feelings. Sandra came for counseling because she felt overwhelmed by her feelings of grief and her loneliness in that grief. One of Sandra's sisters was planning a large christening party for her new baby, and she expected Sandra and Michael to attend.

Sandra dreaded the event, and yet she and Michael felt that they were obligated to attend. We counseled her to share her feelings with her family, but she felt that wasn't possible. So they did attend. As Sandra later told the story, they drove to the church with her stomach lurching and her inner voices screaming at her not to go. Sandra told herself to be brave and to stop acting childish. She told herself that she was "obligated" to go to the ceremony and that her family would worry if she and Michael did not attend. So she denied her inner voice and her bodily feelings and made herself go on.

The christening was a community service, not only for Sandra's young nephew, but also for seven other infants, all under three months of age. Sandra and Michael were overwhelmed by the presence of so many babies, the joyous celebrations, the chattering toddlers present. Again, Sandra wanted to leave, to retreat home to her comforting living room and the quiet music she had so often used to bring calm to herself. Again, the voices of "obligation" won out and Sandra forced her body to remain present, although, she recalled that spiritually and emotionally she had faded out.

Then Sandra felt compelled to look at the infants' faces. She saw the baby she so desperately wanted in every one. Her heart ached, as never before, and she began to tremble. She left the church, drove home alone, and cried. She sobbed alone in her living room, letting go of the pain and the deep sorrow for her lost children.

No one in her family called. No one came to her door to offer support. Sandra felt too "proud" to let anyone know she was in such need. Finally, Sandra recovered herself and drove to the christening party. No one asked her where she had gone or how she was. Everyone stared, helplessly, at her reddened eyes and felt too afraid to confront her pain.

Suddenly, Sandra was simply unable to endure her tortured feelings. She took several of her family members aside and told them how sad she had been feeling. Michael and others joined the group. Before they were finished, the entire family had gathered around them, and there were many wet eyes.

With great awkwardness, several family members reached out and touched Sandra and Michael. One great-aunt said that she'd been alive for eighty-three years and had never seen the family so truly involved with each other before.

Perhaps not all families would be capable of such a decent and supportive response. Many people are still too frightened of death, or of emotion, to be so open. However, our tasks, as grieving parents, are to remain "supportable": to pass by those unable to be with us in our pain and to reach out to those who can.

### 3. Anchor Yourself in Self-Acceptance

If we do not accept ourselves, we cannot accept and effectively express our feelings. We will suffer endlessly, without reaching healing. In October 1982, we received the following letter from a bereaved mother who could not accept herself:

> *To Offspring:*
>
> *My daughter died almost a year ago. She was born with multiple birth defects that could not be corrected by present day medical technology. She lived for almost three weeks, in a small glass box in the intensive care unit. Her name was Jenny.*
>
> *My husband and I knew all along that Jenny would die, but we could not let ourselves fully face the reality of her death. I watched her day after day without touching her or comforting her. And this is why I'm writing to you.*
>
> *You see, I feel that I should have taken her off all those machines and held her and mothered her instead of just watching her die. But, if I did pick her up, I would have had to face the reality of her death, and I wanted to hope. The hope was for me, it really never existed for Jenny, so I was being selfish, and I had no courage. Now, I am ashamed that I could not help her. I can't believe that I had her for such a short time and failed her so.*
>
> *My husband doesn't want to hear me complain anymore. He says it's over and we should forget it. I can't forget it.*
>
> *Sincerely,*
> *Janice*

We responded:

> *Dear Janice,*
> *Thanks so much for telling us about Jenny and about you. It is so hard to face ourselves and our perceived shortcomings. We are not going to tell*

you to stop hurting and punishing yourself, because if you could do that you would have done so by now. We are going to ask you, however, to find a way to accept yourself without suffering. It probably would have been better for Jenny and you to have been physically close. It's sad that our medical system was so unable to help you and your little girl to do that.

Yet, they didn't and you couldn't. Now, however, your task is to find a way to live gracefully with yourself and honorably with Jenny. So, we're going to invite you to write to us every day. Write all of your feelings, all your thoughts, all your pain. Write to us; write to Jenny; write to yourself. Write until you can look in the mirror in the morning and say "Janice, I love you. Jenny was so very fortunate to have you as a mom."

Today, that might seem like it could take forever. You probably think it's easy for us to suggest out here in Arlington, Massachusetts, with you a thousand miles away. You're right, it is easy to suggest and much harder to do. But, we must encourage you to let go of the pain you've shared—slowly in your time. You and Jenny, both, deserve a connection founded in love and joy, not pain and suffering.

Thank you for the privilege of knowing you, and may peace be in your heart.

And the letters came, day after day, letters of anger, shame, sorrow, guilt, hurt, fear, and then love and devotion and fierce protection and then of compassion, understanding, and forgiveness. Then one day:

Dear Janice,
I forgive you for everything. Jenny was so fortunate to have you as a mom. You did all you could

*do. You wanted her to live because you loved her.
I'm sorry I punished you.*

> *Love,
> Janice*

It's so easy, so human to bog ourselves down in the flood of pain we attempt to release. Kubler-Ross (1980-83) believes that the emotion of grief will run free and pure, except when we block its flow with guilt, blame, resentment, bitterness, or other adulterations of pure sorrow.

Suffering unnecessarily only increases our pain and blocks our growth. Genuine sorrow, hurt, and anger are real, deep, and at times feel bottomless. Yet, even these painful emotions can be released when freed from the bonds of endless self-punishment or unforgiving bitterness. In order to *stop* punishing ourselves and release our bitterness, we must somehow anchor ourselves in self-love, self-acceptance, and self-responsibility. Emotions are never adequately honored when we believe we are worthless, or when we view ourselves as victims and tragic figures. We must begin to see ourselves as good, as capable of reaching healing, and as deserving of support on our way. We often suggest that those who profess not to accept themselves begin a process of affirmation. Sondra Ray (1981) writes that "An affirmation is a positive thought that you consciously chose to immerse in your consciousness to produce a certain desired result." So begin to use an affirmation such as this one: "I am *good* and *lovable* and fully deserving of acceptance and support—especially my own."

Thinking it, saying it, writing it—these are all ways to use affirmations. Repetition is what works, so use it often.

If you continue to find yourself judging or punishing yourself for some specific actions, try a process of self-forgiveness. Ask yourself, as Anne was asked in therapy, if you can forgive your baby. If you can, can you offer yourself any less, for if you do, doesn't that dishonor your relationship with your child? You do deserve your most sincere self-forgiveness and your most supportive self-acceptance.


## LETTING GO

So now the framework is there. You have anchored yourself in self-acceptance in order to release emotion without suffering; you have become a supportable person; and you do assume all your feelings are sane and valid. So what now? How do you release feelings?

Some people, like Janice, will write. Buy a notebook and use it to record your thoughts and feelings. Write to yourself, or your lost child. Write to anyone and everyone: spouse, relatives, friends, physicians. Some people actually send their letters; most do not. The important aspect of writing is releasing feelings *from* your body, where they could do harm if trapped.

Some people need to vocalize their feelings. If your throat feels tight or constantly sore, perhaps that is a physical indication of your need to speak out your emotions. You may only feel safe talking to a professional counselor, as Anne did, or a clergy person, or loved ones, as Sandra did, or even to yourself alone. Women we've worked with have gotten in their showers with both taps streaming so they could muffle screams they had to let out. Others have gone for solitary drives so they could privately speak aloud their grief or pain. Still others have asked friends for help with child care so they could go home alone, or with their spouses, to speak freely and cry without restraint.

Tears are a particularly effective form of release. Tears offer a gentle, cleansing bath for our whole beings—body, mind, heart, and soul. If there are tears inside, find safe places and times and ways to release them. Only if they are dammed up inside can they drown you in sorrow.

Some people express their feelings in their art or their hobbies. One grieving mother, a professional dancer, created an intensely moving dance program in memory of her stillborn son. Another woman painted a portrayal of her feelings after a miscarriage. Others sing or play instruments; still others feel release through exposure to the art or the expression of others. One father commented that when he attended the symphony and heard the music he loved, he was able to let go and cry for his dead son.

Exercise is another form of release. As the perspiration and energy flow from your body, so too can some of the stored-up pain. One grieving woman told us she swam several times a week at a local pool. The water absorbed her tears and provided a safe place for her to vent her anger. "I poured out my rage into that water," she said. "My arms and legs would just *slice* through it. When I climbed out of the pool, I'd feel so spent, but much more peaceful."

Others pound their fists on beds or pillows. One grieving father, whose emotions were normally held in tight check, suddenly picked up a pillow and flung it. Then he grabbed another pillow and held it while he pounded it with a balled fist. "Why is this happening to us?" he cried. "Why? Why?" His wife calmly reassured their children that Daddy was releasing his great anger and pain, but that he did so in a safe and healthy way, without hurting anyone. What a valuable lesson for his children!

Perhaps if more and more of us are able to let go—to talk, cry, rage, exercise, pound pillows, write, create, sing, dance, *be*—then more and more of our world will be healthy, and healed, and at peace.

# ELEVEN

# SUFFER THE LITTLE CHILDREN

In her achingly beautiful book, *A Parting Gift* (1982), pediatrician Frances Sharkey relates the story of her young patient, David—his valiant battle with leukemia, his heart-piercing wisdom, and his gentle death. One of the most poignant passages describe Sharkey's intense desire, fueled by all her medical training, to help David and his family, and then her ultimate lonely helplessness to "make every-thing all right." Doctors aren't the only people who feel helpless and lonely and thwarted. So do children—our other children, our "healthy" children. In many ways, their health is just as threatened by loss as is our health—maybe even more threatened, for as Nancy Berezin, author of *After a Loss in Pregnancy* (1982), reminds us, children are often "the forgotten mourners." When we don't know what to say to our children, we often avoid confrontation; thinking to protect them, we may say nothing at all. That awful quiet, that lonely isolation, is terrible for children of all ages to bear. Desperate for answers and for recognition, children will do anything to be noticed; often negative behavior draws the quickest parental response.

Sharkey tells how stressed David and his parents were during David's progressing illness. They just couldn't handle the additional stress of their younger son, John's, accelerating misbehavior. John alternated between sullenness and mischieviousness. He teased and hit his younger sister. He disturbed everyone around him. John's parents had been unable to confront John with his misbehavior; their guilt at "neglecting" him in favor of David paralyzed them. Nor could they tell him, in their own emptiness devoid of answers, that David was dying. Yet, Dr. Sharkey guessed that John *knew*. She makes a lovely analogy: she describes children as the true weathervanes in the family. "When things are steady, they turn without effort in the right direction. When problems make life stormy, they spin out of control." In an effort to help John and his parents, Dr. Sharkey requested permission to meet with John alone. Sitting close and holding John's hands, she asked him if he understood the problem of David's needing so much of his mother's time. With a five-year-old's breathtaking directness, John replied, "David's sick," and then asked, "Is he going to die?"

When Dr. Sharkey gently responded, "Yes, John, he's going to die," John's response was instantaneous and heartrending. As tears gathered in his eyes, he asked, "Did I do it to him? Is it my fault?"

Therein lies much of the suffering of our healthy children. Children often assume blame for the loss, feeling themselves in some way responsible. If a child had to deal with separation from her parents and that separation was due to a new sibling being born or requiring extended care, it would be natural and normal and *healthy* for the child to feel resentful. Dr. Lee Salk (1976-78), who is a pediatric psychologist, and other child care professionals ask us to imagine how *we* would handle this scenario: Your spouse sits down with you one day and says, "Sweetheart, I love you so very much! So much, in fact, that I'm going to bring home a new mate to share your life!" How do you feel? What do you feel? Anger? Shock? "Am *I* not good enough?" Fear? Pain? Loss? Imagine then that you probably bear that interloper no good will at all—even if only in your mind and heart and even if you manage "proper" cheerfulness on the surface. Then imagine that if loss strikes, you just might feel responsible. Children *do*. They do feel at fault—so universally, in fact, that Elisabeth Kubler-Ross (1980-83), Rabbi Earl Grollman (1976-83), Lee Salk (1973), and others advise us to *tell children they didn't cause the loss*, even if they have never shared with us their own horrified thoughts of responsibility.

There are many aspects of loss wherein we feel helpless, but we are not totally helpless with children: we can take away their self-inflicted suffering by telling them the truth about what happened. That truth will set our children free to feel any grief natural to them and free to heal.

Observers and teachers in the fields of psychology, sociology, and medicine increasingly favor including children in *all* major family passages, be they joyous or sad, peaceful or jarring. Kubler-Ross (1975) writes that we "routinely shelter children from death and dying, thinking we are protecting them from harm. But it is clear that we do them a disservice by depriving them of the experience. By making death and dying a taboo subject . . . we create fear that need not be there."

Rabbi Earl Grollman has written and lectured extensively on the positive effects of including children in our loss and in our mourning rituals. His books, *Explaining Death to Children* (1967) and *Talking about Death: A Dialogue between Parent and Child* (1976), plead that children be included, given their own opportunities to express their grief, and offered honest explanations as to why death occurred and what death means. Without adequate inclusion and accurate information, say Grollman, Salk, and Kubler-

Ross, children often assume blame for tragic events, judging themselves responsible because of their behavior or even because of their thoughts. Those of us who try to protect our children from death or sorrow fail miserably. Child psychologists are unanimous in their belief that major life experiences and their residue of feelings cannot be hidden from children of any age. Children *know;* they respond intuitively to our feelings. They are indeed Dr. Sharkey's (1982) weathervanes. Any attempts to spare the children, write nurses Carol Hardgrove and Louise H. Warrick (1974), "build walls between parents and young-sters and set a pattern of withholding talk and expression of genuine emotion. This secrecy can cast a lifetime shadow, creating a fear that the child has no permission to explore."

No permission to explore. Feeling constrained from asking questions and sharing fears can create harmful turmoil for a child. One mother, Carol, came to us for counseling after her third stillbirth. She had four pregnancies, only one of which resulted in a living child, Gretchen. Both Carol and her husband were so frozen in grief that they found it very difficult to communicate with Gretchen.

Gretchen was six years old, at the time of the third stillbirth and had been very consciously awaiting the arrival of a new sibling. When her mother told her that the baby died, Gretchen wanted to know more details. Her parents, paralyzed by grief and counseled by their pediatrician to share as little as possible with Gretchen, did not respond to her questions.

Several months passed and Gretchen said nothing, other than to cry more easily over sad television programs and minor life disappointments. One day Carol received a call from Gretchen's school principal, telling her that Gretchen was not doing her work, was refusing to socialize with the other children, and was responding angrily and disrespectfully to her teachers. Such behavior was in no way characteristic of Gretchen, who was ordinarily quite a good student, responsive to authority, and cooperative with her many friends.

Carol attended several meetings with school personnel, but the school difficulties continued. In addition, Gretchen developed a severe bladder infection that required hospitalization and potential surgery.

At this point, Carol was encouraged to include Gretchen in the family's grieving process. Slowly, Carol gave Gretchen information about her lost sibling. Guided by Gretchen's questions, Carol shared with her daughter the fact that she did have a brother, that his name was Jason, and the circumstances of his death.

Gretchen's infection began to clear enough so that she was released from the hospital. Once she came home, she began to draw pictures of Jason. Carol showed her Jason's footprint and a lock of his hair.

Finally, Carol took Gretchen to the cemetery. Standing over her brother's grave, Gretchen said, "Jason, I've been seeing you in my dreams at night. You were a beautiful baby and I wish you came to live with me. I wondered what the doctors did with you."

Gretchen returned to school. Her bladder infection cleared. Her grades returned to normal, and her previous social life resumed.

Many parents think that they have included their children in their loss and that they have been present and truthful and honest with their children. Yet loss wraps such a dense blanket around us all that feeble efforts at reaching out can seem monumental. Our attempts to reach out to our children may seem quite adequate to us but be less so to our children.

Harriet Sarnoff Schiff, in *The Bereaved Parent* (1977), explains that "many surviving children suffer because their parents were unable to fulfill this responsibility, and the effects of their inability can be lifelong. When Robby [Schiff's son] died, our instinctive thought was to get home and be with our children, who had been left in the care of family . . . because we felt our children needed us. We were right. They did. But six years later, our son who was twelve when his brother died, remembers feeling unloved and alone during the entire grieving period and indeed for several years thereafter.'' Schiff adds that ''Somehow, and I suspect it's true in nearly all families, there is no depth of communication about feelings surrounding the dead sibling.''

Nancy wrote: ''I was two and a half when my twin brothers were born and died. They were premature and very small at birth and lived only for a day or two. Everyone must have assumed that I was too young to understand what had happened, and it is true that I have barely any concrete recollection of that time in my life. But the fact of the matter is that I spent years and years in my life wondering about my brothers—where they were, what they looked like, what it would have been like had they lived, and wishing that they had. I was never satisfied with the short explanations given me by my parents. 'They were just too small.' 'If they had lived, your sister might not have ever been born!' I recall that even as a very young child, I thought about my twin brothers—lovingly, wistfully, regretfully, and sadly—very often.

''At first, I was too young to describe my grief adequately *in words*. Then, and later, I never felt free enough to express all that I felt. Would my grief have been different, would it have released its hold on me, if I *had* talked about it? Would the loss I felt have been easier to bear?

''I don't know the answers to these questions. I do know that I had been grieving all those years, and that even as a two-year-old, I was totally aware of the 'goings on.' I still feel as if I want to stamp my feet in protest, and have a tantrum like a two-year-old, and hit and scratch and yell WHERE ARE MY BROTHERS? YOU PROMISED ME BABIES! WHERE IS MY MOTHER? I DON'T WANT TO SLEEP AT GRAMMA'S HOUSE! THIS PLACE SCARES ME AND I WANT TO HOLD THE BABIES. I WANT TO SEEEEEEE THEM. PLEASE SOMEBODY LET ME SEE

MY BABY BROTHERS, EVEN IF THEY ARE DEAD. THAT'S OKAY; I STILL NEED TO *SEE* THEM.''

We all, no matter what our ages, *feel* loss when it happens. Few of us reach out adequately enough to help support those feelings in each other.

Reaching out isn't easy; trying to bring comfort to a child when you are so in need yourself is enormously difficult. We can only promise you that reaching out to your children is worth the effort. Your children will be whole and healed because of your reaching out in love, and, then, so too will you.

## CHILDREN'S NEEDS

The very first need of surviving children is to be told that they are loved. The second is to be shown that they are not responsible for the loss. And then, they need *truth:* accurate information about what happened.

Whatever the event—a birth, a death, a fearsome upset— it is reality. Those not part of the event can only imagine it, and as Grollman and Salk and others have shown, children's fantasies are almost universally more alarming than the reality ever was. We know from numerous psychological observations that the mind tends to fill in unknown data with alarming possibilities. Imagine such a common situation as expecting your spouse home at a certain time and then having that time pass by. Rather than thinking "How wonderful! He (or she) is probably stopping to buy me a present—maybe flowers!" most of us imagine the worst instead and worry about what harm may have befallen our loved one. Children are not immune from such negative fantasizing, and they are supremely susceptible to fill-in-the-blanks nightmares after a powerful event like birth or death. Children deserve to hear the truth about what happened. Lewis Mehl, Carol Brendsel, and Gayle Peterson, in their study *Children at Birth: Effects and Implications* (1977), describe the "fantastic notions" of birth that children *not* present at the event concoct; these children "seemed mystified and found the idea of birth puzzling and inconceivable." Salk, Grollman, and others tell us that children often feel so fearful of their fantasies, so transfixed by them, that they do not share them with us. Thus, children not present during a time of loss may indeed suffer great anxiety from their own fantasies of what happened—and suffer without telling us that they do. In attempting to shield our children, then, rather than protecting them, we may be cutting them adrift to navigate alone a sea of nightmarish imaginings.

## INCLUDING CHILDREN IN LOSS

Perhaps we *can't* protect our children from upset or sorrow, even if they were not present at the actual event. Some of our children may indeed have been present at the moment of loss. What next? Can children integrate death or loss in a healthy way? They can, according to a 1973 study by R.A. Furman, *if they are given prompt, accurate information about what happened, are allowed to ask all sorts of questions and get answers, and participate in the family's grieving process.*

One family shared with us their story of loss and of how their son handled it, and it lends positive testimony to Furman's findings. Jeffrey was two when his brother Mark was born. Mark lived only two weeks and then died of acute leukemia. Despite his age, Jeffrey was told the truth about what happened. His questions, then and later, were always answered honestly and directly. Over the years Jeffrey's parents honored Mark's memory in their family prayers and in periodic visits to the cemetery. Jeffrey was always included. As Jeffrey reached significant milestones and as each of his two sisters was born, he would ask how old Mark would have been at that time. He occasionally expressed longing for his brother; his complaints about his sisters were accepted with understanding. When Jeffrey was six his mother gave birth to another boy, Steven. Normally quiet and restrained in group situations, Jeffrey stood up to tell his first-grade class about his new brother. His voice electrified with feeling, Jeffrey said that he had had a brother who died and that he was "really glad to have a brother again." His teacher and classmates were all deeply touched. "I think the children all felt how much Jeffrey cared," his teacher said. "You could have heard a pin drop in the room while he was speaking."

Jeffrey's parents gave him far more than a new brother and the special healing Steven's birth brought. They gave him a safe and supportive environment in which to work through the family's loss—to understand it, to be included in it, to express feelings about it, and to grow from it. The growth he attained, along with the memory of Mark, will be a part of him always.

Children can gain a great deal from being part of any powerful life experience, even part of a crisis, part of the depth of loss. The most important gift of all may be an awareness, for them, of how totally we respond when a loved one is in distress or in danger. That awareness certainly builds greater security for the child. Some children present during the moment of loss (such as at a traumatic birth) may have seen frantic, even hysterical, action. A response to crisis with action, even frantic action, can be very comforting to a child, who wants to believe, as psychologist Arthur Janov (1973) tells us, *that people will respond when he's in need*. Most children, present during times of great loss, learn how deeply people care for one another. What a wonderful lesson! Children included in mourning gain a deep respect for life and death and our feelings about both. They add to their own stock of coping techniques. And family ties are often strengthened by the sharing of intense emotions.

So, the gifts are there. How do we guide our children to find them, especially if the experience is one of deeply felt loss? To help resolve an experience of loss, death, or any other, we've successfully used several exercise techniques with children. We offer them now to you, with the hope that these healing techniques will make reaching out to your children less difficult and more effective.

## ARTISTIC EXPRESSION

First, encourage the children's *artistic* expression of their loss. Ask them to draw how they're feeling. If appropriate, ask them also to draw the scene of loss, even if they weren't present. Know that children tend to draw as they perceive, not necessarily as life actually presents itself.

Sarah was four years old when her mother gave birth to a severely brain-damaged child, Alex, who lived for six weeks. Alex never came home but remained in intensive care at a perinatology unit.

Sarah's parents spent every day at the unit while she was cared for by her grandparents. Because Alex had several physical deformities, Sarah's parents were advised not to allow Sarah to visit her new brother.

After Alex's death, Sarah's grandmother attended one of our grief seminars and went home to encourage Sarah's expression of grief. She gave Sarah some crayons and asked her to draw some pictures of Alex.

At first Sarah drew a big yellow ball in the middle of the page, a symbol, Sarah's grandmother thought, for his soul.

Then she began to draw his face with an enlarged head and big purple mouth. Alex had a cleft lip, a condition that was never discussed in Sarah's presence. Drawing allowed her to share what she intuitively knew and felt about her brother.

Kubler-Ross (1980-83), Salk (1974), and Anderson and Simkin (1981) all rely on children's drawing to unlock their hidden feelings. You may choose to invite your children to express their feelings in art; just allow yourself to respond *intuitively,* not critically, to what they put on paper. Notice the colors they choose, the interrelative sizes of people or things, the feeling the drawing calls up in you. You might see, as we have in some drawings, representations of two parents holding an overly large baby, while the artist has drawn himself much tinier than the others, crouching in a corner of the page. What do you feel? Let your heart tell you that your little son feels lost, unnoticed, unimportant, dwarfed by his infant sibling's death. You can't change the death but let your son know that *he* is important and noticed and deeply loved. He needs to hear those things; he needs to hear *you* say them.

## RECALL PROCESSING

Recall processing, a technique we've described in previous chapters, can be used effectively to help children deal with loss. You can guide your children through recall processing in this way:

1. Eliminate any possible distractions.
2. Ask your child to sit or lie in a comfortable position, with her eyes closed to reduce distracting stimuli.
3. Ask your child to place herself in the situation you want to recall. Ask her for *lots of detail:* time of year, day, weather, place. Begin with general questions and then gradually narrow down to the more specific: time of day, room, colors, scents, textures, people present, clothes worn.
4. If she says she can't remember, ask her to tell the story anyway, making up whatever she forgets.
5. If she wasn't part of the scene but is troubled by it, ask he to tell it the way she imagines it.
6. When she seems sufficiently "grounded" in the scene (sensory details do that grounding), ask her to begin telling the story as *though it is happening now,* in the

present time. ("Mommy is leaning on Daddy and breathing hard to help the baby out and moaning.")

7. If you notice bottled up emotion, try to stimulate its release—not by saying, "I know how you feel," but rather with words like "That must have felt really lonely," or "How frightening that sounds."

8. Ask questions for more detail, but don't needlessly interrupt. Honor your child's feelings.

9. Bring the recall to some completion. Often, just the releasing of feelings works a healing. Sometimes, you need to do more; perhaps asking if your child needs to forgive anyone or asking if she feels in need of forgiveness will seem right. Or it may help to *role play* the scene the way the child would have liked it to be.

To reach a deeper healing, we use a lovely and effective process we've taken from the Senoi tribe of Malaysia. The Senoi are sensitively attuned to their dreams, their "dream life," as they call it. They believe that every life experience and every dream can *teach* something and therefore offers some "gift," something of value gained or learned, experienced or felt.

We believe that even the deepest, most painful loss can offer some such gift, that *every* child comes with a gift, no matter how short her stay. So ask your child to imagine her dead sibling (or whatever loss she experienced) before her. Direct her to open her heart and feel what *her* gift has been.

Then you might decide to, somehow, manifest this gift in a physical way, so that your child will have, forever, a reminder of the special gift received from her brother or sister. Five-year-old Jessica felt a greater awareness of the gift of love, from her brother's stillbirth, so she then chose two hugging koala bears for her bedtime companions. Eight-year-old Ian pictured his family as a beautiful tree with spreading, sheltering branches as the gift he received, so his parents planted a young tree to grow along with the family.

Most children respond with positive eagerness to the concept of recall processing. They often instinctively understand the power of sharing feelings; in this as in so many ways, they are our teachers.

## TELLING THE TRUTH—AND FAITH

During recall processing with your children, it may be evident that they have lots of unanswered questions. If you can offer accurate and truthful explanations for your loss, do so. If you have no clear understanding yourself, be honest and say so! Say that you may understand at some later time, or you may not, but talking about uncertainties usually helps all of us.

Children often have questions about God's role in loss. So do we adults. Beth remarked that after her miscarriage, she had very great difficulty talking to her son about God because *she* was upset with God. We think that children, if they feel supported, can handle upset pretty well. They experience it, after all, themselves. We *can* share our very great sadness and pain. We *can* be truthful about any lack of certainty we feel as to why loss and suffering exist or where *exactly* the souls of dead loved ones are. We can mention that clergymen grapple with the same feelings. The world is uncertain for our children, too. Pretending otherwise will only build walls Hardgrove and Warrick (1974) so poignantly describe. According to Nancy Berezin (1982), "clergymen of all denominations who have studied children's responses to death are in agreement that it is not necessary for parents to claim to have all of the [spiritual] answers."

Explanations such as "This is God's will," or "God wanted your brother," or even, as Berezin states, greatly romanticized or fanciful visions of an afterlife can threaten the healthy development of a *child's* spiritual beliefs. Berezin cites the example of the three-year-old who was told that her dead baby brother was an angel "looking down at her." The little girl became terrified whenever it rained, thinking her brother would be washed from the sky.

Kubler-Ross (1980-83) refers to the case of a little girl who had been told that God so loved little boys that he took her younger brother to heaven. The child never resolved her great anger with God or her feelings of powerlessness and helplessness. Thirty years later, when her own son died, she plummeted into a serious psychotic depression.

Telling a child that God dictates the moment of death is asking a lot of a child's immature understanding. A child's view of loss, in that framework, might be something like this, "If God took my baby brother away, God must be very, very mean, because now everyone's so sad. I don't like God at all. I'm really afraid of him. Maybe he'll get *me* next." Living with that dread and fear of God, despite what we adults say about His goodness, can be a pretty difficult task for a small child. Children are simplistic; they live in the here and now, not looking ahead to the hereafter. If *we* are feeling "let down" by God, imagine how your child, who doesn't grasp the full spectrum of divinity, must feel. Children may indeed be so transfixed by their present fear of, or anger with, God that they may be unable to share those feelings, especially if we adults appear accepting.

Heidi traced her atheistic upbringing to her father, Michael, and his childhood. Michael's mother had died when he was only six years old; the little boy's grieving father explained that God must have wanted Michael's mother. But Michael wanted her, too, *desperately,* and he felt a hatred of God grow within him that he never shared with his father, for he sensed such feelings would have met with great disapproval. When Michael grew up, he turned the ultimate insult in God's direction—denial of his existence. "My sister and I," Heidi writes, "were given no hope in God's presence, no faith to call our own. For my father, it was a dead issue."

Kubler-Ross (1980-83) believes that under normal conditions our spiritual quadrants, our spiritual natures, don't develop until we reach adolescence. It might be wiser to wait until your children reach that stage in their growth before expressing a belief, if you hold it, that God ordains death. We can share the truth about what happened, we can share our grief and pain and faith and accept and support that of our children, and we can share that we don't always understand *why* things happen as they do, without making God, in our children's eyes at least, the ultimate scapegoat.

## LITTLE DEATHS

Artistic expression, recall processing, forgiveness release, role playing, and the Senoi gift process can be applied to any situations where children feel loss. Helping our children recover from loss builds their store of coping mechanisms for dealing with death. In their book *Responsible Parenthood* (1980), Gilbert Kliman, M.D., and Albert Rosenfeld say that "No child should have to deal with the overwhelming experience of bereavement without prior exposure to small doses of ideas and feelings about death."

Kubler-Ross (1980-83) speaks of all the "little deaths" we face throughout our lives: skinning a knee, losing a favorite toy, failing an exam, losing a game, having a pet die, losing a friend, moving away from home, losing a job, and on and on. We can help our children learn how to grieve and resolve their small losses (although they may not feel "small" to our children) more effectively. How much better prepared they will be to deal with more serious loss! We can turn those "little deaths" into opportunities for growth.

John and I (Cathy) had just such an opportunity when our third child was born, and her birth was not at all what our older children had anticipated. In fact, Sharon and Paul felt Allison's birth *as a loss,* so we used several of the exercises previously described to help them resolve their feelings.

We had envisioned a peaceful birth at home with Sharon,

then eight, and Paul, four, actively involved. Instead, labor was breathtakingly brief—forty minutes—chaotic and tense, with an emergency ambulance transfer to the hospital when Allison was born without a heartbeat. Our call for the ambulance brought the entire local '911' emergency team: a fire engine, a police car, the ambulance, and a following of at least a hundred people. Our peaceful, safe and personal birth felt like a Hollywood disaster film. Sharon and Paul, who had anticipated leading roles, were relegated to walk-on parts. Not only did they "lose" the active involvement they had practiced, they also felt shunted aside as the EMTs rushed into the house, and then they felt great fear as they watched Allison and me being wheeled out on a stretcher.

Our story did have a happy ending: Allison began to breathe and continued to improve even before we reached the hospital. Yet Sharon and Paul were left with a residue of feelings about their personal losses. Afterward, when I was back home and in bed, I began to give horrified thought to my older children and their reactions to Allison's birth. I hadn't even reassured them, or said good-bye to them, as I had left in the ambulance; all my focus had been on the child I perceived in need. Would they understand that? They barely responded when we asked how they felt. So we decided to hold a family resolution evening. Sharon and Paul were at first reluctant and then, when recall processing enabled them to get in touch with their feelings, increasingly eager to share. They let us see the birth through their eyes; they shared their disappointments and fears. ("I never got to wipe your forehead or run for juice or rub your back!" "At first I was really scared when the policemen rushed in...." "You didn't even say good-bye; I thought you were *dying;* I thought you and Allison wouldn't come home!")

There were wonderful. We could see the buried emotional "charges" rising to the surface, being released and then melting away. And then we did it their way, role playing Allison's birth the way they had dreamed it would be. And we all saw how much we wanted to help each other, to be together, share what is important. I let them know, as did John, how their very presence had helped us, and how their excited exclamations had helped their little sister to feel loved and welcomed and strong enough to breathe. Sharon and Paul were awed and pleased by that new awareness of the importance of their caring and love.

When they talked about what they had gained, they now spoke with excitement of "all the people and the fire engine—awesome!" "You and Daddy worked really hard—I never knew that before." "Allison was like a star of a movie; everyone really tried to help her. Was it like that when I was born?" "Being there with her when she was born and needing help makes me feel so close to her."

John and I saw Allison's birth in a new light, too—the children's light—and we could no longer hold our memories of her birth in quite the same places as before. All of us, together, added the bits and pieces that make up the mosaic of our family experience.

Allison lived. It might have been our inclination, or it might understandably be yours now to brush aside the older children's feelings since "everything had turned our OK." How unfortunate that would have been! It is in the resolving and healing of each little death that we learn how to heal each major one. Helping Sharon and Paul work through their feelings of loss around Allison's birth was more than worthwhile. We believe it was necessary. How very much more vital it is, then, to help our children who lose more than expectations, who lose a sibling, to resolve their pain.

Our dream is that every family will find its won best way to nurture each other through life's passages—especially the difficult ones—so that every passage becomes an honoring and a celebration of those who together are family. Our children especially need our help in unloading from their baggage of grief the heavy rocks of guilt, self-blame, resentment, and feelings of being unloved and unimportant. We can help free them of that heaviness so that each child may lift her lightened burden of loss and carry it on until she can put it down in her own place and time of healing.

# TWELVE

# SPIRITUAL RESOLUTION

C.S. Lewis, noted author of *The Chronicles of Narnia, The Screwtape Letters,* and other works, wrote of his intense spiritual turmoil after his wife's death: "Meanwhile, where is God?... The longer you wait, the more emphatic the silence will become" (*A Grief Observed* 1976).

As Lewis discovered, the full healing of loss demands spiritual resolution, for we are indeed more than physical, emotional, and intellectual beings. We are spiritual beings as well. We must, therefore, go beyond any therapeutic traditions that ignore spirituality in each of us and face the reality of our own inner yearning for some "soul" consolation, some meaning in the haze of sorrow, conflict, and pain.

Many of the letters and stories of those we have counseled indicate such a search for spiritual meaning in loss and death and even in existence. We do not claim in any way to have found the ultimate truths or spiritual answers, but we do believe we must all bravely face our own spiritual questions if ever we are to find any genuine peace.

In the previous chapters we have approached loss by inviting parents to begin to view pain and death as a part of life. We encouraged the embracing of pain—not unnecessary suffering but the real heartfelt human pain that loss and extreme disappointment cause us to face. We have encouraged parents to see that pain is healthy, normal, and sane, and that it should be honored, not medicated or ignored.

Now we suggest a spiritual context for that pain so that it is not only honored and respected but is also used as pathway to greater personal growth and peace. Kubler-Ross, throughout her work, reminds us that we can never go back to things the way they were before our children died. It is not possible to "return to normal" as life once was because the consciousness has been jolted by the unexpected and must rearrange itself accordingly. Most parents with pregnancy- and birth-related losses will confirm this view as they attempt to seek such an impossible return only to find that death has closed the door.

We believe that a choice to grow through our disappointment and sorrow and to reach spiritual resolution is the only path to ultimate healing and that anything else will cause continued physical, emotional, and mental debilitation. Spiritual resolution is such a personal process that we offer only some possible avenues for expression. Since each of us must ultimately answer our own inner quest for truth, our ideas of spirituality may not be right for every reader. However, they may serve as points from which to begin.

## FAITH

The Bible tells us that "faith is the assurance of things hoped for, the conviction of things not seen" (New American Standard Bible, Hebrews 11:1). *Webster's New World*

*Dictionary* defines faith as "complete trust, confidence, or reliance." Faith is often shattered by loss. In our work with bereaved parents, we have discovered two areas of faith that seem to require spiritual resolution.

## *God*

The first is one's relationship with God. We accept God as the Source of our universe; others may not hold that belief, but spiritual resolution will be just as necessary for nonbelievers. Any spiritual philosophy is shaken to its roots by loss. And so, we who thought we knew God or knew our spiritual faith, or we who never tried to know before, or we who were convinced in any spiritual belief are all suddenly confronted with the unprovable, the supernatural—at a time when *to know* is paramount. Lewis described his formerly strong faith as nothing more than a house of cards when confronted with his wife's death (1976). The Reverend William Sloane Coffin, Jr., in a sermon following his son's death said, "The reality of grief is the absence of God—'My God, my God, why hast thou forsaken me?'"

The ended beginning of a new life impales our spiritual beliefs on a supranatural sword. Life is our natural state, our reality, our expectation, and our hope. Few of us view death in the same way. The death of a child who has not yet lived is unnatural, unreal, and in opposition to our every expectation. Most of us have faith in life, but few of us have faith in death.

Although noted writers on death such as Kubler-Ross, Grollman, and others have attempted to teach us a new approach to the dying process, one that views death as a part of life rather than a polarity to life, death is still experienced as an unnatural, isolated state. The cultural treatment of those who have been touched by death is all too often consistent with this position. Hundreds of letters have come to us over the past few years written by women who have experienced pregnancy losses and who are suffering not only the pain of these losses, but also the nightmare of isolation as friends and family react to their own inner fears of dying with suppression and denial. Bereaved parents are often aware of being an embarrassment to everyone they meet. These reactions and the resulting pain of isolation are due, at least in part, to our failure to respect our own spiritual natures, which *can* make sense of what seems incomprehensible.

For years parents with pregnancy losses had nowhere to go, no one to turn to, because all of us, lay people and professionals alike, have been too uncomfortable with death. Miscarriages, stillbirths, infant deaths, abortions, and lost dreams open the tightly shut windows on our own deaths. As we look through these windows, we look into our own souls and awaken our common need for meaning in life and in death.

## Soul Connections

The second area in need of spiritual resolution is one's relationship with a lost child's soul. Lewis wrote, "Kind people have said to me, 'She is with God.' In one sense that is most certain. She is, like God, incomprehensible and unimaginable" (1976). Bereaved parents we've counseled after loss have commonly described both God and their lost children's souls as out of their reach and incomprehensible, and they speak of those voids as more painful than anything they had ever known. Parents who experienced the death of a dream report similar spiritual loneliness, questioning and searching.

Although it would be impossible to demonstrate, in any

visual form, the existence of a human soul, it is equally impossible to disprove the existence of such spiritual energy. Most bereaved parents we've counseled search desperately for some connection with their children's souls. The powerful and innate instinct to protect one's child is thwarted by death and, at times, by surgical deliveries and traumatic births. Many parents agonize over whether their children are in need in death. As described in previous chapters, many parents, especially women, feel a pull toward death that can so easily be misinterpreted as suicidal urge instead of as a mother's need to know that her child is safe. Such women need full and continual support and our understanding of a mother's normal natural desire to know that her child is cared for. The resolution of this suffering and of feelings of alienation from God can only occur through some form of spiritual reconciliation.

For most parents we have dealt with, this reconciliation has not come overnight or without emotional pain and mental conflict. The process unfolds gradually, as does the moon in its lunar cycle. We see no stark changes from one day to the next. The crescent moon is illuminated a bit more each day, until the full moon shines in resplendent glory. Spiritual resolution is human glory, and to begin the process, one needs only to be willing.

## ANALYZING GOD

A willingness to face one's spiritual beliefs is the first step. The foundation for spiritual beliefs is begun in childhood; early spiritual impressions may live in us unexplored or unchallenged for years. The shock of loss, however, is a great challenge, and oftentimes childlike beliefs cannot meet it. For example, many of our clients report having once held a spiritual view of life that depended on ''good'' being rewarded and ''bad'' being punished. For those people, the death of a newborn or an unborn child, or the birth of an infant afflicted with a handicap, or the loss of a dream of parenthood caused great spiritual turmoil. Former faith and spiritual beliefs simply could not bear the loss, so parents began to question their beliefs.

Rabbi Harold Kushner faced such spiritual questions. Shortly after becoming rabbi of a congregation, Kushner learned that his three-year-old son, Aaron, was suffering from a rare and fatal disease and would not live past his early teens. Trained to counsel others through pain and grief, Kushner nevertheless found his theological background and his personal faith unequal to his spiritual crisis. And so began a personal groping for spiritual resolution that finally culminated in peace for Kushner: his spiritual odyssey is sensitively documented in his book, *When Bad Things Happen to Good People* (1981). It is a tribute to Kushner's son. It offers one man's reconciled view of God and faith and why pain and suffering exist. And most of all, it invites each of us in need of resolution to begin the search: to explore, to analyze, to set out all the pieces of the puzzle; to question faith; to cross-examine God. So many of us are afraid to begin. Who are we to dare to question God or the laws of the universe? How dare we even *feel* angry with God, let alone tell God so? Yet there is Rabbi Kushner, a man deeply committed to his faith and the service of God—and he dared to question; he dared to ask, to seek, to analyze. So too, did the Reverend Biebel who wrote of *his* agonized spiritual searching after the death of his young son (1981).

Joan wrote of how she came to analyze God: "While I was dealing with the grief of infertility, I went through the first serious faith crisis of my life. I had been praying and believing that God would end this awful time and allow me to get pregnant. I used to kneel at the side of my bed every night and pray so hard. My hands would be so tightly clenched, and I would beg—oh would I beg. I bargained, too. I used to write letters to St. Jude and to God. I'd date them and seal them and put them in my dresser drawer. I would promise that if I became pregnant, I would take the letter out and show everyone that it's true—prayers are answered. But my prayer was *not* answered. Finally one night, in such frustration, hurt, grief, and anger, I took our crucifix off the wall and hurled it across the room. I told God how I felt—that I was so angry with Him for not allowing me to get pregnant while letting others conceive children by mistake and still others abuse their children. That release of anger was such a turning point for me. I thoroughly shocked myself, but I also recognized that it had been the first totally honest communication I'd had with God in months. It was the beginning of my looking at God to really learn who He was and what prayer was. It took a while—a long while— for me to feel His love again, but when I did, it was more real and meaningful to me than it had ever been.''

At first the analyzing is really just the recognition of need, the knowledge that here is a great rent in the fabric of our lives—a rent that needs repair. It becomes an examination of one's beliefs. Is God involved with death? Who is God? What power does God, or the universe, or whatever, hold? It might help to search backward through time for your earliest impressions of God and your first spiritual beliefs. When you were young, how did you imagine God? Parent figure? Disciplinarian? Judge? Protector? Healer? Pretend that you are seven years old and write a brief essay entitled ''Who Is God?'' Take the time to locate yourself in your childhood before you begin this exercise. Close your eyes; visualize a time of year and a day when you were seven or eight; see yourself in your home, surrounded by familiar childhood toys and possessions; notice as many sensory details as you can; recall favorite friends and activities of that time; if you went to Sunday school, try to visualize yourself there, too. Then *be* that child, and write the essay.

When you're finished the essay, put it aside for a bit. Later read it with love for and acceptance of your childlike self and your heritage of faith. Know that when a child's faith matures into adult understanding without spiritual crisis, it tends to evolve within the same basic framework. Even those of us who stop practicing a family religion often maintain the same general beliefs about God. Thus, by evaluating faith from our past point of view, we often get a clear and simplified picture of our most basic beliefs and expectations. So now draw your child's faith out to meet your present loss. Using that context, speak directly to God—in writing, in thoughts, or in words aloud. Allow your honest feelings full expression. Whether you feel let down, cheated, misled, unsupported, abandoned, unloved, or anything else, say so. Speak to God, or to your inner spiritual beliefs, even if only in anger. Anger, bitterness, and resentment are normal human emotions. However, if we don't release those feelings but rather keep them locked inside, churning away, then they can hurt us. Continuing to hold anger or bitterness toward God usually means we are holding the same hurtful emotions toward ourselves as well. If we believe God is punishing us, we are probably still punishing ourselves, feeling guilty for that which we could not control. If we continue to feel resentful, we hold this bitterness deep in our physical bodies, running the risk of long-term "disease." We deserve no such punishment or pain. Yet, to be at peace, we must be honest with ourselves and with God. A resolved spiritual relationship is a *whole* one, not just the parts dressed up in Sunday best. The following letters were written by two women who speak honestly to God about their spiritual beliefs.

> *Dear God,*
> *Two months ago my son Joshua was stillborn. I have trusted the strengths and teachings of Judaism since childhood. However, I could not comply with tradition and place my son in a nameless grave site. I was once taught that a "soul" has lived only after thirty days of life. But Joshua lived for months inside me. He moved. He kicked and survived until his birth. To place my baby in a name-*

*less grave would deny my belief in his very existence. Surely, You don't want me to do that. I'm angry with You. I'm so divided inside. With all this pain, I don't want to feel guilty too. I'm so confused.*

*Sandra*

*Dear God,*
*I'm afraid to write to you, because I'm afraid you'll punish me. I feel punished already, though, so maybe writing will help. My twins died at five and a half months of pregnancy. They weren't baptized. When I was a child I was told that unbaptized babies went to Limbo. My priest now says that Limbo doesn't exist. I don't believe they could be in some in-between place. They were pure. They had no darkness or evil. They were babies. Yet my childhood beliefs haunt me. What is the truth? Where are they? Whey did they die? Where are You? I believed, and I prayed. There is nothing to console me—nothing I believed in as a child, and nothing now. I'm alone. I'm empty. I feel so misled and so abandoned.*

*Julia*

Analyzing God and spiritual beliefs may be frightening, for we may feel cut off from the comfortable and the familiar. Many of us are frightened by the unknown. Yet deep within us all are reserves of strength and courage that can lead us on.

## THE PASSAGE

Every act of birth requires the courage to let go of something, to let go of the breast, to let go of the lap, to let go of the hand, to let go eventually of all certainties, and to rely on one thing: one's own power to be aware and to respond; that is, one's creativity. To be creative means to consider the whole process of life as a process of birth, and not to take any stage of life as a final stage.

Erich Fromm

In 1620, a band of brave souls set sail from England to found a colony in America, a land where they could worship God in their own chosen way. The process of spiritual resolution is much like that famous journey. It is, indeed, a passage from a known, often comfortable, and basically undisturbed faith into strange and uncharted waters. What a challenge this passage represents! To hoist sail and *let go,* to feel fear and uncertainty requires a very special courage. And yet for many of us to hold on tight to what was no longer brings peace or security. Death and loss have already begun the transformation, and to resist the process is to block peace. As Marilyn Ferguson wrote in *The Aquarian Conspiracy* (1980), "The known has failed us too completely."

Many parents report that they considered themselves "religious" until the loss of a child. "But then," Susan wrote, "I realized that my new questions had *no* answers in my faith. Nothing I ever believed before could comfort me. God abandoned me when I needed Him most. It was all useless, so I just stopped believing. I didn't trust God anymore, so I couldn't share any of my pain with Him. I couldn't pray. But the void was just as painful as the unanswered questions were. I try not to think about any of it, that's all." Sadly, Susan won't be able not to think about it either.

Some may feel deeply threatened by this phase of passage. You may most fear losing the faith that brought you comfort and sustenance in past years, the faith of your childhood, your parents, and other loved ones. Know that *losing* your faith is not the goal. *Transforming* your faith is.

Faith, if allowed to stagnate, will surely die. Transformed faith may indeed be childhood faith dramatically matured to its fullest, deepest, most beautiful expression. Letting go and moving ahead, just as the early Pilgrims did, can be an act of supreme faith. Those of us in need of spiritual resolution, then, might give ourselves permission to let go—to let the questions rise, to air the doubts, to explore the possibilities.

Some people choose to begin "spiritual direction" with a trusted pastoral counselor or even a good friend or psychotherapist. Spiritual direction is often just a series of dialogues in which ideas and questions are offered and discussed. Suggestions for follow-up reading might be given. To be effective, spiritual direction must be absolutely *safe;* in other words, one must feel totally free to express whatever thoughts or feelings crop up, without concern for blame or judgment.

Others choose to explore alternative faith systems or support groups within a religious body. A particular retreat experience might seem to beckon, or a book on faith structures might appeal; or even quiet, personal meditation might uncover a new approach to faith. You might begin a personal journal. Choose a title that expresses your willingness to let go and to grow. And then write any thoughts or feelings you observe in yourself, questions about faith, disagreements with old concepts. If you feel inhibited, begin by writing a letter to God, or even to your pastoral leader. Here is a sample that might put you in touch with your own thoughts:

> *Dear God and Bishop,*
> *I feel so awkward and silly writing to you in this way. Yet I must do it. Please understand my need; feel compassion for my pain; and accept what I write here as a cry for help, guidance and peace. I ache to know and understand. I hope to set out all my doubts and questions that I may come to find acceptance and answers. My faith is trying to*

*grow, and so I will loosen the seams, let down the hems, and fashion a new garment. I may need to work and rework it before it fits. I seek your blessing and your understanding before I begin.*

*Jean*

## CLARITY

As we release the past and are willing to be open to new thoughts, feelings, and experiences of spirituality, we may share much in common with each other. Those we have counseled often report first a sense of spiritual emptiness. Lewis described turning to God and finding an empty house with a bolted door and no lights in the windows (1976). Coffin described the reality of grief as being the absence of God (1983). Yet most of us, as did Lewis and Coffin, move beyond that emptiness to see a great deal.

Fear can block our passage to clarity. We may fear that we won't like what we see. Perhaps we won't. Yet, falling in love with a fantasy will get us nowhere. Learning to live with reality can help us move mountains! There are no magic words to make clarity appear. A desire to understand is the first step into spiritual clarity. Then ask your inner wisdom to show you whatever you need to see.

Barbara wrote: "All my life I believed that if I lived a good life and didn't harm others, then I would be rewarded. I thought that tragedy befell only those who deserved punishment. I knew the world really doesn't function that way, but my inner belief system told me that it *should*, so I just didn't let myself *see* what contradicted my beliefs. But then when our son was born so handicapped, I couldn't believe that anymore. I couldn't *not* see. There he was, so innocent, and so stricken. I couldn't even think about God, much less pray *to* Him, for months. Then, after I released my anger and hurt and pain and told God how betrayed I felt, I felt empty—less ready to scream with pain and rage, but so empty. I don't know which was worse. I had let go of everything I ever believed and trusted. But then, I began to see the truth—and the truth was that I had been misleading myself. *God* never promised what I chose to believe about life. As I looked around the world, I saw so many millions suffering or stricken, and most of them were good, caring people. Was I still angry with God? What I really felt was anger with myself; disappointment and disbelief that I had deluded myself all these years. I never let myself *see* before, so I had left myself wide open, vulnerable and defenseless to tragedy. Of course it *could* happen to me; my 'goodness' couldn't guarantee that it wouldn't. I don't know how understanding this helped, but it did. Thank you. . . ."

Clarity *does* help. Understanding truth—whatever is truth for each of us—is a freeing experience. Lewis, who once felt that God was an empty, barred, dark house, came to see with clarity that perhaps his own reiterated cries for help deafened him to the voice he hoped to hear. "After all," he wrote, "you must have a capacity to receive, or even omnipotence can't give" (1976).

One woman we counseled wrote:

> The growing was painful, but the gifts of growth for all of my family, especially for me, are exceedingly precious. I believe I now know my own spiritual nature, through my own eyes, in a new and mature way. I am more real to me than ever before. I feel a sense of spiritual assistance so actively in my life. I still love my church; I view its errors sometimes with anger or sorrow, often with compassion and forgiveness, and its desire to sustain and inspire with deep gratitude. I believe in the need of people to come together to support love and caring in each other.
>
> I now have faith in me, too; in my own intuitive understanding of and relationship with God. I'm

*willing now for God to be God—not a spirit made to my image and likeness, but a spirit unto Himself, or maybe even Herself! I not only accept the mystery of God's divinity—I embrace it. The mystery excites and challenges and draws me, as a moth is drawn to light. I feel eager to know more of God as He is, not as I had fantasized Him to be. My immature and genuine, yet often manipulative, love for God has blossomed into a mature, deeply satisfying, noncontrolling, unconditional love. With that love in my heart, I feel so much better about myself too!*

*Mary*

Being willing to love, accept, and forgive God clears the way for us to offer those same gifts to ourselves. And then the path to spiritual peace is open before us.

## PEACE

### *GOOD-BYE KIM*

*I've carried you in my mind for five long years.*
  *Haunting me.*
  *Waking me at night in tears.*
  *Asking why—no answer given.*

*Wanting to be with you,*
  *yet*
*ties that hold me here not always stronger than you.*

*Living with the fear*
  *of having let you go too soon.*
  *But for whom was it too soon?*

*Learning that you won't be back.*
  *But knowing you are here*
  *in different things*
    *in wind,*
    *in light*
    *in faces of friends who care.*

*I'm finding you a place to stay*
  *that's soft and warm and safe.*
*A place where we can be together without hurt,*
  *without the tears and terror and screams.*

*It's in my heart, my firstborn child,*
  *this place where you can go.*
*Where we can visit*
  *and share the love we felt before.*

*So leave my mind and find my heart,*
  *where a welcome awaits your soul.*
*So we can dream of beautiful things,*
  *like flowers in the snow.*

                              *Peggi Barnicle*

Finally, each of us must somehow find a way to bring our relationships to rest. It is impossible to forget about our pregnancy losses, particularly about children we've loved and lost. Grieving is ultimately an opportunity for us to remember, to visit with the souls of our children and with the memory of our experience. We hope that our memories will not be burdened with unnecessary suffering and guilt. In order to allow ourselves and other parents the dignity of a continued relationship that offers peace, we have developed a visualization process that may allow for the soul contact we all pursue. The process is based on the work of psychologist Jack Johnston, who studied the dreamlife of the Senoi culture in Malaysia, and of others who have researched the significance of dreaming—both daydreaming and night dreams.

The Tibetan Buddhists, centuries ago, suggested that lucid dreaming is a first step toward illumination and enlightenment, toward accepting death and optimizing the conditions of rebirth. In modern times, psychotherapists beginning with Sigmund Freud, whose *Interpretation of Dreams* appeared in 1900, were at least partly aware of the healing available to the consciousness on the dream plane. Gestalt psychotherapist Fritz Perls saw dreams as a projected vision of all parts of the self—parts that must be accepted as a whole (1969).

Here, we do not take such an analytical view of dreams but rather view dreamlife in accordance with the Tibetan approach—as a spiritual plane, free of the conflicts and anguish common to physical and emotional levels.

As a physician, Gladys McGarey has found that "Dreams have had a highly important role to play in my life, and particularly in my care of obstetrical patients. Dreams can reveal the health or illness of a baby, the sex, the time when it's to be born, etc." (*Born to Live*, 1980). Many parents, mothers especially, report dreaming of their children who die—either before of after the child's death. They often describe their visions in much the same manner that Raymond Moody, author of *Life After Life* (1975), reported from his work with those who had had near death experiences. Moody's subjects, as well as many people we have counseled, described visions of being with souls on another plane.

Whether one believes in afterlife, reincarnation, or something else, the following meditation/visualization is offered as an opportunity for parents to create a safe, supportive space for "visiting" and grieving with another soul. It is a day dream that may become or resolve a night dream. This exercise can be applied to any loss. It may be used as a means of connecting with lost children. It may also serve as a means of honoring lost dreams. As a way of reaching peace with whatever you have lost, we invite you to meet what is gone here, in the safe haven of a visualization you create. You may first want to read this exercise through and then do it with closed eyes.

> Find a place where you can be quiet and undisturbed. You may want to play a favorite piece of music that you find particularly peaceful. Follow a realization process that works well for you, or simply breathe slowly and rhythmically, allowing yourself to let go of tension, pain, or anxiety through your breath. The oxygen in your breath reaches every cell in your body without your even having to think about it; you might pretend that your breath can bring peace to every part of your body as well.
>
> When your body and mind are more peaceful and calm, allow yourself to drift off to some place in the world that you feel would support a meeting once again between you and your child. You may have visited this place many times, or perhaps you've never been there before. Take your time and locate yourself in a place that will truly honor this meeting—a beach, a forest, a meadow, a special room. You are creating a sanctuary, a haven of

*perfect peace, acceptance, and understanding. Your sanctuary is a place which no one can violate and where no one can interfere. Breathe evenly. Remember that all is safe here; all is understood. Blame and cruelty cannot exist here, for unconditional love reigns. No performance ratings; only complete acceptance. Lean into those feelings now; let them fill you and heal you. Breathe.*

*Now imagine that you are surrounding this place with complete protection. Perhaps you may envision the protection in the form of white healing light, or perhaps you will choose guardian angels or spirits who may already seem to be protecting your child. Breathe.*

*When you feel ready, look off into the distance and see your child in some physical form. (Or you might choose to envision your lost dream, somehow manifested in physical form.) This is a meeting beyond the body; it is a meeting of love and of the essence of each person. You may see your son or daughter as an infant or as a young child. Allow your loved one to take any age or appearance that feels right. Follow the vision intuitively, not intellectually. Whatever physical image you envision, remember that it is a meeting of one essence with another. Allow the image to come closer, close enough so that you are able to communicate with one another. Breathe.*

*If you feel tears, welcome them—for tears are the rivers of life that cleanse the heart and soul. They are signs of sorrow but also of love.*

*Please give your child the power to communicate in a way that you will be sure to understand. The essence of one's soul may communicate regardless of whether he or she has language. Take some moments to be fully with each other, experiencing each other's deepest capacities for love and understanding. Breathe.*

*Ask your child if there is anything she needs from you in order to be at peace. Allow all the time you need for an answer. If you do feel some need in your child, take the time now to provide for her. Remember that in this space everything is possible, and all wishes may be granted. Breathe. If there is anything further you need to learn, share, or say, allow it to be freely communicated. Take all the time you need.*

*You might then choose to offer a gift to your child, a gift that represents your eternal love. Then ask your child for a gift as well—an essence gift. An essence gift is a present that symbolizes some deeper meaning. Open your heart to receive this gift, even though you may not understand it fully.*

*Take the gift into your possession—keep it always as a sign of the permanent and indestructible bond between you and your child. Stand together in your sanctuary and see a star (or any other symbol of peace) above your heads, gently raining down peace, healing, and love on the two of you.*

*Now it is time to begin to slowly leave this place. Before you do, bless your child. As you bless her, the star above you both melts into two stars—one will follow each of you wherever you go. Allow your child to drift away just as she appeared, remembering that you may visit with her at any time on this plane.*

*Bring with you the gift you received. See that gift as a symbol and draw from it new strength and healing. Make a commitment to find for yourself some actual, physical manifestation of what you've received. It need not be an exact replica but a symbol that feels right—trust yourself to know when you have found it.*

Over the past several years, we have been using this meditation/visualization with grieving parents.

We have no technological or scientific explanation that can adequately describe its effects. Parents consistently report a greater sense of peace. Some have shared stories that can only be explained in a spiritual context. Here is such a story.

## NINA'S ANSWER

Nina's twin sons were delivered prematurely at six and a half months. They were stillborn, and Nina's grief shaped her life for many months. She willingly agreed to the visualization exercise, searching for some connection with the sons she had lost. She asked her boys to join her on a beach. They appeared, in her visualization, as young children. They each clutched a shell and held it throughout her mental imagery. Nina envisioned playing with her boys, fully feeling their presence, and then she asked them for gifts that she could keep with her as ever present reminders of their love for and connection with each other. Nina told us later that she thought the boys would give her the shells they held, but to her surprise, they didn't. Instead, one son gave her a flower, and the other, a piece of driftwood. Nina cried and smiled and felt closer to her sons than she ever had before. "I couldn't believe," she says, "how it all *worked*! I didn't consciously think any of it, it just unfolded before me like a movie. It was one of the most beautiful experiences of my life." When asked to find some manifestation or symbol, on the physical plane, of her sons' gifts, Nina smilingly replied that she didn't even need to do that. She thought he might, anyway, but she knew that the flower and the driftwood were forever ensconced in her heart.

Nina was so delighted with her newfound pathway to her sons that she couldn't wait to share it with her husband. However, rather than just telling him about it, she asked him to experience the visualization himself. She did not share her experience but instead guided him through the relaxation until he too chose a sanctuary—also a beach—and then asked the boys to be with him. Nina could barely speak when he told her, through his tears, that they each gave him a shell.

# THIRTEEN

# TRANSFORMED!

*THE SITTING TIME*

> Don't listen to the foolish unbelievers
> who say forget.
> Take up your armful of roses and
> remember them
> the flower and the fragrance.
> When you go home to do your sitting
> in the corner by the clck
> and sip your rosethorn tea
> It will warm your face and fingers
> and burn the bottom of your belly.
> But as her gone-ness piles in white,
> crystal drifts,
> It will be the blossom of her moment
> the warmth on your belly,
> the tiny fingers unfolding,

> *the new face you've always known,*
> *That has changed you.*
> *Take her moment, and hold it*
>      *As every mother does.*
>          *She will always be*
>          *your daughter*
> *And when the sitting is done you'll find*
>      *bitter grief could never poison*
>      *the sweetness of her time.*
>
> *—Joseph Digman*

In the scientific field of optics, the term resolution means ''to make visible the individual parts of an image.'' Imagine setting off from a lake shore in a rowboat; as the boat moves farther out onto the lake, you look back and see more and more of the shoreline. The shore stretches far to both sides. You see things you never saw before, never knew were there. A boathouse, hidden by an outcropping of rock and trees. An inlet filled with graceful sailboats. And rising up behind the tree-lined shore, you see a mountain. The trees had obscured your view, and you never saw this magnificent natural backdrop before.

So it is with the resolution of loss. Loss thrusts us from the relatively sheltered lives we once had known. Although the passage through grief is infinitely painful, ultimately our eyes are opened wider by the newness—and the goodness—around us. The Reverend Biebel wrote, ''I will never accept the idea, or even the implication, that there was anything good about what happened to Jonathan. It was an utter, abject, absolute evil. But good has come of it, because God is able to take even the evil, the suffering, and the pain of our lives and transform . . . them. . . . All things are not good, but all things can have a good result'' (1981). One day, or bit by bit on many days, we reach peace and healing.

The final stage of healing is transformation—a profound change of inner nature. It is much like the metamorphosis of the sluggish, earthy caterpillar into an incredibly lovely and delicate butterfly—so beautiful would be human transformation if we could but see its entire form. We *can* see the outer glow reflected from an inner peace. We can see the pulsing of a renewed life force, as though we had been disconnected from, but then plugged back into, the source of life, the current of power. We can often see other changes as well—new jobs, new friends, new activities, new passions. New life. Transformation is life matured and threshed and squeezed and shaped and reborn. It may include an awakening of eagerness. It rests on the awareness that we cannot return to what we were before There is peace in that awareness—peace reached after the long uphill climb from despair. More than all this, transformation is perhaps what we are all about and why we are here.

Our healing knows no boundaries, for the effects of inner peace spread like ripples to others, and so we contribute to the world's evolution. All together we generate *such a power,* the power of defeat transformed into victory—the victory over death itself, the victory of life with purpose.

If this power is to be felt in greatest force, we must be willing to reach for maximum transformation from within. We cannot close our eyes on any aspect of childbearing losses. We must seek peace and resolution for our own inner restoration. For too long, women have been treated as incompetent, dependent hysterics. For too long, men have had to hide their tears behind facades of macho strength. For too long, we have failed to value ourselves, our resources, and our needs.

At last, we are reclaiming ourselves. We can all begin, together, to build a new age of interaction with each other, a new age of relationships. Our new age must be marked not by strife, but rather by acceptance; not by blame and judgment, but by forgiveness and love. If we share fully with our loved ones who and what we are, and if we accept ourselves and each other, then death or loss cannot leave us in such guilt, such self-recrimination, such blame, or such self-pity. For we can all know that we and our children have been our very best for each other.

We will still feel grief, to be sure, but its cleansing path through our bodies, minds, hearts, and souls will not be hampered by the adulterations or sieves through which most of us now filter grief. We will be left with grief but with no "grief work." When death comes to a loved one, we will be free of the burdens of so many unsaid words and unshared feelings, of "unfinished business" as Elisabeth Kubler-Ross (1980-83) terms it.

Leonard Clark's sensitive poem "Stillborn" (1981) ends with the lines:

> *I know that for me you are born still;*
> *I shall carry you with me forever,*
> *My child, you were always mine,*
> *You are mine now.*
> *Death and life are the same mysteries*

Life and death *are* intrinsic parts, one of the other. And so, if we can unravel a little of the mystery of life, we can know and understand a bit more of death. We can begin to recognize and honor our eternal connections with our children—connections that begin with their conception. We can consciously share ourselves with our children, from the moment we know they exist. The richness of relationship we begin to build will only enhance and grace the ties that endure beyond death, whenever it comes. Death cannot destroy that which always lives.

We cannot recall our children from their new lives in death, nor can we recover other childbearing losses now gone from us. Yet we can honor the eternal love we feel for our children, and they for us, by transforming our ended beginnings into new beginnings. Beginning today.

> *And to Elizabeth and for all our Children . . .*
> *Whom I've never held or physically seen.*

*For years, now, I have talked to you in that old rocker. I have seen you sitting there. I've told no one. Today, I am free to give the old rocker to someone I truly love. And you, my child, live in my heart forever. I am free to let you go, to find your way.*

*I am grateful that you could stay so long on this plane, to guide this work before beginning anew your purpose. God bless you always.*

*Love,*
*Mom*

*And to the Dreams*

*I cradled you in my heart for so long. When I felt you crumple within me, a part of me was lost too. But now I'm whole again—and there are new dreams in my heart. And so, I let you go—and bless the gifts the loss of you brought to my life. And bless yesterday, tomorrow, and most of all, today.*

*Love,*
*Me*

# RESOURCES

*Support Groups*

*Local chapters exist for several of the groups listed below and can be found by contacting the central agency.*

AMEND (Aiding A Mother Experiencing Neonatal Death)
  Los Angeles Chapter
  4032 Towhee Drive
  Calabassas, CA 91302

HOPE (Help Other Parents Endure)
  c/o Susan Harrington
  South Shore Hospital
  55 Fogg Road
  South Weymouth, MA 02190
  (617) 337-7011, Ext. 332

THE COMPASSIONATE FRIENDS, INC.
P.O. Box 1347
Oak Brook, IL 60521
(313) 323-5010
self help organization for parents who have lost children of all ages

AMERICAN MASSAGE THERAPY ASSOC.
Albert Hunt
P.O. Box G-36
Wakefield, Mass. 01880
(617) 665-9588

C-SEC, INC. (Cesareans/Support, Education & Concern)
22 Forest Road
Framingham, Mass. 01701

THE CESAREAN PREVENTION MOVEMENT
Box 152
University Station
Syracuse, N.Y. 13210

RESOLVE INC.
497 Common Street
Belmont, Mass. 02178
(617) 484-2424
for people with problems of infertility

LA LECHE LEAGUE INTERNATIONAL
9616 Minneapolis Avenue
Franklin Park, IL 60131
(312) 455-7730
for breastfeeding mothers including those nursing handicapped and premature infants

## NATIONAL SUDDEN INFANT DEATH SYNDROME FOUNDATION
310 South Michigan Avenue
Chicago, IL 60604
(312) 663-0650
for support regarding crib death

### *Cookbooks and Nutrition Information*

---

*The Brewer Medical Diet for Normal and High-Risk Pregnancy* by Gail Sforza Brewer with Thomas Brewer, M.D. 1983. New York: Simon and Schuster.

*Diet for a Small Planet* by Frances Moore Lappe'. 1971. New York: Ballantine Books.

*Herbs for Women—A Guide for Lay Midwives* by Valerie Hobbs. 1981. Self published: 308 Highland Ave., Athens, Ohio 45701.

*Moosewood Cookbook* by Mollie Katzen. 1977. Berkeley, CA: Ten Speed Press.

*Whole Foods For The Whole Family*. Recipes compiled by La Leche League International. 1981. Franklin Park, IL: Leche League.

# BIBLIOGRAPHY

Anderson, Sandra Van Dam, R.N., M.S., and Penny Simkin, R.P.T. *Birth—Through Children's Eyes*. Seattle: The Pennypress, 1981.

Arms, Suzanne. *Immaculate Deception*. New York: Bantam Books, 1975.

————. *To Love and Let Go*. New York: Alfred Knopf, 1983.

Brezin, Nancy. *After A Loss In Pregnancy*. New York: Simon and Schuster, 1982.

Berne, Eric. *What Do You Say After You Say Hello?* New York: Grove Press, 1972.

Biebel, David B. *Jonathan: You Left Too Soon*. New York: New American Library, 1981.

Bittman, Sam and Sue Rosenberg Zalk. *Expectant Fathers*. New York: Ballantine Books, 1978.

Blavatsky, H. P. *The Secret Doctrine*. Russia, 1888. Two Volume Series.

Boerstler, Richard W. *Letting Go*. Watertown, MA: Associates in Thanatology, 1982.

Bombardieri, Merle. Written statement regarding physical effects of infertility. 1983.

Borg, Susan and Judith Lasker. *When Pregnancy Fails*. Boston: Beacon Press, 1981.

Bowlby, John. *Loss*. New York: Basic Books, 1980. Brazelton, T. Berry M.D. *On Becoming a Family*. New York: Delacorte Press, 1981.

Brazelton, T. Berry M.D. *On Becoming a Family*. New York: Delacorte Press, 1981.

Breckenridge, Kati Ph.D and Lyn Delliquadri M.S.W. *Mother Care*. New York: Pocket Books, 1979.

Brems, Marianne. Ongoing long term study of "some physiological changes that resulted from exercise," Western Illinois University. Cited in *Swim For Fitness*. San Francisco: Chronicle Books, 1979.

Brewer, Gail and Tom Brewer, M.D. *What Every Pregnant Woman Should Know, The Truth About Diet and Drugs in Pregnancy*. New York: Random House, 1977.

Clark, Leonard. "Stillborn". Pat Schwiebert, R.N., and Paul Kirk, M.D. *When Hello Means Goodbye*. Portland, OR: University of Oregon Health Center.

Coffin, Rev. William Sloane Jr. A sermon delivered at Riverside Church, NY and printed in *The Boston Globe*, December 30, 1983.

Cohen, Nancy Wainer and Lois J. Estner. *Silent Knife: Cesarean Prevention and Vaginal Birth After Cesarean*. South Hadley, MA: Bergin & Garvey, 1983.

Colen, B. D. *Born At Risk*. New York: St. Martin's Press, 1981.

Colgan, Dr. Michael. *Your Personal Vitamin Profile*. New York: Quill, 1982.

Cousins, Norman. *The Anatomy Of An Illness As Told By The Patient*. Toronto, Canada: N.W. Norton, 1979.

D'Arcy, Paula. *Song for Sarah*. Wheaton, IL: Harold Shaw, 1979.

Davis, Elizabeth. "Energy Cycles in Pregnancy And Childbirth." *Yoga Journal*, Vol. 32 (May-June, 1980).

Denning, Melita and Osborne Phillips. *The Llewellyn Practical Guide To Creative Visualization*. St. Paul: Llewellyn Publications, 1981.

Deutsch, Helene. *The Psychology Of Women Volume II*. New York: Bantam Books, 1945.

Digman, Joseph. P.O. Box 14864. Portland, OR 97214.

Dill, Barbara. Written statement on physical effects of childbearing loss. 1983.

Featherstone, Helen. *A Difference In The Family*. New York: Penguin Books, 1980.

Ferguson, Marilyn. *The Aquarian Conspiracy*. Los Angeles: J.P. Tarcher, 1980.

Fox, Margaret. *Unmarried Adult Mother: A Study Of The Parenthood Transition From Late Pregnancy To 2 Months Postpartum*. Unpublished dissertation. Boston University, Boston, 1979.

Freeman, Roger M.D. and Susan C. Pescar. *Safe Delivery*. New York: McGraw Hill, 1982.

Freud, S. "The Occult Significance of Dreams." *Psychoanalysis and The Occult*. G. Devereux. International Universities Press, 1970.

Friedman, Rochelle M.D. and Bonnie Gradstein M.P.H. *Surviving Pregnancy Loss*. Boston: Little, Brown, 1982.

Friedmann, Lawrence W., M.D. and Lawrence Galton. *Freedom From Backaches*. New York: Pocket Books, 1976.

Furman, R.A. "A Child's Capacity For Mourning". *The Child in His Family: The Impact Of Disease And Death*. (E.J. Anthony and C. Koupernik, Eds.) New York: John Wiley, 1973.

Gass, Robbie. *Trust and Love*. Record Album, Cassette, Lyric Booklet. Ashby, MA: Spring Hill Music, 1981.

Gawain, Shakti. *Creative Visualization*. Mill Valley, CA: Whatever Publishing, 1978.

Grollman, Earl A. from his lectures on talking with children about death, 1976–1983.

————. *Explaining Death to Children*. Boston: Beacon Press, 1976.

————. *Talking About Death: A Dialogue Between Parent And Child*. Boston: Beacon Press, 1976.

————. *What Helped Me When My Loved One Died*. Boston: Beacon Press, 1981.

Hardgrove, Carol and Louise H. Warrick. "How Shall We Tell The Children?" *American Journal Of Nursing,* 74:3, March, pp. 448–450.

Harrison, Mary. *Infertility: A Guide For Couples*. Boston: Houghton Mifflin, 1979.

Hendin, David. *Death As A Fact Of Life*. New York: Warner Books, 1973.

Hickey, Isabel. *It Is All Right*. Self published, 1976. To obtain: Helen Hickey, 103 Golden Crest Ave., Waltham, MA 02154.

Hodson, Geoffrey. *The Miracle Of Birth*. Wheaton, IL: The Theosophical Publishing House, 1981.

Holmes, T.H. and R.H. Rahe. "The Social Readjustment Rating Scale." *Journal Of Psychosomatic Research,* pp. 213–218, 1967, Vol. II.

James, Muriel and Dorothy Jongeward. *Born To Win*. Reading, MA: Addison-Wesley, 1973.

Jameson, Beth. *Hold Me Tight*. Old Tappan, NJ: Fleming H. Revell, 1971.

Janney, Peter Ed. D. *A Vision Of Eternity: The Phenomena Of A Life Reading By George Tiffen And Its Therapeutic Value In Psychotherapy*. Boston University, Boston: 1982.

Janov, Arthur, Ph.D. *The Feeling Child*. New York: Simon And Schuster, 1973.

Jiménez, Sherry Lynn Mims. *The Other Side Of Pregnancy*. Englewood Cliffs, NJ: Prentice Hall, 1982.

Kitzinger, Sheila. *The Complete Book Of Pregnancy And Childbirth*. New York: Alfred Knopf, 1980.

Klaus, Marshall H. and John H. Kennell. *Parent-Infant Bonding*. St. Louis: C V. Mosby, 1982.

Kliman, Gilbert W. and Albert Rosenfield. *Responsible Parenthood: The Child's Psyche Through The Six-Year Pregnancy*. New York: Hold, Rinehart and Winston, 1980.

Knapp, Ronald, and Larry G. Peppers. *Motherhood And Mourning*. New York: Praeger Publishers, 1980.

Kubler-Ross, Elisabeth, M.D. *Death-The Final Stage Of Growth*. Englewood Cliffs, NJ: Prentice-Hall, 1975.

————.*On Death And Dying*. New York: MacMillan, 1969.

————. From her lectures and tapes on death and dying, 1980-1983.

Kushner, Harold S. *When Bad Things Happen To Good People*. New York: Schocken, 1981.

La Leche League International. *Whole Foods For The Whole Family*. Franklin Park, IL: La Leche League International, 1981.

Lappé, Frances Moore. *Diet For A Small Planet*. New York: Ballantine, 1971.

Lewis, Emmanuel. "The Management Of Stillbirth, Coping With An Unreality". *Lancet*, Vol. 2, 1976.

Lindemann, Erich, M.D. *Beyond Grief: Studies In Crisis Intervention*. New York: Jason Aronson, 1979.

Littlefield, John W. and Jean DeGrouchy. *Birth Defect*. New York: March Of Dimes, Amsterdam, Holland: Excerpta Medica, 1978.

Lowen, Alexander. *Bioenergetics*. New York: Penguin Books, 1975.

Mandell, Frederick M.D., Elizabeth McAnulty, R.N., M.P.H., and Robert M. Reece M.D. "Observations of Paternal Response To Sudden Unanticipated Infant Death". *Pediatrics*, Vol. 65, No. 2, 1980, pp. 221–225.

Manners, Ellia, M.S. Comments recorded during an interview in Arlington, MA, 1983.

McGrath, William. *Common Herbs For Common Illnesses*. Provo, UT: New Life Publishing, 1977.

McNamara, Joan. *The Adoption Adviser.* New York: Hawthorne Books, 1975.

Mehl, Lewis E. M. D., Carol Brendsel R.N., and Gayle H. Peterson, M.S.S.W. "Children At Birth: Effects And Implications." *Journal Of Sex & Marital Therapy,* Vol. 3, No. 4 (Winter, 1977), pp. 274–279.

Meltzer, David. *Birth.* San Francisco: North Point Press, 1981.

Mendelsohn, Robert S. M.D. *Mal(e)Practice: How Doctors Manipulate Women.* Chicago: Contemporary Books, 1981.

Meyer, Linda. *The Cesarean(R)Evolution.* Edmonds, WA: Chas. Franklin Press, 1979.

Mindell, Earl. *The Vitamin Bible.* New York: Warner Books, 1979.

Moody, Raymond A., Jr. *Life After Life.* New York: Bantam, 1975.

Morningstar, Jim. *Spiritual Psychology.* Self Published Work, 1980.

Naisbitt, John. *Megatrends.* New York: Warner Books, 1982.

Norman, Charles. *E. E. Cummings The Magic-Maker.* New York: MacMillan Company, 1958.

Oleksiw, Carol, M.S.T. Quoted in interview, 1983. Business address: P.O. Box 173, Acton, MA 01720.

Palinski, Christine O'Brien and Hank Pizer. *Coping With A Miscarriage.* New York: New American Library, 1980.

Parkes, C.M. " 'Seeking' and 'Finding' A Lost Object: evidence from recent studies of reaction to bereavement." *Social Science And Medicine.* Vol. 4 (1970 B), pp. 187–201.

Peels, Fritz. *Gestalt Therapy Verbatim.* Lafayette, CA: The Real Press, 1969.

Peterson, Gail H. *Birthing Normally: A Personal Growth Approach To Childbirth.* Berkeley: Mindbody Press, 1981.

Raphael, Dana. *The Tender Gift: Breastfeeding*. New York: Schocken Books, 1973.

Ray, Sondra. *Loving Relationships*. Millbrae, CA: Celestial Arts, 1980.

————. *The Only Diet There Is*. Millbrae, CA: Celestial Arts, 1981.

Rees, W. D. "The Hallucinations Of Widowhood". *British Medical Journal,* No. 4, pp. 37–41.

Rogers, Carl R. *On Becoming A Person*. Boston: Houghton Mifflin, 1961.

Ryan, Regina Sara and John W. Travis M.D. *The Wellness Workbook*. Berkeley: Ten Speed Press, 1981.

Salk, Dr. Lee, from his lectures on parenting, 1976–1978.

————. *Preparing For Parenthood*. New York: David McKay, 1974.

————. *What Every Child Would Like His Parents To Know*. New York: Warner, 1974.

Samuels, Mike, M.D. and Hal Z. Bennett. *Be Well*. New York: Random House, 1974.

Schiff, Harriet Sarnoff. *The Bereaved Parent*. New York: Crown, 1977.

Selye, Hans. *The Stress Of Life*. New York: McGraw-Hill, 1956.

Sharkey, Frances, M.D. *Parting Gift*. New York: St. Martins', 1982.

Sherfan, Andrew Dib. *The Nature Of Love*. New York: Philosophical Library, 1971.

Simonton, O. Carl, M.D., Stephanie Matthews-Simonton, and James L. Creighton. *Getting Well Again*. Los Angeles: J. P. Tarcher, 1978.

Singh, Bruce, and Beverly Raphael, M.D. "Postdisaster Morbidity Of The Bereaved." *The Journal Of Nervous And Mental Disease,* Vol. 169, No. 4, 1981, pp. 203–212.

Steiner, Claude. *Scripts People Live*. New York: Grove Press, 1974. Lectures, Boston, 1975.

Stevenson, Nancy Comey and Cory Higley Straffin. *When Your Child Dies: Finding The Meaning In Mourning*. Cleveland Heights, OH: Philomel Press, 1981.

"Stress: Can We Cope?" *Time*, Vol. 121, No. 23, June 6, 1983, pp. 48–54.

"Stress". *The Boston Globe,* May 30, 1983, pp. 39 and 41.

Sutherland, R. L., M.D. "East, West and Psychotherapy". *Main Currents In Modern Thought,* Vol. 23, No. 1 (Sept./Oct. 1966).

Webster. *New Collegiate Dictionary*. Springfield, MA: G & C Merriam, 1976.

*Websters New World Dictionary*. New York: World Publishing, 1957.

Williams, Roger. *Nutrition In A Nutshell*. New York: Doubleday, 1979.

# INDEX